Waiting for

The Spiritual Explorations of a Reluctant Atheist

by **Lawrence Bush**

Ben Yehuda Press
Teaneck, New Jersey

Published by Ben Yehuda Press
430 Kensington Road
Teaneck, NJ 07666

http://www.BenYehudaPress.com

For permission to reprint, please contact:
Permissions, Ben Yehuda Press,
430 Kensington Road, Teaneck, NJ 07666.
permissions@BenYehudaPress.com.

Segments of this book have appeared in various versions in *Jewish Currents* magazine, *Reconstructionism Today*, *The Reconstructionist*, and *Tikkun*.

Cover photo © Lawrence Bush

Library of Congress Cataloging-in-Publication Data

Bush, Lawrence.
 Waiting for God : the spiritual explorations of a reluctant atheist /
by Lawrence Bush.
    p. cm.
Includes bibliographical references and index.
ISBN-13: 978-0-9789980-5-9
ISBN-10: 0-9789980-5-7
 1. Spirituality. 2. Baby boom generation--Religious life. I. Title.

BL624.B885 2007
204--dc22

                                    2007033440

08 09 10   / 10 9 8 7 6 5 4 3

In memory of
Morris Babushkin,
1910-1981

"to thine own self be true"

Contents

Introduction

The Atheism that Failed

> Pozzo: (*peremptory*). Who is Godot?
> Estragon: Godot?
> Pozzo: You took me for Godot.
> Vladimir: Oh no, Sir, not for an instant, Sir. . . .
> Estragon: Personally I wouldn't even know him if I saw him.
> Pozzo: You took me for him.
> — Samuel Beckett, *Waiting for Godot*

MY MOTHER LOVES TO TELL of a time from my childhood in the 1950s when she eavesdropped on a conversation I was having with another young kid. "Do you believe in God?" I asked, to which the girl earnestly replied:

"Yes, and in Mighty Mouse, too."

Like a snapshot in a photo album, Mom's repeated telling of this story has preserved, or perhaps implanted, a shred of "remembrance" in me: I see Little Larry sitting side-by-side with somebody in a semi-enclosed space, and I feel my question to be risky and intimate — an effort to find someone complicit in my family's atheism, which, I was only then learning, was not a mainstream view.

My "memory" dissolves as soon as the girl answers my question. I have no idea of whether I found her reply funny or disappointing. "It was so cute" is all that my mother says — yet her delight in the anecdote goes well beyond its charm. In fact, the story is highly ideological, with a double moral that sums up the content of my family's atheism:

1) God is just another version of Mighty ("Here I come to save the day!") Mouse.

2) People who believe in God are childish.

This is the atheism with which I was raised. It acknowledged no theology more sophisticated or subtle than the "God with a white beard" variety, and it gave no respect to 20th-century religious thinkers who were grappling with modernity to produce modern theologies. So what if Martin Buber or Dorothy Day or Paul Tillich or Mordecai Kaplan were shaving off God's beard and expressing religious insights born of their own struggles with science, materialism, and the disillusioning horrors of the two world wars? My parents and their peers of the radical left were not in the least interested in the progressive renewal of religion, but in making religion itself obsolete through socialist uplift of the world. They basically saw religious people as weaklings or charlatans — or, at best, as sentimental addicts unable to wean themselves off what Karl Marx so famously called the "opiate of the people."

"The fool has said in his heart: There is no God," intones Psalm 14. Perhaps it should be easy for me to dismiss my parents' hard-headed atheism that way, as foolery — a ministering angel to their Marxist-Leninist "God that Failed."[1] Certainly, I have permitted the plain evidence of contemporary history to penetrate my skull when it comes to communist ideology: At best, I view it as sadly doomed to failure because of human nature, at worst, as terribly destructive because of its own nature. Still, the capitalist system that my parents sought to replace, especially in its ugliest outcroppings of colonialism and militarism, has been just as destructive of human (and non-human) beings as the communism they advocated. My parents' critique, if not their solution, therefore still has real currency for me, while many of the causes for which they and their peers struggled — workers' rights, racial amity, peace and social justice, a more equitable division of wealth — remain righteous to my mind, some even uncomplicatedly so.

Likewise their atheism: While perhaps consigned to marginality thanks to some human religious "instinct," atheism has yet to suffer "disproof," for me, by miracle, by gulag, by history or by personal experience. The rejection of God still carries implications of an empowering humanism (the belief that we can and must do it all for

---

1. The phrase is Arthur Koestler's, from his 1950 memoir, *The God That Failed: Six Studies in Communism.*

ourselves, by ourselves) and of opposition to the violent, misogynistic and suppressive role played by fundamentalist religious forces around the globe. Therefore atheism still carries its white plume, still shines with a bohemian patina, and it still has tremendous intellectual and cultural significance — for me.

Apparently that makes me an old-fashioned guy (though, at fifty-five, a young baby boomer). Having a real taste for atheism today is rather like having a real taste for men's hats or Lucky Strike cigarettes or the music of Frank Sinatra, whose peak of artistic success and iconic power was in my parents' heyday, not mine.

Especially among the intellectuals and trendsetters of my parents' generation, loss or lack of faith seemed almost a prerequisite to open-mindedness, creativity and non-conformity. It was atheism that marked them as proud heirs to two or more centuries of Enlightenment, to the heresies of empiricism, humanism, materialism, rationalism and "freethinking" that had shattered the chains of superstition, fueled the motors of Western progress, and would ultimately (or imminently) be vindicated, they believed, through the application of "scientific" principles to human society. But as their fellow-socialist Helen Keller once observed, "The heresy of one age becomes the orthodoxy of the next." For many freethinkers of my own generation, the "heresy" of atheism seems peripheral to radicalism and is taken as a symptom of an unimaginative mind and a dour personality, more than anything else. Instead, the riotously anarchic decade of the 1960s yielded adulthoods soaked through with "spirituality," especially with the ideologies and lingo of the "New Age" and "human potential" movement. Todd Gitlin , a perceptive chronicler and active participant in the revolutionary '60s, reports that in subsequent years:

> no ex-movement household was complete without med-itations, tarot cards, group therapies, the *Tao Te Ching*, and the writings of Alan Watts on Zen, Fritz Perls on gestalt therapy, Wilhelm Reich on the recovery of the body, Idries Shah on Sufism, R.D. Laing on the truths of madness, Baba Ram Dass's invocation to *Be Here Now* — and most of all, Carlos Casteneda's parables of an intellectual's skeptical yieldings to the

Yaqui shaman Don Juan. . . . [I]ndividual subjectivity promised to reinvent a shattered world . . . Thus
the fascination with past lives, spiritual 'auras,' extrasensory perception, suppressed goddesses, 'women's
knowledge' (believed to have been the true basis of
'witchcraft' in the Middle Ages), and the like.[2]

Today, Gitlin's list would have to be updated to include Feng Shui,
spirit-channeling, past lives regression, homeopathic medicine, Buddhist meditation, Deepak Chopra's writings on "quantum healing," and
any number of other spiritual and "alternative" teachings that have become so imbedded in American culture as to seem uncontroversial and
unremarkable. The trend that Gitlin observes among "ex-movement"
households would also have to be extended way beyond the shriveled
worlds of the political left and the '60s counterculture.

Across the entire American landscape, the scales of public sentiment
have been tipping away from rationalism and the scientific worldview
for half a century. Despite mind-boggling scientific achievements,
heightened college attendance, and numerous well-publicized scandals and tragedies featuring the hypocrisy, insanity or criminality of
religious leaders (including the terrorism of Al Qaeda, pedophiliac
outrages by Catholic priests, the Jim Jones murders in Guyana, and
the sexual abuse, misconduct and/or hypocrisy of Jim Bakker, Swami
Satchidananda, Ted Haggerty, Jimmy Swaggart, Rajneesh Chandra
Mohan and numerous other religious figures), nearly as many Americans today as in 1957 say that religion plays a "very important" role in
their lives.[3] More than two thirds of Americans describe themselves as
more or equally religious as their parents; more than four fifths express
belief in an afterlife; more than half believe in the existence of hell;
nearly a third have meditated or practiced yoga.[4] Somewhere between

---

2. Todd Gitlin, *The Sixties: Years of Hope, Days of Rage*, 1987.

3. In a 2002 survey by the Pew Global Attitudes Project, 59 percent of Americans made this avowal, compared to only 33 percent in Great Britain and
   smaller and smaller minorities in other developed countries.

4. Statistics from a nationwide poll conducted by the *New York Times* and reported in the *New York Times Magazine*, May 7, 2000. Other polls show

Lawrence Bush

20 and 40 percent attend religious services on a weekly basis, according to Harris polls and other sources, and fully 90 percent say that they engage in private religious experience. A majority even believes in miracles — including, it seems, more than 70 percent of people with postgraduate degrees![5]

This widespread religiosity is accompanied by widespread animosity towards nonbelievers. A telephone survey of 2,000 Americans in March, 2006, for example, found that despite the attacks of September 11, 2001 and the sudden worldwide visibility of Islamic fanaticism, people rate atheists below Muslims (and below gays and lesbians, recent immigrants, and other minority groups) in "sharing their vision of American society" — and that atheists are the minority group Americans are least happy to see their children marry.[6]

Some atheists have mounted a spirited self-defense for the past couple of years, with books about atheism that climb the best-seller lists. These writers (Sam Harris, Richard Dawkins, Christopher Hitchens and several others) have brought skepticism and atheism out of the closet and onto the airwaves, but their work has not so significantly influenced America's marketplace of ideas, which remains far more saturated with religion and spirituality than with psychology, sociology, feminism or other humanistic topics that were the rage in the 1960s and early '70s. Even with the current atheism publishing boomlet, religious books dominate the conversation: At this writing, Amazon.com, the online bookstore, offers 233,916 selections pertaining to the search word "angels," 125,545 pertaining to "spirituality," and 217,187 pertaining to "Jesus," compared to a mere 26,724 for the search word "atheism" and 39,393 pertaining to "humanism." Popular movies and television shows also play constantly on themes of synchronicity (deeply meaningful coincidence), life after death, supernatural mystery, and

---

variations in the numbers, but most of them reveal markedly high levels of religiosity in America.

5. See George H. Gallup, Jr., Religion in America, 1996, as quoted in Winifred Gallagher's *Working on God*, 1999.

6. Research conducted by Penny Edgell, associate professor of sociology at the University of Minnesota, who published her findings in American Sociological Review. Edgell has a website at http://blog.lib.umn.edu/edgell/home/contact.

personal spiritual revelation, and only rarely on themes of skepticism, religious fraud, and the power of rationalism.

It seems, then, that my parents' radical atheism is largely a broken-down relic on the American landscape. *Waiting for God* is my effort to pick through the wreckage and make sense of the religiosity that has flowered wildly in the ruins during the past forty-odd years.

I DO SO FROM MY OWN PECULIAR PERCH as an atheist who has nevertheless worked intimately within Jewish religious institutions as an essayist, editor, speechwriter and interpreter for much of my adult life — editing national religious magazines, leading workshops at religious conventions and retreats, and writing books, essays, and speeches that have been awash with biblical metaphors and appreciated by thousands of religious people.

In the course of this work, I have developed an admiration for liberal faith communities and liberally interpreted religious teachings that my parents would have found unthinkable. Far from providing a mere prettification of human reality ("the sigh of the oppressed creature," said Marx of religion; a "childhood neurosis," scoffed Freud), many of these religious communities offer their members tools with which to cope with life's challenges, celebrate the most meaningful moments, struggle with egotism (or the unhealthy lack of it), and aspire to powerful virtues of discipline, generosity, humility, joy, compassion, mindfulness and more. And rather than merely supporting "the system" of unjust power and wealth distribution ("I am waiting for them to prove that God is really American," wrote Lawrence Ferlinghetti in *Coney Island of the Mind*), many of these communities actively embody social, economic and ethical perspectives that strongly dissent from the status quo.

I have also come to understand how religious language can permit entry into significant conversations about meaning and metaphor, love and death, morality and ethics, self and community, and other subjects that can be difficult to access through wholly rational language. Religiously conversant people, therefore, sometimes seem able to achieve the "buzz" of deep conversation more readily than irreligious people. As philosopher Mitchell Silver notes in his fascinating study of contemporary Jewish humanistic theology, *A Plausible God*, "God-talk," for many people, "may be the only language adequate for the expression of certain emotions. . . . Saying 'God' describes how one feels and how one wants to feel." For many modern theologians, therefore, it is "not important what, if anything, it [the word "God"] refers to; what is important is what it achieves."

From this perspective, prayer's main function is to shape the one who prays, as Silver observes:

> [I]t might teach us to appreciate sheer being; it might reinforce our appreciation of the wonders of person- ality; it might firm our resolve to do better; it might deepen introspection and self-knowledge; it might increase identification with other humans or with the entire universe itself; and it might help to create ex- traordinary experiences of calm, bliss, relief, ecstasy, or self-transcendence. . . . [P]rayer can function as an outlet for emotions seeking an outlet. Prayer allows us to get it off our chest, whatever *it* is . . . Prayer makes one's suffering, one's joy, one's love part of the world. . . . All of these self-transformations are achieved by talking to God, by praying.[7]

On the more intellectual side of things, I myself have been very at- tracted to some of the psychological, social and ethical insights of the Jewish religion. I especially love to read the Talmud (in translation) and encounter the civilizing spirit of the majority of its conversations. Whereas Jewish secular humanists of my parents' generation rarely bothered to look past the most bloodthirsty passages of the Torah (Bible) to confirm their anti-religious scorn, I have learned that the soul of Judaism resides much less in those passages than in the centuries

---

7. Mitchell Silver, *A Plausible God: Secular Reflections on Liberal Jewish Theology*, 2006. Silver, who identifies as a skeptic and an atheist, takes a philosopher's scalpel to the theologies of three influential rabbis: Arthur Green, a leading scholar of Jewish mysticism; Mordecai Kaplan, the founder of Jewish Re- constructionism; and Michael Lerner, founder of *Tikkun* magazine. These three share an essential definition of what Silver calls the "new God" — a naturalistic, depersonified "baseline God" that comprises "whatever there is in nature that makes good things possible . . ." For more discussion about prayer and humanistic God concepts, see Chapter Six.

of commentary and discussion embodied in the many volumes of the Talmud. Those texts, at their best, reflect a superb effort to design a community of minimal suffering and maximal amity.

In particular, Jewish economic teachings, which emphasize the collective nature of wealth yet acknowledge the fear, greed and status-seeking that drive human economic activity, have inspired me to consider a "third way" between the destructive paths of both communism and capitalism.[8] I have also found the Jewish concept of "idolatry," the worship of "false gods," to be a useful tool of cultural critique that helps me define what seems "authentic" and worthy of my passionate attention and what seems "false" and out of step with reality.

In my family life, too, I have been uplifted by such rituals and disciplines as sabbath candle-lighting, Passover seders, charitable giving, and *tashlikh*[9] — rituals that we shamelessly interpret and transform to make our own, that is, to take them out of God's hands, out of the realm of "commandment," and into the realm of celebration, commemoration, conscience, moral discernment, and family connection.

In short, it is Marx's "soul of a heartless world" that I have come to associate with liberal religious life, far more than opiatic or addictive qualities.[10] Still, I remain an atheist, an outsider to the communities I

---

8. Martin Buber described the Jewish view of economics as "a genuine third alternative. . . leading beyond individualism and collectivism, for the life decision of future generations" (quoted in *The Way of Response: Martin Buber, Selections from His Writings*, edited by Nahum N. Glatzer, 1966). Judaism emphasizes the "Divine ownership of wealth" ("The earth is the Lord's, and all its fruits," begins Psalm 24) as its cornerstone principle — which readily translates into an entirely nontheistic apprehension of the collective effort involved in the generation of wealth. This concept is elaborated in Chapter Eight.

9. *Tashlikh* is a Jewish folk custom of "casting your sins on the water" that takes place during Rosh Hashanah, the Jewish New Year. My family has elaborated the ritual into an intensive communication in which we praise each other, express our grievances, make our apologies, and sum up the year's impact on our relationships. See *Sh'ma*, September 2005, for details.

10. Here is the full quote from Karl Marx's *Toward the Critique of Hegel's Philosophy of Law*, 1844: "Religious misery is in one way the expression of real misery, and in another a protest against real misery. Religion is the sigh of the afflicted creature, the soul of a heartless world, as it is also the spirit of

L a w r e n c e   B u s h

serve, in my discomfort with prayer, in my wistful alienation from even the most metaphorical God concepts, and in my general disappointment with my own generation's endless search for self-actualization and a spiritual high. Sure, I recognize the fineness of the line separating my atheism from some modern theologies, and I periodically hop across that line in a burst of enthusiasm. I also recognize the utility of cultivating human virtues by associating them with a "sacred" sensibility. Nevertheless, I have been unable to embrace any systematized spiritual practice or sustain any sense of faith in a meaning-filled universe — and I am reluctant to concede the cultivation of human virtue to the exclusive provenance of religious traditions. No matter how therapeutic religious faith might be for individuals, no matter how nurturing to a sense of dignity, community and responsibility, no matter how beguiling the symbols, metaphors and sancta, there is something in the surrender to God — something in the very *idea* of God — that simply offends my arrogant soul.

This book is therefore also an exploration of the far dimensions of my own atheism — an effort to determine if my resistance to faith is, in fact, primarily a product of egotism and fear or composed of worthier stuff. "Fervid atheism is usually a screen for repressed religion," wrote the Austrian psychiatrist Wilhelm Stekel. If my exploration seems to be more of an apology than an apologia for my faithlessness, let that serve as an antidote to the self-satisfaction and ironic pretensions of most anti-religious testimonies. Surely the religion of our day has undergone enough renewal to warrant a more soulful and self-examining response! —and surely the atheism of our day has endured enough loss of momentum and vilification to require a renewal of its own.

WAITING FOR GOD IS ORGANIZED in three parts. Part One is a four-chapter discussion of some of the unique factors that have helped to "convert" so many of my generation into passionate spiritual seekers. Chapter One speculates about the psychological and cultural impact of

---

spiritless conditions. It is the opiate of the people. The abolition of religion as the illusory happiness of the world is the demand for their real happiness. The demand to abandon the illusions about their condition is the demand to give up a condition that requires illusions. Hence criticism of religion is in embryo a criticism of this vale of tears."

the nuclear bomb. Chapter Two explores the influence of psychedelic drugs, and offers a workable definition of "spirituality." Chapter Three examines how baby-boomer spirituality has been fueled by contemporary environmental issues and has helped shape our response to them. Chapter Four grapples with recent efforts to synthesize science and mysticism, mostly through the metaphysical interpretation of scientific theories, especially those of quantum physics.

Throughout these chapters, my discussion focuses principally upon that sector of the baby-boom generation that Todd Gitlin identifies as "ex-movement" — those who were mostly, like me, middle-class, college-educated, and committed to the culture of "drugs, sex and rock 'n' roll" in the 1960s and '70s and to an anti-Establishment, social-change identity. They were also, as Mitchell Silver observes, "the relatively unalienated . . . [who] control the conditions of their labors far more than have most traditional working classes," and have therefore been attracted, as we shall see, more to a theology of celebration than a theology of salvation.[11] These fortunate folks are the ones I have related to most closely throughout my adult life, and it is their varieties of religious experience that have called out to me with the most allure. "Hippies," "freaks," "Movement people," "New Agers" — we had as many monikers as members. Abbie Hoffman dubbed our aggregate "the Woodstock Nation," and it is this name that I have adapted to "Woodstockers" for the purposes of my discussion.[12]

In Part Two, I wrestle with the alluring writings of three influential radical theologians of our day — the liberationist Christian, Matthew Fox, the founder of Jewish Reconstructionism, Mordecai Kaplan, and the modern feminist witch, Starhawk — all of whom have responded to modernity by pushing the Deity towards abstraction. In my approach-avoidance interactions with their theologies, I am forced to confront some of the psychological dimensions of my "religious autism" and to wonder: Are there some *affirmative* beliefs that derive from atheism,

11. Mitchell Silver, *A Plausible God*, as cited.

12. The 1969 Woodstock Festival itself, of course, took place in Bethel, New York, a good fifty miles away from the village of Woodstock. The term "Woodstockers" has particular appeal for me, given my present residency in the Woodstock area, where unconventional forms of spirituality amount to a local industry.

L a w r e n c e   B u s h

or is it simply a negation, as philosopher Gershon Weiler posits, "an intellectual position derivative of and parasitic upon theism"?[13]

I press that question further in Part Three. Having whacked around some of the favored spiritual belief systems of my fellow Woodstockers, I try to articulate what I myself believe about human beings, about our social relations, even about metaphysics. Can human beings satisfy their religious needs for community, reverence, ethics and meaning *without* resort to God and transcendental explanation? Is the striving for a deep sense of interconnection with other living beings achievable without a leap of faith? Is there a positive value in resisting or restraining our religious instinct, or is the more important task to give liberal, modern expression to it? These are among the fundamental questions that inform this entire book of "spiritual explorations."

I use that phrase, "religious instinct," because, unlike my parents and their peers, I cannot view religion as a purely cultural artifact, foisted on the human race by priesthoods and powerbrokers and therefore capable of being overthrown through education and political action. In his wonderfully wide-ranging book, *Consilience* (1998), entomologist and sociobiologist Edward O. Wilson takes note of a 1945 anthropological study by George P. Murdock that "listed the universals of culture . . . for every one of the hundreds of societies studied to that time." Of the 67 universals in Murdock's list, I count at least ten that are "religious," including divination, soul concepts, religious ritual, propitiation of supernatural beings, eschatology, food taboos, magic, luck superstitions, faith healing, and cosmology. Others, including puberty customs, funeral rites, weather control, dream interpretation and incest taboos, might also be counted as "religious" in inverse proportion to the scientific sophistication of each culture. Wilson concludes from this that "religion has an overwhelming attraction for the human mind" because "ethical precepts" and "religious faith" have, for "more than a thousand generations . . . increased the survival and reproductive success of those who conformed to tribal faiths. . . . Indoctrinability became an instinct."[14] Instinctual or not, religious behaviors that ap-

---

13. Gerson Weiler, "Atheism," in *Contemporary Jewish Religious Thought*, edited by Arthur A. Cohen and Paul Mendes-Flohr, 1987.

14. Edward O. Wilson, *Consilience, The Unity of Knowledge*, 1998.

pear in human cultures at every level of economic, technological and social development cannot be attributed simply to the machinations of society's entrenched "powers that be."

Unfortunately, however, the religious "instinct" does far more than simply "increase the survival and reproductive success" of believers. In more conservative or fundamentalist form, religions also reinforce human traits of submissiveness, conformity, irrationalism, aggression, xenophobia, sexism, sexual repression, mass delusion, and worse. Even progressive theologians who have shaved off God's beard, or given God breasts, must acknowledge their kinship to regressive religious movements — a kinship based on shared scriptures, shared sacred traditions, and a shared perception of a God who is coherent enough, communicative enough, and in relationship enough with the human race, to warrant naming and worship. Such kinship may not provide sufficient ground for condemning efforts to renew theology and imbue it with a liberationist spirit. Still, given the frequency with which conservative religion trumps progressive religion (or reform movements descend into new orthodoxies), my own stubborn instinct seems to favor abolition over reform — even while I recognize the Sisyphean nature of the abolitionist cause.

WAITING FOR GOD is written without the benefit of an advanced degree in theology, psychology, sociology or any other subject. While my professional experience with religious communities has been deep and rich, it has been limited to the liberal movements of North American Judaism, and my personal experience does not range significantly further afield. These and other limitations have led me to rely on autobiographical anecdote, amplified by other people's writings, as my springboard for discussion, speculation, and — heaven help me! — gross generalization. I therefore join the ranks of premature memoirists among the baby-boomers, and stand prepared to receive my share of criticism as a member of a self-important and solipsistic generation.

More charitably, though, my resort to speculative and confessional writing might be attributed to the breathtaking pace at which the world has changed during my short life. When my kids (21-year-old twins) ask about my childhood, it makes me feel grandfatherly, not fatherly, to consider all those elements of change I have experienced. It would require an awfully comprehensive intellect to make sense of the past half century *without* resort to personal history as a kind of experiential touchstone.

History has simply moved more quickly than our individual lives. We've witnessed advances in science and technology as profound as those of any previous breakthrough era. We've seen the apparent triumph of corporate capitalism while communism has slipped into a coma. We've helped to provoke the collapse of centenarian systems of colonialism and legalized racism. We've induced a radical shift in the status of American women, seen the inauguration of a gay and lesbian liberation movement, and enjoyed the advent of sexual permissiveness — and its sudden constriction by AIDS. We've lived under the shadow of the mushroom cloud, wondered at the growth of religious fundamentalism, and suffered the spread of terrorism as a political tool. We've endured the acceleration of communications from rapid to instantaneous, and the rise of visual media to cultural dominance. Like Moses in the book of Exodus (33:18-23), the baby-boom generation has witnessed (repeatedly!) events analogous to the passing "presence of God." Such experiences may not grant wisdom — but they certainly fill us with questions to ponder and tales to tell.

Part One

Spirituality and the Baby Boomers

Lawrence Bush

Chapter One

Taking Shelter

"Ooh, the storm is threatening my very life today.
If I don't get some shelter, oh yeah I'm gonna fade away.
War, children, it's just a shot away . . ."
— Mick Jagger and Keith Richards, "Gimme Shelter"

IN MY EARLIEST PUBLIC EXPRESSION OF ATHEISM, I used to skip over the phrase, "under God," when my elementary school classes recited the Pledge of Allegiance each morning. Sometimes I would just fall silent; sometimes I would hum: "One nation, mm-mm-mm, indivisible . . ." I knew from my parents that Congress had inserted the phrase in 1954, when I was three years old, and that I was upholding, through my silence, the Constitution's principle of separation between church and state[15] — though it was less a sense of civic duty than elitism and mischief that I remember enjoying by straying in this way from the "flock."

When I was 11, my protest was symbolically vindicated: On June 17, 1963, Madalyn Murray won her suit against the public schools of Maryland before the Supreme Court in an 8-1 decision. Bible-reading in public school was thereby banned, and "under God" was dropped from the Pledge for several years, at least in my school district.

In truth, this was a Pyrrhic victory for our mostly Jewish student body at P.S. 196 in Forest Hills, Queens, which gained protection from

---

15. The Pledge itself was written by a Christian socialist, Francis Bellamy, in 1892. Bellamy, a Baptist minister, was cousin to Edward Bellamy, author of the utopian novel, *Looking Backward*. As John W. Baer notes in his essay, "The Pledge of Allegiance: A Short History" (http://history.vineyard.net/pledge.htm), Francis Bellamy was "pressured into leaving his church in 1891 because of his socialist sermons. In his retirement in Florida, he stopped attending church because [of] the racial bigotry he found there." The 1954 insertion of "under God" came after Congressional lobbying by the Knights of Columbus, as a Cold War response to "Godless communism."

the religious impositions of an abstract Christian majority yet lost the thrill of hearing our Jewish principal's sonorous reading of the 23rd Psalm ("The Lord is my shepherd . . .") at the start of our weekly assemblies. Sadly, instead of replacing his Bible readings with poetry or other inspirational but constitutionally permitted material, he resorted to clearing his throat and tapping a key on a wooden auditorium chair to call us to attention.

Stripped of Bible readings and public prayer, elementary school nevertheless became the site of religious "awakening" for me and my peers, due to a purely secular ritual, unique to our generation: the nuclear air-raid drill.

It came in two forms, classroom drills and all-school exercises. Drills in the classroom were rare, perhaps because our teachers found them as absurd as we did, and completely disruptive of classroom decorum. "All right, class: Take cover!" came the command, and we were to dive to the floor beneath our desks, facing away from the oversized classroom windows and covering our heads with our arms. Once the drill ended, the clatter subsided, and the complaints about dirtied clothes and "So-and-so hit me" were registered, we would be left with a feeling of very compromised trust in our teachers and our school — for *we* were deadly certain that an exploding nuclear bomb would evaporate us into shadows.

In our all-school drills, we would make exodus to the school basement and line up in silence, facing the walls in two rows. Compared to the "duck and cover" routine in the classrooms, the basement manueuvers seemed less patently ridiculous, since we'd been trained to think of basement shelters as offering some hope of survival in a nuclear attack. These drills were most distinctive as *crowd* experiences: Pressed nose-to-scalp, feeling the rise and fall of each other's breathing and the twitching of our own muscles, we would envision Armageddon for a few minutes in that enforced silence. After, we would return to our classrooms and resume our lessons without so much as a discussion — never once, a discussion! — of the radically disruptive meaning of the Bomb.

That silence still prevails. The dearth of public discussion about the impact of the Bomb on the psyche of the baby-boom generation has been a wonder to me, given the enormous nostalgia we express for the culture of our childhoods. We've made movies out of every mediocre cartoon show of the '50s and '60s, turned our toys, dolls and comic books into vintage collector's items, and kept Elvis alive long after his drug overdose — yet the images of human extinction that pervaded those same precious childhoods are hardly acknowledged. Do we not remember (we boys especially) jostling together and exchanging Bomb "stats": how close the thing would have to fall to melt our sturdy school building; how we'd want to spend the final fifteen minutes between the sounding of the air-raid sirens and impact; what survival would be like in a toxic, monstrous world? Do we not recall our private yearning for the Bomb, how we wanted to behold its face, see its power, resolve all our adolescent ambivalence in one planetary blast? Have we forgotten the sense of radical absurdity engendered in us by the notion that millions and millions of human beings, including each of us, our families and our best friends, might be annihilated due to a political argument, a failed communication, a stupid technological glitch?

For me, memories of life in the shadow of the mushroom cloud have long seemed causally linked to a whole range of character traits that marked the Woodstockers: our attraction to spirituality and "alternative" (i.e., non-scientific) beliefs, our love of irony and absurdity in art and politics, our desire to "turn on, tune in and drop out" from strivings that seemed doomed to transience and meaninglessness. Such connections between the surreal nuclear nightmare of our childhoods and the psychological character of our adulthoods have rarely been explored — perhaps because the profound threat represented by the Bomb impaired our ability to confront it.

That is the belief of at least one expert, Robert Jay Lifton, emeritus professor of psychiatry at John Jay College of Criminology in New York, who is one of the few writers who has discussed the psychological impact of the Bomb upon the baby boomers. In his 1982 essay, "Imagining the Real,"[16] Lifton reports on interviews conducted in the

---

16. "Imagining the Real," in *Indefensible Weapons: The Political and Psychological Case Against Nuclearism*, by Lifton and Richard Falk, 1982. Lifton's other books include *The Nazi Doctors: Medical Killing and the Psychology of Genocide, Hiroshima in America: A Half-Century of Denial*, and *The Future of Immortality and Other Essays for a Nuclear Age*.

1970s with a small sampling of college students about the psychological impact of their elementary school nuclear air-raid drills. The subjects described "frequent [childhood] dreams or fantasies of people and neighborhoods and cities destroyed by explosions and fires," he writes, but also a subsequent period of amnesia, a "phase of sustained numbing," marked by "the disappearance of these conscious images with little remembered awareness" of the Bomb.

"Sustained numbing" does not mean we have been healed of the Bomb's impact — not by a long shot. To the contrary, Lifton enumerates several interconnected psychological outcomes of what he calls "nuclearism." Perhaps most damaging is the equating of death with absolute human annihilation: the ending of life, culture, mommy, daddy, everything. According to Lifton, this equation disrupts the "symbolic immortality" of the individual (the "appropriate symbolization of our biological and historical connectedness"), which normally enables us each to function and seek a future and participate in the flow of human culture despite death's existential reality.

The identification of one's own death with mass destruction was especially acute for a generation that began its hypnotic romance with television by watching the live telecasts of the Adolf Eichmann trial. In 1961, "How to punish Eichmann" was a major topic of lurid conversation on the school playground, especially in my Jewish neighborhood. The Bomb, which we knew to have been created, at least in part, by Jewish refugees who had fled from Eichmann, became even more enshrouded in mythic symbolism — both as the machine of righteous revenge and as a "portable Auschwitz."[17]

With our "symbolic immortality" destroyed by the Bomb, Lifton continues in his essay, we find our relation to life also altered. Among the psychic effects he cites are:

• a "new ephemeralism," which he describes as "doubts about the lasting nature of anything and similar doubts about the authenticity of virtually all claims to achievement";

• "nuclear fundamentalism" — the effort to regain our stolen connections to life, community, our past and our future by establishing an

---

17. The phrase, "portable Auschwitz," was coined by Rabbi Arthur Waskow, director of the Shalom Center, a Jewish anti-nuclear and environmental resource center in Philadelphia. See footnote 22.

Lawrence Bush

inviolate stubborn, true-believer mindset and "doctrinal restatement[s] of those connections";

- the pressing urge to seek "transcendence as an *alternative* to extinction" — an urge that extends, Lifton argues, to our perception of the Bomb itself: "Our sense is that a force capable of *destroying* human history must not be of it but beyond it. "

GRANTED, MUCH OF LIFTON'S DISCUSSION is speculative (and suffers greatly from my summarization, which strips it of both subtlety and passion). Writing in 1982, with the benefit of hindsight about the baby-boom generation and at the height of a renewal of anti-nuclear activism stirred by Ronald Reagan's ascent to the presidency, he adopts a pained, hortative tone but offers little clinical evidence of nuclearism and its effects. Yet his dire, apocalyptic view of nuclear weapons was shared, as I can testify, by nearly all of us kids in the classrooms and basement of P.S. 196 back in the late '50s and early '60s.

Terror and awe formed the core of our perception of the Bomb. We had all repeatedly viewed and discussed grade-B sci-fi movies about mutant insects, behemoth lizards, crawling eyeballs, 50-foot humans, and other monstrous outcomes of radiation. We had all watched *Twilight Zone* episodes dealing with nuclear war, each of which lent it a sense of fateful meaning.[18] We all knew real Bomb facts and figures: that just one nuke, and a little one at that, had flattened the city of Hiroshima and killed at least 100,000 Japanese, and that we and the Soviets had thousands more to throw, each one a thousand times more powerful than the original! We had all lived, moreover, through the Cuban Missile Crisis of 1962, during which we sat in school awash with feelings of existential fear, despair and detachment that were truly unnatural and bizarre for self-centered adolescents.

---

18. At least three episodes during the show's five-year run, 1959-64, dealt directly with nuclear holocaust — most memorably, the first season's "Time Enough At Last," with Burgess Meredith as a bookworm bank teller who lunches in the vault and emerges into a world devastated by a nuclear exchange. He soon discovers an intact stockpile of classic books — but as he's whooping for joy, he breaks his reading glasses. Rod Serling's show had an enormous influence on us kids. Every Monday morning found us gathered in school, recounting the highlights and debating the merits of the previous weekend's episode.

Worst of all, we knew that our parents, our teachers, our religious leaders and even "bigger" authorities were helpless to do anything but deny the danger.

I do think it plausible to link many of our most distinctive characteristics as Woodstockers to these unique experiences. The generational arrogance expressed as "Don't trust anyone over 30" may have had roots in our childhood perception of our elders' helplessness and hypocrisy. The hippie scorn for work and materialism might be seen as a manifestation of the "new ephemeralism" that Lifton identifies with nuclearism. Psychedelic drug use and involvement with Eastern mystical practices can be taken as evidence of what he calls the "drive for transcendence." The growth of hard-nosed religious and political cults during the 1970s and early '80s seems to embody "nuclear fundamentalism." Etcetera.

WITH THE ADVANTAGE OF 25 MORE YEARS of hindsight since Lifton's analysis was first published, I would extend that "etcetera" to make at least one explicit link between the Bomb and my generation's distinctive cultural profile — a link that proved to be a catalyst for the Woodstockers' widespread embrace of religion during the past four decades.

It was the splitting of the atom that first split my generation away from the humanistic faith in science and rationalism that our parents favored. For their generation, science was a Promethean quest that resulted in the polio vaccine and the eradication of smallpox, the refrigerator and the television, Albert Einstein's socialist humanism and Bertrand Russell's pacifism. For the baby boomers, by contrast, science was a Frankenstein-like overreaching that brought Mutually Assured Destruction and neutron bombs, Chernobyl and Bhopal, pesticide-poisoned foods and toxic waste sites.

Our parents' scientist was a world citizen, a messenger of prosperity and household ease, a crusader for truth against superstition, and a conqueror of hunger, disease and fascism. To the Woodstocker, the scientist appeared to be a corporate citizen, an idolater tampering with the very forces of creation for petty purposes, an amoral technician, and, in anthropologist Loren Eiseley's words, an "extreme reductionist . . .

so busy stripping things apart that the tremendous mystery has been reduced to a trifle . . ."[19]

This shift in the perception of science can be encapsulated by comparing two science fiction movies, each popular and representative of its era. When Klaatu, an alien from an advanced civilization, comes to Earth to warn humanity about our militarism in Robert Wise's 1951 film, *The Day the Earth Stood Still,* he reveals his mission first to a man of science, an Einstein look-alike named Professor Barnhardt. Our parents believed such a man of science would prove a contact superior to any president, military general, or simple man-on-the-street. When the alien E.T. is accidentally stranded on Earth in Steven Spielberg's 1982 sci-fi hit, *E.T., the Extra-Terrestrial,* he reveals himself first to a boy, innocent and full of wonder. My generation believed that such a choice would prove to be a contact superior to any president, military general . . . or scientist.

Of course, there is plenty of historical precedent for the Woodstockers' distrustful reaction to science. The advent of the scientific method and modern scientific discovery in the 18th century gave rise to a grand countermovement of Romanticism, as voiced philosophically by Jean Jacques Rousseau, mystically by William Blake, and in tones of gothic horror by Mary Wollstonecraft Shelley, author of *Frankenstein* (1818). Yet the Romantics found themselves caught up in their era's excitement about science, technology and the "progress of man." Johann von Goethe, to cite one outstanding example, was not only the genius of German Romanticism but a naturalist and director of scientific institutions in the court of Saxe-Weimer. "Without my attempts in natural sciences," he wrote, "I should never have learned to know mankind such as it is. In nothing else can we so closely approach pure contemplation and thought, so closely observe the errors of the senses and of the understanding."[20]

By contrast, well-educated American baby boomers are likely to be scientifically illiterate — and ideologically proud of it. Gerald Horton,

---

19. Loren Eiseley, "Science and the Sense of the Holy," published in *The Star Thrower*, 1978.

20. J.W. Goethe, *Conversations with Eckermann*, 1829, quoted in Gerald Horton's *Einstein, History and Other Passions*, 1996.

a Harvard professor emeritus of science history, points out that in many leading American universities, science and mathematics comprise from zero to six percent of the typical student's overall course requirements. Nearly two-fifths of recent American college graduates, Horton adds, have not taken a single course in the physical or biological sciences. The trend began with the baby boomers and has carried over to our children: CUNY's Andrew Hacker notes that the number of people actually receiving bachelor's degrees in the physical sciences fell between 1970 and 1994 from 21,439 to 18,400, and in mathematics from 24,937 to 14,396. According to William R. Brody, the president of Johns Hopkins University, less than 15 percent of U.S. students have taken the prerequisite courses necessary to pursue scientific or technical degrees in college. Not surprisingly, only 11 percent of bachelor's degrees in the U.S. today are in the sciences or engineering, compared with 23 percent in the rest of the world and 50 percent in China.[21]

Our scientific ignorance has been buttressed, moreover, into something willful and prideful by a whole set of "alternative" ideologies that have flourished, like those mutated creatures of atomic sci-fi movies, in the Bomb-poisoned landscape of our mental life. As the split atom was taken as a metaphor for all that is allegedly wrong with scientific thinking — its perverting power, its irreverence for mystery and boundaries, its obsession with causality, its lack of concern for social consequences — the attraction of "holistic" notions about reality became almost irresistible.

Rabbi Arthur Waskow, a highly creative anti-nuclear activist, writer and theologian, described this attraction eloquently when he and I engaged in a "secular/religious dialogue" in July, 1985, during a conference of New Jewish Agenda, a Jewish activist organization. Waskow

---

21. See Gerald Horton's *Einstein, History and Other Passions*, 1996, Andrew Hacker's *Money: Who Has How Much and Why*, 1997, and national statistics from the Davidson Academy of Nevada (http://presskit.ditd.org/Davidson_Academy/pr2006_Academy_National_Statistics.html). The statistics indicate that scientific illiteracy extends to the generation for whom the baby-boomers serve as parents, professors and role models. Even while science makes a comeback in public popularity — thanks especially to a decade of consumer-friendly computer science and medical innovation — the number of Americans capable of serving the cause of scientific innovation falls far short of the number of job openings in scientific fields.

framed the tension between science and religion as one between "splitness" and "wholeness." "In our generation," he said, "the world needs more than ever to be made whole. Scientific analysis is not a fully effective way to sustain that kind of healing." He continued:

> Science says that there is no such thing as mystery, only ignorance. Ignorance, it says, needs to be conquered, and we will conquer it with more knowledge. But the search for wholeness . . . is rooted in the understanding that there is mystery which will never be solved, a yearning which will never be satisfied by increasing knowledge. . . . Just as the heart of the candle is dark, just as its light grows from its darkness, our real light as human beings comes from that sense of mystery in the world and in ourselves.[22]

"Splitness" and "wholeness": These words resonate powerfully for a generation terrorized by the Bomb. Never mind that Waskow's characterization ignores the integrative theories of modern physics, the role of metaphor and imagination in scientific discovery, and the vital role that scientific analysis has played in generating "holistic" environmental

22. New Jewish Agenda was a progressive Jewish organization active during the 1980s. The texts of our "secular-religious dialogue" were excerpted in *Genesis 2*, April/May, 1986. Waskow heads the Shalom Center, a Jewish anti-nuclear and environmental center, and is the author of *Godwrestling, Down-to-Earth Judaism, Seasons of Our Joy*, and numerous other books. He was ordained a rabbi in the 1990s, years after achieving prominence as a theologian. Waskow often strives to integrate scientific and religious perspectives. The scientific revolution, he said in our same dialogue, "was one major sign that God-power was moving deeper into the world, suffusing the world. . . . But the religious people of that era . . . so deeply feared the abandonment of that wholeness for which they yearned that first they fought against Galileo, Darwin, Marx, Freud, Mill; and then they simply ruled physical, psychological, and social science out of the religious enterprise. . . . I believe there was a spark of truth in their fear, for they saw the danger of becoming only analytical, of abandoning that yearning for wholeness. But by turning away from the new modes of scientific thought, they split the world in their own way. They also chose reductionism, by reducing the domain of God into a tiny private zone, giving up wholeness in their quest to preserve it."

understanding. Never mind the fuzzy meanings embodied by that very word, "holistic," in application to a wide range of undertakings. It has nevertheless become an ideological password. "Holistic" is the mark of an evolved consciousness and an open heart, a word of faith by which people pledge to look beyond the rational, embrace mystery, and promote life-giving alternatives to death-dealing science. At bottom, it is an incantation meant to protect us from the split atom.

YET THE SCIENTIFIC QUEST that split the atom was itself driven by a "holistic" sensibility, as embodied by Albert Einstein. "Einstein explicitly and frankly hoped for a theory that would ultimately be utterly comprehensive and completely unified," writes science historian Gerald Horton. "This vision drove him on from the special to the general theory, and then to the unified field theory. . . . Without doubt, something like an Ionian Enchantment, the commitment to the theme of grand unification, was upon Einstein."[23]

Einstein himself expressed it this way: "The eternally incomprehensible thing about the world is its comprehensibility." This led him to what he described as "a cosmic religious feeling" aroused by this "deep conviction of the rationality of the universe."[24] Corresponding in 1936 with a sixth-grade Sunday school student in New York, he elaborated: "Everyone who is seriously involved in the pursuit of science becomes convinced that a spirit is manifest in the laws of the Universe — a spirit vastly superior to that of man, and one in the face of which we with our modest powers must feel humble. In this way the pursuit of science leads to a religious feeling of a special sort, which is indeed quite different from the religiosity of someone more naïve."[25]

How ironic that this brilliant synthesizer of scientific knowledge and religious wonder should be responsible for facilitating the creation of the Bomb, the terrible "splitting" that would alienate an entire generation from the sciences!

---

23. Gerald Horton, *Einstein, History and Other Passions*, as cited.

24. See Einstein's *Ideas and Opinions*, translated by Sonja Bergmann, 1954, referenced in Horton's book.

25. See *Albert Einstein, the Human Side*, edited by Helen Dukas and Banesh Hoffman, Princeton University Press, 1979.

Lawrence Bush

Still, it was not Einstein, nor even the Bomb itself, that betrayed the Promethean spirit of science and replaced it with the Frankenstein monster. As Einstein explained in a 1945 Voice of America broadcast, "We helped in creating this new weapon [only] in order to prevent the enemies of mankind from achieving it ahead of us, which, given the mentality of the Nazis, would have meant inconceivable destruction, and the enslavement of the rest of the world."[26] Redeemed from that fate, the world, as he envisioned it, would take the next step and abolish war altogether — though this, he acknowledged, would "demand distasteful limitations to national sovereignty." In 1946, Einstein became chair of the newly formed Emergency Committee of Atomic Scientists. Throughout the next decade, he and several of his fellow scientists consistently spoke out in support of the United Nations, for mediation between the superpowers, and against the Cold War and nuclear proliferation. Ultimately, it was the political and military handlers of the communist-capitalist struggle, far more than his scientific peers, who scorned and betrayed Einstein's vision of science as a force for international redemption.

That betrayal went way beyond the Bomb and the 1950s. The radicals of my generation perceived clearly the enthrallment of science and scientists to the "military-industrial complex" of Eisenhower's description: how scientific research and development is largely funded and controlled by the Pentagon, weapons manufacturers, and corporate giants in pharmaceuticals, energy, chemicals, food, transportation and communications. The commingling of superpower militarism, profit motive and scientific quest has been highly effective and highly problematic — problematic, especially, for the integrity of some scientists, for the well-being of the environment, and for those who face, merciless weaponry if they dare to resist American political policy.

We have also been correct in criticizing the scientific world's insularity and lack of social vision: the lack of structured ethical discussion and decision-making about such potent and dangerous innovations

---

26. The Nazi onslaught has been viewed by some as the swan song of modernism and proof of the failure of humanism's promise. To view Nazism as humanistic, however, requires ignoring the occultism and mysticism that were blended with pseudo-scientific racial theories by Nazi ideology. See Dusty Sklar's 1977 book, *Gods and Beasts: The Nazis and the Occult* (Cromwell).

as genetic engineering or nuclear power; the lack of alternative to the profit motive and the anarchic marketplace as guardians of the scientific Pandora's Box; the lack of integration of "what we *can* do" with "what we *should* do."

The folly of the Woodstockers, however, has been to mistake the demonic visage of the mushroom cloud for the face of science itself. Fearfully shunning that face, we have fixed our gazes instead on "alternative ways of knowing" that are empowered simply by our yearning and our anger. These range from pre-modern astrology and faith healing to post-modern academic critiques of the very concepts of "objectivity" and "truth"; from political analyses that conflate science with capitalism and patriarchy[27] to mystical religious systems that conflate metaphor and reality. To me, our involvement with these enterprises seems little more than a latter-day version of our classroom air-raid drills: We are still pursuing fantasies under our desks, while outside the window, the "military-industrial complex" harnesses science to transform and rule the world.

AS I INVOKE ALBERT EINSTEIN'S NAME and make skeptical pronouncements about "holism," it is impossible for me not to hear echoes of my father's voice. Dad kept a bust of the great physicist in our home and claimed to share in Einstein's sense of wonder at the exquisite workings of the universe. All through the heady 1960s and '70s, the generational split in the perception of science that I have described in this chapter would play out in my family, as I challenged my father's rationalism with various mystical rumors and intimations: Wasn't it *possible* that the Maharishi Mahesh Yogi could levitate,[28] couldn't my dad be *open-minded* about extrasensory perception, couldn't there be imperceptible influences beyond scientific measurement that might account for miraculous cancer cures? He would shake his head, throw

---

27. A full and provocative discussion of the academic post-modern and feminist critiques of science is found in Paul R. Gross and Norman Levitt's *Higher Superstition: The Academic Left and Its Quarrels with Science*, 1994.

28. Teacher and millionaire proprietor of Transcendental Meditation, the Mahareshi Mahesh Yogi briefly became guru to the Beatles and ended up the lead character in their song, "Fool on the Hill." In the early 1980s, TM began offering instructional classes in levitation to advanced practitioners.

the burden of proof back onto the shoulders of the irrationalists, and then speak rhapsodically of his own sense of awe and mystery. The ecology of the universe, and the inner workings of the human being, Dad would say, were so fantastically complex as to be belittled by all simplistic schemata — but I should rest assured that a commitment to atheism and skepticism did not mandate a lack of joy or a lack of feeling for nature and for fellow human beings.

In fact, my father was a curmudgeon, irritable and morose, who clung addictively to his intellectual life to avoid intimacy and escape the frustrations of his marriage, his family and his work. Dad did not fish or play the violin like his hero, and his sense of awe and wonder seemed to be an intellectual construct more than a deeply felt response to the natural world. To this day, more than twenty-five years after his death, when I encounter nature most intensely — in viewing the Northern Lights, or camping and hiking in the Pacific Redwoods, the Grand Canyon or other astounding spots in America — I miss my father acutely, not for the loss of a shared bond of rapture, but for our having never shared such rapture at all.

"The soul of man does not thrive on godlessness," wrote philosopher Harry Wolfson in the *Menorah Journal* in 1921. For my father, at least, Wolfson's observation seemed painfully true. Humanism offered my dad a belief system — or, perhaps more accurately, a counter-belief system — but no program for the thriving of his soul, the thawing of his personality, the heightening of his inner peace and contentment. To my knowledge, there was simply no analogy in the humanistic communities of his day to the Catholic sacrament of confession, the Jewish practice of prayer and *teshuvah* (repentance), the Buddhist discipline of meditation, or other religious traditions' regularly scheduled rituals of self-revelation, mental training and emotional expurgation. Psychotherapy, in all its variations, is the closest he might have had to a humanistic equivalent — but unlike religious rituals, therapy has no context of communal bonding and social approval,[29] no mystique of

---

29. To the contrary, psychotherapy remains heavily stigmatized in our culture. During the presidential primary campaign for president in 2000, for example, Sen. John McCain proudly pointed to his lack of psychotherapeutic care following seven years of torture and imprisonment in Vietnam as evidence of his emotional fitness to serve as president!

virtue and piety, no fixed place on the calendar, no formal, prescriptive structure, and little ideological imperative beyond "know thyself." Therapy, moreover, is expensive — and, as a marketplace transaction, it lacks something in the way of dignity.

Of course, I cannot personally attest to the actual therapeutic power of religious rituals, since I have generally used my atheism to excuse myself from pursuing any of them with discipline and regularity. In fact, I distrust the sense of instant intimacy and community that can be generated through the *gestalt* of communal prayer, song, or confession; too often we have seen it exploited by religious and political cults (and governments!) to break down individuals' personalities and create a dangerous state of enthrallment and codependence. Nevertheless, the lack of transformative rituals in humanistic movements seems to me one of their major weaknesses, for when I envision the good and just society, I see not only a chicken in every pot, but a therapist on every corner. Without that presence, without the embrace of processes of psychological healing, we will be unable to break the cycle of abuse and mean-spiritedness that trap so many of us, from generation to generation, in angry, punitive attitudes — attitudes that breed violence, abuse, and political reaction and make social progress almost impossible.

There is a leap of faith implicit in this vision of mine: faith in the human capacity to change, faith in the validity and usefulness of at least some therapeutic theories and modalities, and faith in the superior value of the "examined life" over the "unexamined life" for the individual and for society at large. Perhaps such "faith" even marks me as something other than an atheist; as we will see in my chapter on Mordecai Kaplan in Part Two, belief in the potential for human goodness and redemption is sufficient to mark you as a "believer," according to some of the favored theologies of the Woodstockers. As a committed skeptic, I should unpack these articles of faith and determine if there's any real evidence to support them. Are my suppositions merely those of a Woodstocker titillated by the "human potential" movements of the 1960s and '70s (who happens to have a lot of good friends who have participated in psychotherapy both as clients and therapists)?

Whether my concept of a "therapeutic society" is valid or fantastic or somewhere in between, the fact remains that my parents' generation of radical activists largely conceded the field of personal transformation to religious communities. Marxists, in particular, tended to exile the idea of personal growth to the revolutionary hinterlands, where it would have to wait for the economic reordering of society. Since Marxist theories of economically driven culture and consciousness are directly challenged by psychological perspectives on human behavior, those who made a religion of Marxism would have had reason to denounce psychological perspectives as "bourgeois" theories.[30]

Communists were not alone among humanistic communities in their failure to deal with "personal growth" issues. The American Humanist Association, for example, in its "Humanist Manifesto II" (1973), got no closer than to say that rationalism should be "balanced with compassion and empathy and the whole person fulfilled" and that "Practicing humanists should make it their vocation to humanize personal relations." Their original "Humanist Manifesto" (1933) declared "the complete realization of human personality to be the end [goal] of man's life," yet failed to parlay the idea into a set of rituals or techniques. The eloquent "Humanist Manifesto 2000" similarly fails to wrestle with this need, instead restricting itself to the affirmation of "empathy and caring" as "essential for ethical conduct," and of "the core principle" that "each person should be afforded the opportunity to realize his or her own personal fulfillment" — with the disclaimer that "this actual realization depends on the individual and not on society." Nowhere is there mention of confession, self-examination, forgiveness, reconciliation, renewal, intimacy, meditation, or other tools of personal growth. Even while the Humanist Manifesto 2000 holds forth a detailed plan

---

30. Communists often found their own needs for engagement and identity met by the verve and camaraderie of their activism. As my fellow red-diaper baby (child of communists) Vivian Gornick writes in *The Romance of American Communism* (1977): "When these people sat down at the kitchen table to talk, Politics sat down with them, Ideas sat down with them, above all, History sat down with them . . . the more each one identified himself or herself with the working-class movement, the more each one came individually alive. The more each one acknowledged his or her condition as one of binding connectedness, the more each one pushed back the darkness and experienced the life within." However, excitement and fervor do not necessarily add up to personal growth or psychological wholeness. One of Gornick's contacts confessed: "I associate my years in the Party with years of not knowing who or what the hell I was. I associate them with guilt, conflict, apprehension, divided feelings, a fatal kind of unknowingness."

"for peace, dignity and freedom in the global human family," it leaves, by default, rituals of personal growth entirely in the hands of religious institutions and psychotherapists.[31]

Intellectualizations were therefore all that humanist movements seemed to be offering at the time when the baby boomers, destabilized by the nuclearism of the 1950s and '60s, and reshaped by whirlwinds of social change, came questing for transcendence and emotional peace. Deeply uncomfortable with ritual, most humanist organizations and their representatives, like my father, could only talk the talk. But we wanted also to walk the walk. We wanted transformation. We wanted rapture.

31. The Humanist Manifesto 2000 was drafted by Paul Kurtz and published in the Fall, 1999 issue of the magazine he edits, *Free Inquiry* (Vol. 19, No. 4). Signatories include Edward O. Wilson, Richard Dawkins, Arthur C. Clarke, nine Nobel Laureates, and scientists, activists, writers and academics from twenty-five countries.

L a w r e n c e   B u s h

Chapter Two

The Psychedelic Seed

"Timothy Leary's dead.
No, no, no, no, he's outside
looking in."
— Ray Thomas, "Legend of a Mind"

HERE WAS OUR RAPTURE: to lick a piece of chemically stained blotter paper and spend the next six to eight hours in a state of exaltation, hallucination and altered consciousness that religious mystics down through the ages have achieved only through years of prayer, meditation, isolation, or self-mortification.

Under the influence of LSD, I suddenly apprehended cubism as a form of realism. I spent a full hour examining the exquisite symmetry of a dew-hung spiderweb. I stayed up all night and watched the daylight spread through a stony, littered New York cityscape. I wept about the pain that I perceived in the faces and body language of passersby. I even became Jesus Christ for one night, and emerged from this minipsychosis with insights into the roots of my own egotism and messianism that might have taken years of therapy to uncover.[32]

The creative metaphysics of LSD trips were wondrous and alluring — but also totally unnerving to me. So much of the psychedelic experience seemed tinged with madness! The greatly intensified sense of metaphor, and the blurring of distinctions between symbol and reality; the powerful "perception" of what was real and illusory, natural and artificial, holy and profane, and the manic longing to organize these insights into a redemptive system; the intimations of an ethically and aesthetically structured universe, in which human decisions would

---

32. The experience is more fully described in Chapter Five. Readers can refer to my articles, "Drugs and Jewish Spirituality" in *Tikkun*, May/June 1999 (anthologized in *Hallucinogens: A Reader*, edited by Charles S. Grob, 2005), and "Messiah and Me," *Genesis 2*, Winter 1988/89.

have ultimate measure — each of these "insights" wrought by LSD presented a powerful challenge to my young and immature mind, and I would wrestle with what I had "seen" or intuited for days after, worrying about its existential meaning.

Is there a Cause to serve beyond personal aggrandizement?

Is it possible that illness is a metaphor, a revelation of inner psycho-spiritual distress?

Could it be that the smiling dog who crossed my path was actually a messenger — with a message sent, and simply not received? Might there be a coherence to the universe that our brains are simply too stunted to apprehend — the way a dog cannot comprehend arithmetic? Is my rationalism simply the barking of a dog? (And why is "God," "dog" spelled backwards?!)

Perhaps most worrisome of all was the dissolution of ego borders that I experienced repeatedly on LSD, the perception of my "self" as a construct, less than fully real. "Bouncing ego can't be free, boundless ego won't be me," I fretted in a poem written at age 16 (by which time I had already tripped half a dozen times), in response to these intimations of mystical union that the drug induced.[33]

In the late 1960s, similar experiences were landing my contemporaries in ashrams, cults, and mental hospitals by the thousands. Fortunately, I lacked the faith to make any such "commitment." Because of my personal wiring and family history, I could not surrender my rationalism to the seduction of LSD. Instead, like the Hebrew people

---

33. "Protoplas me in a cell.
   If it bursts my life is gone . . .
   Harry Christmas, Harry Christmas,
   Christmas Christmas, Harry, Harry.
   Karma keep me safe in hell.
   Burning womb, I am reborn.
   Harry's grandma, Harry's grandma,
   Grandma grandma, Harry Harry.
   Bouncing ego can't be free.
   Boundless ego won't be me.
   Eeny meany miney moe
   Catch a tiger by the toe.
   Ever since I ate my shit
   I've been afraid of losing it.
   My mother says to pick this one
   And out goes Y-O-U."

at the foot of Mount Sinai, I "fell back and stood at a distance" ("Let not God speak to us, lest we die," they say in *Exodus* 20:15-16). By age 20, I had left psychedelic drugs behind, less with a sense of relief than with a sense of failure, incompleteness, and envy for those free spirits who *could* safely ascend the mountain.

In truth, the biblical imagery I've just used would not have occurred to me during my psychedelic days, when I identified far more with the Woodstock Nation than with the Jewish People. During my subsequent years of work as a writer and editor in the Jewish community, however, I began to suspect that many of the most innovative and influential theologians and teachers of my own generation of Jews — folks who were not only reviving Judaism, but revitalizing and reinventing it — had been initially inspired in their religious activism by psychedelic drug experiences. In a series of interviews a few years ago, I confirmed this hunch.

I spoke to Rabbi N., for example, an executive within Jewish congregational life, who turned out to have tripped on LSD and mescaline several times annually for a twelve-year period before entering rabbinical school. Rabbi N. told me that his drug experiences (he is still a regular user of marijuana and hashish) had opened him up "for prayer experiences and a relationship to God — there are even similar feelings of community in getting high with people and praying with them. There should be a way," he added, "to allow marijuana and psychedelics to expand people's spiritual consciousness in a safe environment."

Rabbi C., a prolific author, never took LSD during the '60s heyday but waited two decades until he was in his late forties. With his own rabbi serving as his (drug-free) "guide," C. spent some six hours rapturously experiencing the Revelation at Sinai. He had an overpowering sense of oceanic union with God; he could "see" the entire cosmos, micro and macro, and experienced what he described to me as "an unbearable feeling" of having his own boundaries stretched to encompass it all. This piercing perception of the infinitesimal yet infinite nature of his individual identity was accompanied by an overpowering infusion of faith, a certainty about there being meaning in the universe and interconnection among all life. The experience has served as the bedrock of Rabbi C.'s theology for the rest of his influential career.

"What I encountered and felt," he reported to me, "was not unreal or less real but *more* real than my daily perceptions. I've never felt any other way about it."

B., a Jewish educator and day school principal, told me that she took psychedelic drugs about a dozen times, "always with a sense of spiritual mission." She remembered with particular fondness a Shavuot (the festival that celebrates the giving of the Torah at Mt. Sinai) some thirty years ago, when she and three other women, all prominent in Jewish religious life today, "borrowed" a Torah scroll from a day school, took it to a state park, ate hallucinogenic mushrooms and spent the day "reading Torah along with woodland creatures, frogs and deer" who "came out and participated!" B. admitted that "the fact of connectedness or 'oneness' that the *Shema*[34] expresses first became clear to me on LSD."

F., a successful writer and editor of religious books, told me that he had numerous psychedelic experiences in the 1970s. "I look back on nearly all of them with great awe and respect," he said. "Each time was a 'big occasion' with a consistent teaching: that there are all kinds of things going on in the spectrum that our normal waking consciousness doesn't pick up. It's like a dog whistle. Your ear doesn't hear all the frequencies. But with each 'awakening' there is some residue left in the senses."

Rabbi S., who heads a vibrant congregation in the Northeast, underwent two LSD trips, one during college and one shortly after graduation. He told me that they strongly influenced his later rabbinical practice. "I remember sitting outside my apartment in the snow," he said, "drawing a circle in the snow to make a pie, putting jelly on it, cutting up slices and eating them. Looking through the patio doors of the next apartment, I saw a very fancy cocktail party." Rabbi S. was struck by the ways in which both his "party" and the cocktail party were contrivances. "I realized at that moment that every social interaction is a construct, a kind of pretense. The perception didn't require me to 'drop out,' but it did help me become radically unregimented as a rabbi. I saw that there is no particular activity or time that has a

---

34. The *Shema* is the fundamental Jewish avowal of the unity of God, which is recited at many junctures in life, including at the point of death. It is translated as, "Hear, O, Israel, the Lord our God, the Lord is One."

Lawrence Bush

meaning beyond that which we humans have attached to it. Nothing is sacred, in other words, except when we choose to make it sacred — which is something I really value and love doing."

GRANTED, THESE ARE AMONG the more radical leaders in contemporary Jewish life, both theologically and in their orientation towards ritual and liturgy. They are hardly alone among Woodstockers, however, in their experiments with psychedelic drugs and their positive associations between those experiments and their spirituality. According to statistics from the U.S. Department of Justice, in 1975, 16 percent of high school seniors reported having using LSD at least once; by 1980, the total rose to 25 percent. On college campuses, where students had much more freedom, autonomy, and dynamic identification with the counterculture, the rate was undoubtedly as high or higher.[35] Factor in the use of other psychedelic drugs, as well as the very widespread use of marijuana and hashish, and you have among the baby-boom generation a large plurality that has experienced the psychedelic, i.e., "mind-opening," impact of drug use.

Not all of this impact was religiously-oriented, of course. Once the substances were removed from the psychology laboratory and placed on the list of banned narcotics (LSD was fully outlawed in 1967), their recreational use at parties, concerts, festivals, and other social events predominated. According to researchers Walter N. Pahnke and William A. Richards, "As mystical consciousness is seldom entered [under the influence of LSD] without serious preparation and a quiet, reverent atmosphere, we may suggest that the experiences of most people at 'LSD parties' are of an aesthetic [sensual, not mystical] nature."[36]

Yet even for those who never approached the most exalted plateaus

---

35. In 1974, 17 percent of all Americans reported having used an hallucinogen at least once in their lifetime. Statistics from "Rise of Hallucinogen Use," by Dana Hunt, October, 1997, National Institute of Justice, U.S. Department of Justice, www.serendipity.li/dmt/166607.html.

36. Walter N. Pahnke and William A. Richards, "Implications of LSD and Experimental Mysticism," *Journal of Religion and Health*, Vol. 5, 1966, available online at: www.druglibrary.org/schaffer/lsd/pahnke4.htm. At the time of his death in 1972, Pahnke was Director of Clinical Sciences at Maryland Psychiatric Research Center.

of LSD mysticism — including that bulk of baby boomers who experimented with marijuana and hashish without "graduating" to LSD — "getting high" certainly included potentially transformative experiences. People stoned on marijuana, for example, often are seized by powerful emotions such as uproarious laughter or loving feelings or deep sadness or uneasy paranoia. There can be a therapeutic aspect to these outbursts, as they provide a refreshing perspective on the scripted quality of our normal mental states and a mother lode of thoughts, feelings and associations worthy of analysis. Pot also tends to induce a moment-by-moment self-consciousness, a stream of metacognition and self-commentary that challenges our constructs of "personality." By wading in this stream, people may become aware of the fears and inhibitions that keep them clinging to roles, attitudes, and schedules. They may escape depression or anger or other immobilizing feelings long enough to revitalize other dimensions of their inner lives. They can then reintegrate themselves with a renewed energy for their relationships and their lives.

Many people would describe the mental excitement of the marijuana/hashish experience as "spiritual." Their sense of metaphor, symbol and meaning may become enlarged in engrossing ways that point to patterns of interconnection. The inner voice of metacognition may seem an outer voice, a voice of guidance "from the universe." To borrow my editor friend's metaphor, people on pot are alert to the dog whistle: "all kinds of things going on in the spectrum that our normal waking consciousness doesn't pick up."

It was really as a generation, therefore, that Woodstockers experienced their rough-and-tumble religious awakening. Drugs provided a widespread experience of spirituality and even mysticism on a par with the "Great Awakening" of early American Methodism or any other wave of evangelical revivalism that has swept the country. Drug use took place within a unique social context of general promiscuity and license, and was viewed as a sign of enlightened membership in the pace-setting community. Even those baby boomers who never took psychedelics were influenced by the creative culture and utopian philosophies of the psychedelic community, and in particular by the music and art of the '60s, which often communicated the perceptual impact of the drugs.[37]

THE CORE ELEMENTS of that impact were neatly detailed in the article by Pahnke and Richards cited above, published in 1966, which cited, in nine compact categories, the types of mystical consciousness associated with LSD use. In brief, these are:

1. "Unity" — "the empirical ego [i.e., the sense of self] seems to die away or fade away while pure consciousness of what is being experienced paradoxically remains and seems to expand as a vast inner world is encountered."

2. "Objectivity and Reality" — "Insightful knowledge or illumination about being or existence in general" is "felt at an intuitive, non-rational level and gained by direct experience, " and there is "certainty . . . that such knowledge is truly or ultimately real," not "a subjective delusion."

3. "Transcendence of Space and Time" — "a radical change in perspective in which [the subject] suddenly feels . . . outside of time, in eternity or infinity, beyond both past and future."

4. "Sense of Sacredness" — "a nonrational, intuitive, hushed, palpitant response in the presence of inspiring realities. . . . a profound sense of holiness and sacredness that is felt to be at a more basic level than any religious or philosophical concepts held by the experiencer."

5. "Deeply-Felt Positive Mood" — described by one of their research subjects as "cosmic tenderness, infinite love, penetrating peace, eternal blessing and unconditional acceptance on one hand, and on the other . . . unspeakable awe, overflowing joy, primeval humility, inexpressible gratitude and boundless devotion."

6. "Paradoxicality" — "significant aspects of mystical consciousness are felt by the experiencer to be true in spite of the fact that they violate

---

37. "One pill makes you larger, and one pill makes you small," sang Grace Slick in the Jefferson Airplane's retelling of the experiences of Alice in Wonderland. "Picture yourself on a boat on a river, with tangerine trees and marmelade skies," suggested the Beatles in "Lucy in the Sky with Diamonds." (John Lennon insisted the song was not about LSD, but ooh, those first initials!) "We have all been here before, we have all been here before," chanted Crosby, Stills, Nash and Young on "Deja Vu." "Electrical banana is bound to be the very next phase," suggested Donovan in "Mellow Yellow" — which prompted me and friends to try smoking dried banana peel, just to find out.

the laws of . . . logic."

7. "Alleged Ineffability" — "When a subject attempts to communicate mystical consciousness verbally to another person, he [sic] usually claims that the available linguistic symbols — if not the structure of language itself — are inadequate . . ."

8. "Transiency" — "the mystical state of consciousness is not sustained indefinitely," which "marks one of the important differences between it and psychosis."

9. "Positive changes in attitude and/or behavior" — "Increased personality integration is reported, including a renewed sense of personal worth coupled with a relaxation of habitual mechanisms of ego defense."

Generic descriptions of mystical union such as these could apply equally to the experiences of Abraham Abulafia (13th-century Jewish kabbalist), and Theresa of Avila (16th-century Roman Catholic saint), Milarepa (10th-11th-century Tibetan Buddhist), and al Ghazali (11th-century Islamic theologian), Black Elk (20th-century Oglala shaman), and Starhawk (contemporary Witch). With the advent of LSD, however, what was once available, after years of practice and dedication, only to a disciplined, questing elite, was "democratized" and made accessible to an entire privileged generation.

It was this capacity of LSD to induce mystical experiences that elicited, according to Richards and Pahnke, "the most enthusiastic interest as well as the most indignant rebuttal from both psychiatric and theological spokesmen . . ." Respectful though they were towards these "indignant rebuttals," the two researchers could not restrain their enthusiasm about the religious potential of psychedelic drugs. The easy accessibility of drug-induced mystical consciousness, they suggested, might even make it a superior path to the time-honored tools of asceticism, sensory deprivation, meditation, fasting and so on; the rapid, transformational impact would enable people to "enjoy the enriched life," to use "the inner strength to cope with suffering and struggle in society," and to "serve other persons during the greater part of [one's] life" rather than spending a cloistered life in pursuit of a "natural" mystical high.

Pahnke and Richards were similarly positive about the potential use of psychedelic drugs in psychiatry.[38] They prophetically argued that the legal suppression of psychedelics would only heighten black-market usage and attract "more interest and curiosity from the very people who should not take the drugs," people who would use them "without psychiatric screening, preparation, supervision, or follow-up therapy." Ultimately, Pahnke and Richards wished for the scientific community to embrace LSD as a tool of awesome potential for human understanding and transformation. Their article represents the most positive and mature sector of opinion about psychedelics from the heyday of baby-boomer experimentation.

FORTY YEARS LATER, psychedelic research is now enjoying a small comeback. In 2005, Harvard University approved a research project investigating the impact of MDMA (proscribed in 1986, MDMA is known on the street as Ecstasy) upon the anxieties of terminally ill patients. Israel is also investigating MDMA, which is a serotonin-up-take inhibitor, as a treatment for post-traumatic stress disorder, and other universities in the U.S. and Europe are engaged in psychological

---

38. In the 1971 edition of *Psychedelic Review* (Number 11), Pahnke wrote about the therapeutic use of LSD with terminally ill patients. "Our experiments have indicated," he wrote, "that deep within every human being there are vast usually untapped resources of love, joy and peace. One aspect of the psychedelic mystical experience is a release of these positive feelings with subsequent decrease in negative feelings of depression, despair and anxiety. But this shift in mood is not enough to account for our most dramatic finding — loss of the fear of death. . . . Our data show that these feelings are released most fully when there is complete surrender to the ego-loss experience of positive ego transcendence, which is often experienced as a moment of death and rebirth. At this point, unless the patient . . . becomes intensely aware of completely new dimensions of experience . . . he [sic] now knows that there is more to the potential range of human consciousness than we ordinarily realize. This profound and awe-inspiring insight sometimes is experienced as if a veil had been lifted and can transform attitude and behavior. Once a person has had this vision, life and death can be looked at from a new perspective. Patients seem able to meet the unknown with a new sense of self-confidence and security."

research involving psychedelics and psychopathology.[39]

In November, 2005, I investigated this trend by interviewing four leading psychedelic researchers for *Jewish Currents*, the magazine I edit. I spoke to Dr. Charles Grob, UCLA professor of psychiatry and pediatrics, who is investigating the therapeutic use of MDMA, psilocybin and other psychedelics for the treatment of alcoholism and for palliative use by terminally ill patients; Howard Lotsof, who advocates the use of ibogaine to treat opiatic drug addiction; Dr. Julie Holland, a psychiatrist at Bellevue Hospital, who believes that MDMA may be a highly effective tool for psychotherapy; and Rick Doblin, founder and president of the Multidisciplinary Association for Psychedelic Studies (MAPS), a research, activist and funding group.

As researchers dealing with alcoholism, terminal illness, and psychopathology, they were reluctant to endanger their work by publicly speculating about the value of psychedelics as tools of mystical elevation or social transformation. "Many people had experiences that positively influenced the course of their lives," conceded Charles Grob. "But we can't lose sight of the fact that there were people who went off the deep end and never came back." Rick Doblin, however — who operates independently of any university or hospital — indicated that his goal with psychedelic drugs is, indeed, "to transform society."[40] "I do think

---

39. The *New York Times* on March 12, 2001 reported a resurgence of interest among neurologists and psychiatrists in psychedelic drugs as possible tools for treating mental disorders. Purdue University's Dr. David E. Nichols, wrote Sandra Blakeslee, "said there were reports that symptoms of obsessive compulsive disorder . . . subside under the influence of psilocybin, a hallucinogen derived from mushrooms. . . . Dying patients given LSD have reported less pain and less fear, he said. Ayahuasca (a Brazilian plant extract) and peyote (derived from cactus) have reported helped alcoholics stay sober." Blakeslee continues: "Much has changed in the half-century since LSD was first used by psychiatrists and then found widespread recreational use in the 1960s and '70s. Modern psychiatry has embraced drugs that affect the same brain molecules that are tweaked by hallucinogens. . . . Moreover, many of the people who hold political and scientific power today came of age during the 1960s, and they, unlike their parents, are not as afraid of hallucinogens, Dr. Nichols said."

40. "Just Say Maybe: Psychedelic Drugs, Healing and Politics," in *Jewish Currents*, November-December, 2005. "At this point," argued Grob, "it's essential that

L a w r e n c e   B u s h

that large-scale social change can be motivated by that unitive mystical experience," Doblin explained, "because once you have identified 'across boundaries,' it's less possible to get involved in scapegoating or demonizing others . . . "

For all of the transformative potential of psychedelic mysticism, however, there is clearly a cognitive danger associated with the experience — and, I would guess, with mysticism of any variety. Richards and Pahnke identified it in their research as Category 2, "Objectivity and Reality" — the "certainty . . . that such knowledge is truly or ultimately real" — and as Category 6, "Paradoxicality" — "significant aspects of mystical consciousness are felt by the experiencer to be true in spite of the fact that they violate the laws of . . . logic." Rick Doblin described it to me as "the self-confirmatory" aspect of "the unitive experience," which he summarized as: "This is *so* true!" Or, as Rabbi C. the theologian told me: "What I encountered and felt" under the influence of LSD "was . . . *more* real than my daily perception of reality."

Perhaps such a surrender of skepticism and doubt is a critical catalyst to the positive changes among LSD users reported by Pahnke and Richards ("increased personality integration," and so on): Not only do the users have a transportive sensory, emotional and psychological experience, but they grant it the force of revelation. Mystics throughout

---

we focus on their potential utilization in a therapeutic context. If psychoactive drugs are ever to achieve legal status, there will no doubt be credentials that individual practitioners will have to apply for before they could legally administer them in treatment." It was striking that all four of the interviewees were Jewish and that Jews have been disproportionately involved in psychedelic experimentation and research. Grob, who is the editor of *Hallucinogens: A Reader* (2002) and *Higher Wisdom: Eminent Elders Explore the Continuing Impact of Psychedelics* (2006), described himself to me as "a direct descendant of a long line of rabbis going back forty generations to Rashi" and saw his work with psychedelics and MDMA as "coming from the tradition of healing, the tradition of compassion, the tradition of service, the tradition of exploring religious experience, all bound up with my Jewish identity." Rick Doblin observed that "there is a large percentage of Jews in science, but even a larger percentage in psychiatry. I think this Jewish focus on diseases of the mind reflects our own history of being victims of cultural insanity and irrationality for so long. . . . I would say that my work with psychedelics was motivated primarily as a response to the Holocaust."

the ages have affirmed this, that they have not merely experienced hallucinations or altered states of consciousness but have actually gotten in touch with some underlying "super intelligence" or "force of love" or "absolute reality" or "presence of God." They believe that the "unity" perceived while intoxicated, that profound sense of ego dissolution and oceanic union, is actually *more* real, more fundamental to the fabric of reality, than what we daily experience as separateness, boundary and polarity. Mysticism has thus historically served as a form of *personal witness* to God's existence. While mystical testimonials have been both enshrined and repressed, depending on their heretical and populist content, their cumulative effect across the spectrum of world religions has been to give credibility to theological and metaphysical belief systems as the plain evidence of the senses: "The spirit of the Lord has spoken through me,/ His message is on my tongue . . ." (*II Samuel* 23: 2).

The more deeply one investigates the metaphysical beliefs of psychedelic mystics of the Woodstock generation, however, the more skeptical one becomes about interpreting their mystical experiences as the products of divine outreach or as reliable testimony about metaphysical realities. For example, in John Horgan's very adventurous book of encounters with psychedelic investigators, *Rational Mysticism*, we learn about the far-out beliefs of one veteran, the late Terence McKenna, who states that psilocybin mushrooms come "from outside the terrestrial ecosystem" and that "existence emerges from the clash of two forces, not good and evil but habit and novelty," with "novelty winning."[41] Other notable contemporary mystics such as Aldous Huxley, Huston Smith, and Ken Wilbur have all suggested, according to Horgan, that "mystical knowledge may awaken latent paranormal capacities . . . [such as] extrasensory perception, telekinesis, and other

41. John Horgan, *Rational Mysticism: Spirituality Meets Science in the Search for Enlightenment*, 2003. Horgan further quotes Terence McKenna in a somewhat self-mocking vein, speaking about another of his bizarre theories: "The notion of some kind of fantastically complicated visionary revelation that happens to put one at the very center of the action is a symptom of mental illness. [My timewave] theory does that, and yet so does immediate experience, and so do the ontologies of Judaism, Islam, and Christianity. My theory may be clinically pathological, but unlike these religious systems, I have enough humor to realize this." McKenna died in 2000 at age 52.

psychic effects."[42]

Horgan concludes that "belief in extrasensory perception, telekinesis, and other psychic effects" seems "a logical consequence of the mystical doctrine . . . that mind rather than matter constitutes the primary level of reality." His reports reinforce my sense that psychedelic drugs, as well as other tools of mystical access, strongly excite what Edward O. Wilson calls "the symbol-forming human mind"[43] and drive people to systematize new insights into belief systems, however outlandish or lunatic they may be.

Still, even certain scientists engaged in the exploration of the biological foundations of mysticism have construed the mystical experience as an actual "glimpse of God." In *Why God Won't Go Away*, Drs. Andrew Newberg and the late Eugene D'Aquili describe their attempts to map the mystical experience in the laboratory. Newberg and D'Aquili took SPECT camera photographs of devout Buddhist practitioners at the height of their meditations and Franciscan nuns caught up in devotional prayer.[44] These photos, they say, indicate that the state of mystical union involves the quieting of the orientation association area of the brain (OAA), located in the posterior superior parietal lobe — "a small lump of gray matter nestled in the top rear section of the brain." The main job of the OAA, as they describe it,

---

42. There isn't room here to enter into discussion about the lack of reliable scientific evidence for mental telepathy and telekinesis, distant viewing, and so on, but the scientific testimony against the existence of such paranormal phenomena is voluminous. In my experience, however, many Woodstockers either believe in paranormal psychic powers or at least "keep an open mind" about them and feel strong antipathy for people who don't. For discussion of skeptic and stage magician James Randi's unclaimed $1 million offer to anyone who can demonstrate psychic phenomena in his presence under mutually agreed-upon conditions, see Chapter 4.

43. Edward O. Wilson, *Consilence*, 1998.

44. Andrew Newberg and Eugene D'Aquili, *Why God Won't Go Away, Brain Science and the Biology of Belief*, 2001. SPECT stands for "single photon emission computer tomography," an imaging tool that accurately shows blood-flow patterns in the brain. Newberg and D'Aquili's work has been sharply challenged as simplistic by Dr. Jensine Andresen of Boston University and others, according to John Horgan's *Rational Mysticism*.

is to orient the individual in physical space — it keeps track of which end is up, helps us judge angles and distances, and allows us to negotiate safely the dangerous physical landscape around us. To perform this crucial function, it must first generate a clear, consistent cognition of the physical limits of the self . . . to sort you out from the infinite not-you . . .

Newberg and D'Aquili believe that when the OAA is dramatically quieted by spiritual activity such as prayer or meditation, the brain interprets "its failure to find the borderline between the self and the outside world . . . to mean that such a distinction doesn't exist . . ." The brain then perceives the self as "endless and intimately interwoven with everyone and everything the mind senses. And this perception . . . feel[s] utterly and unquestionably real."

Why God Won't Go Away details the structure of the brain and how its "systems," "association areas" and "operators" function during times of spiritual arousal. The experience of transcendence, they speculate, "may have arisen from the neural circuitry that evolved for mating and sexual experience." Despite their belief that they have placed mysticism within the structure of the brain and human evolutionary history, however, Newberg and D'Aquili go on to elevate neurology into neurotheology by speculating that these structural capacities may be an evolutionary gift that permits us, uniquely among the species, to commune with an "absolute, universal reality" that actually may exist outside the boundaries of the brain.

> After years of scientific study, and careful consideration of our results, [we believe] that we saw evidence of a neurological process that has evolved to allow us humans to transcend material existence and acknowledge and connect with a deeper, more spiritual part of ourselves perceived of as an absolute, universal reality that connects us to all that is.

They stay within my boundaries of skepticism by confining their theology to belief in "a deeper, more spiritual part of ourselves." Yet much of the second half of their book is devoted to resurrecting rather classic arguments positing an external-to-the-brain existence of a Deity. While "all spirituality and any experience of the reality of God [can] be reduced," they write, "to a fleeting rush of electro-chemical blips and flashes, racing along the neural pathways of the brain, brain science can neither prove nor disprove the existence of God, at least not with simple answers."

Granted, their research does not and cannot "disprove the existence of God" — but does it not even shift the burden of proof from the deniers to the believers? To me, the research of Newberg and D'Aquili, like so much else in modern science, suggests that seeing (or perceiving or feeling) is *not* believing — that human sensory and mental experience, and especially the interpretations we lend to it, are *not* to be taken at face value. If a small shift in our biochemistry can fool the brain into interpreting "its failure to find the borderline between the self and the outside world . . . to mean that such a distinction doesn't exist," which in turn yields a mystical sense of being "endless and intimately interwoven with everyone and everything," why should we favor this perceptual experience as somehow *more real* than that usually-perceived borderline?

It may be that the experience of mystical union is extremely *valuable* for human society, as I will discuss shortly. But the time-honored interpretation of mysticism as an eyewitness testimonial to an abiding (if coy) Divine presence becomes a lot less than convincing when the same God is making casual appearances at rock concerts or finding his home, in Newberg and D'Aquili's words, within "the mechanism of the sexual response."[45] This is, at best, a déclassé Deity.

THE WIDESPREAD TENDENCY to interpret mystical subjectivity as an actual map of hidden reality had enormous cultural implications for the Woodstockers. It meant that, in addition to experiencing emotional openings, aesthetic awakenings, and radical shifts in their perception of

---

45. "Mystical experiences," writes John Horgan, surveying Newberg and D'Aquili's work in *Rational Mysticism*, "can be induced by rhythmic activities, as orgasms are; orgasms trigger the simultaneous activation of our arousal and quiescent systems, as unitive experiences do. . . Through some evolutionary quirk, perhaps, our orgasmic capacity gave rise to our mystical capacity."

society, thousands of baby boomers were beguiled by LSD into states of gullibility, lack of discernment and otherworldliness. Tingling with drug-induced perceptions of a reality greater than our bounded, material world, and swooning with the will to believe, the Woodstockers quickly attracted a crew of religious entrepreneurs peddling various brews of Eastern and Native American mysticism.

A leading influence was Carlos Castaneda, who weighed in between 1968 and his death in 1997 with a best-selling series of books about his magician teacher, a Yaqui Indian named Don Juan. Castaneda's books treated psychedelic substances as tools for plugging into unseen realities and paranormal powers — including the power to fly. The first of the series, *The Teachings of Don Juan,* was presented as a scholarly, factual thesis in anthropology, yet Castaneda was describing events that totally defied rationality. It was not until his books achieved best-seller status that critics suggested that they were fictional — a charge never disproved, even while Castaneda became a "shaman" in his own right and achieved great wealth and mystique.[46] The question of whether his narratives were fact or metaphor bedeviled me throughout my psychedelic years, until my rationality won out (Don Juan's purported ability to fly went beyond my sense of plausibility), and I became convinced that the books were simply wonderful and engrossing works of the imagination. Millions of my peers who had not been raised as atheist skeptics, however, were bewitched rather than bedeviled by Castaneda.

Meanwhile, the Maharishi Mahesh Yogi (Transcendental Meditation), Guru Maharaj Ji (The Divine Light Mission), Rajneesh Chandra Mohan (a.k.a. Bhagwan), Chögyam Trungpa (Naropa Institute) and many other gurus, yogis and avatars were introducing varieties of Vedic and Buddhist mysticism, meditation and myth to the United States — and meeting with tremendous financial success. These traditions, which encourage altered states of consciousness and are tolerant of fluid images of divinity, provided a more suitable backdrop for the creative metaphysics of LSD than the sin-and-salvation schemes of Western religion. For the majority of my peers, therefore, the leap from psychedelic use to Eastern spirituality seemed hardly even a broad jump.

---

46. An interesting interview in which Castaneda is asked to discuss the views of skeptics can be found at www.castaneda.org/english/interviews.

L a w r e n c e   B u s h

Here again, I was held back by my atheist upbringing. Although my psychedelic experiences made the gurus' promises of enlightenment seem credible and attractive, and although my druggy desire to chart the patterns of reality made the ancient metaphysical systems of the East seem resonant and impressive, I simply could not buy the idea that a 14-year-old boy from India could alter my consciousness with a touch to the forehead[47] or that the dedicated pursuit of Transcendental Meditation would enable me to overcome gravity and levitate. Such miracle stories were not to be believed: They were equivalent, in my mind, to the Virgin Birth, the parting of the Red Sea, and other familiar religious miracle stories, only presented with more contemporary vocabulary and swathed in Eastern religious garb.

Similarly, the gurus' teachings about illusion and dualism, karma, reincarnation, nirvana, and so on seemed another form of "original sin" to me, a punishing idea that our natural human consciousness is somehow benighted and straps us to the "karmic wheel" unless we achieve enlightenment. For all of their benign smiling and giggling, it seemed to me that the gurus of the East were dealing out some harsh, anti-humanistic teachings that bore especially strong resemblance to the punishing spirit of Christian dogma.

Resisting their siren call was no glib experience, however: I spent many teenage hours, both stoned and straight, haranguing myself for keeping aloof from the busy swirl of meditation, yoga, chanting, abstinence, and new dietary discipline that engrossed many of my peers. (*Egotist! Misanthrope! What, you think you're already so enlightened? Can't deal with the idea that someone might know more than you, be more evolved than you? You'd rather hunker down in sour skepticism like your father than do the work of opening your heart to a Love Supreme?*) Eventually, however

---

47. Astronomer and adventurer Bob Berman describes a revealing encounter in India with the 14-year-old Guru Maharaj Ji in his 1998 book, *Cosmic Adventure*, although Berman describes him only as "a chubby boy who, along with his entire family, claimed divine powers. . . . The big deal and main entrée . . . was an initiation ritual whereupon you could supposedly experience the 'clear light.' . . . the orange-clad priest stood before me where I sat, and then he pushed my eyeballs inward with great pressure. Naturally, along with feeling the pain, I saw 'lights.' That was it! That was the whole deal!" In private correspondence with me, Berman identified the charlatan as Guru Maharaj Ji, the "perfect 14-year-old master."

— just in time to preserve my sanity! — the all-too-human nature of America's favorite "enlightened" leaders became evident in a string of sexual and financial scandals.[48] The cultural spotlight shifted to highly controversial religious cults such as the Reverend Sun Myung Moon's Unification Church (the "Moonies") and the Hare Krishna movement. By then, skepticism seemed a cheap alternative to deprogramming.

The boom of eastern mysticism was not the only outgrowth of my generation's psychedelic experiences, however. Within their own religions, creative leaders (such as those Jews with psychedelic experience whom I interviewed) began to overturn what Rabbi Arthur Green has called the "cult of God-as-father" — the "father figure who looms so large that one dare not *try* to look beyond Him."[49] The fruits of

---

48. Mick Brown recounts some of these in *The Spiritual Tourist: A Personal Odyssey Through the Outer Reaches of Belief*, 1998. Rajneesh developed a sexually-oriented cult in India and transferred it to Oregon when the Indian government revoked his tax-exempt status. "From 1981," Brown reports, "he ceased speaking in public altogether, apparently concentrating instead on amassing personal wealth, and adding to his collection of Rolls-Royces (which eventually numbered ninety-three)." Rajneesh was arrested for election fraud in 1984. Deported to India, he died in 1990. Guru Maharaj Ji ended up marrying his American secretary while in his teens. Today he "continues to travel the world, lecturing to private audiences, distributing his teachings on video and tape and politely declining to talk to the media." Chögyam Trungpa, whose best-known student was Allen Ginsberg, exercised "virtual *droit de seigneur* over female students" and died of alcoholism-related health complications in 1987.

49. Arthur Green, writing pseudonomously as Itzik Lodzer in *Response* magazine, Winter, 1968. Green is now a leading scholar of Jewish mysticism. His article in *Response* proceeded to draw four analogies between psychedelic and kabbalistic mysticism. First, he wrote, the "everything-has-been-changing-but-nothing-has-changed" experience of tripping is analogous to "the Kabbalists' descriptions of God as *sefirot*," in which "there is no limit to the ever-flowing and ever-changing face of the divine personality." Second, LSD's "terribly exhilarating liberation . . . from the bondage of all those daily ego problems" has analogy in Judaism's 'stripping off of the physical' (*hitpashtut ha-gashmiyut*)," an "interpretation that some of the kabbalists give to the act of fasting on Yom Kippur." Third, the acid-induced sense of time as a "union of moment and eternity" is parallel to the kabbalistic view that "all future moments were contained within creation, and creation is renewed in every

their activism are visible today in the widespread revival of interest in religious mysticism, especially *kabbalah*; in the embrace of a theology of immanence (God is everywhere, especially within); in the emphasis on healing as a spiritual enterprise; in the growth of syncrenistic or hybrid religion and the emphasis on "spirituality" over organized religion; and in the perpetual search for a spiritual high, with a concomitant disregard for those aspects of religious tradition that seem coercive or repressive. Certainly, other social influences helped to shape these trends among the baby boomers — especially the emergence of feminism as a potent source of religious innovation and energy. Still, the overlap in content and theme between psychedelic mysticism and Woodstocker religious renewal is too obvious to be ignored.

Hardly anyone talks about it, however — at least, not in public! Most books and articles on contemporary spirituality barely reference the psychedelic experience, and most historical writings about the crucible decades of the '60s and '70s tend to ignore or greatly underestimate the impact of drug use upon our generation's consciousness. Public personalities demur and equivocate about their youthful drug use — and the rest of us tend to follow their example.

Perhaps there is a tiny element of reverence at work in this silence about drugs. The Talmud (B. *Hagiga* 13a), for example, warns that "things that are as sweet as honey," i.e., mystical knowledge, "should remain under your tongue," and urges that mystical pursuits not be undertaken before age 40, before marriage, parenthood and the pursuit of livelihood have helped to establish one's personal stability. Veterans of psychedelic drugs understand their destabilizing effect upon the ego and, in some cases, upon sanity itself, and the wise among us might want to "share the secret" only with mature folks able to handle it constructively, when their mental health is at a peak.[50]

---

moment." Finally, Green wrote of the "deepest, simplest and most radical insight of psychedelic/mystic consciousness . . . the realization that all reality is one with the Divine." Despite Judaism's built-in "fears and reservations" about this insight, he declared, "the feeling of true oneness of God and man is encountered with surprising frequency in the literature of the *kabbalah*."

50. The Talmud obliquely pursues this in B. Yoma 76b, in a discussion about wine: "Rabbi Kahana explained an inconsistency: the word for 'wine' is spelled *tirash* but pronounced *tirosh*. If a man merits it, wine makes him *rosh*, 'chief'; if not,

More obviously, the role of parenthood has imposed silence on many of us, as we soberly contemplate the prospect of our own kids experimenting with these powerful substances. Although psychedelics are known for the peculiar virtue of provoking fantastic visions and broad emotional upheaval while nevertheless preserving in the user an objective, "watcher" frame of mind, this sense of objectivity, and the judgment associated with it, can be overwhelmed at high enough dosages. Of course, the criminalization of drugs has made it difficult if not impossible for parents to play the "watcher" role for their teenagers themselves, or even to discuss drug use in as honest and nuanced a way as they might like. Criminalization also assures that if kids do experiment with drugs, their parents are helpless to exercise "quality control" and maximize their children's safety.

Ultimately, however, I believe it is cowardice more than reverence or parental ambivalence that has tied our tongues on this subject. The "War on Drugs" and the "Just Say No" propaganda of the past three decades has made saying "yes" or even "maybe" into a major career and legal risk. The dark underside of drug use — the mental crack-ups attributable to bad or excessive trips, as well as the broader problem of addiction to narcotics, with all its concomitant miseries — has embarrassed us and dissuaded us from advocating even the sanctified use of psychedelics.[51] Religious and cultural leaders have therefore packaged

---

it makes him *rash*, 'a poor man.' . . . Rava explained another inconsistency: as spelled, the text reads, 'Wine that desolates [*yeshammah*]' (Ps. 104:15), but we pronounce the last word, '*yesammah* [that maketh glad].' If a man merits it, wine makes him glad; if not, it desolates him. That is what Rava meant when he said: Wine and spices stimulate my mind." (Translated by William G. Braude in H.N. Bialik and Y.H. Ravnitzky, *Sefer Ha-Aggadah*, reprinted in 1992.)

51. Pahnke and Richards predicted that "the known and unknown uses of these drugs that could prove to be legitimate and beneficial for individual persona and society may be suppressed until some future century when investigation will be permitted to proceed unhampered by popular hysteria and overrestrictive legislation." They drew an interesting analogy to hypnosis, which "is only beginning to recover from the sensationalistic publicity and irrational reactions that surrounded Mesmer and subsequently suppressed its legitimate use for almost a century."

their psychedelic insights in more traditional wrappings and, in the process, gained respectability and influence.

Their choice has facilitated many important innovations in liberal religious life. But it has also left our children to fend for themselves regarding the pleasures and dangers of drugs. It has left tens of thousands of human beings to wallow in prison without protest from our religious institutions. It has left the distribution of psychedelics in the hands of black marketeers and removed all sense of sanctity from psychedelic use. It has left the radical heritage of the 1960s vulnerable to slander, while the "War on Drugs" rages out of control, with inquisitors calling the shots.

WIDESPREAD SILENCE ABOUT PSYCHEDELICS has also left religious leaders free to ignore the challenge posed by the 'God-within-a-pill' experience. Dismiss drugs and you can dismiss the implications they raise: that the miracles and wonders, visions and visitations, raptures and out-of-body experiences to which generations of religiously devoted people have given testimony are simply internal functions of our very versatile and amazing brains. As Rabbi Zalman Schachter-Shalomi, the charismatic leader of the Jewish Renewal movement, admitted in an August, 1966 symposium in *Commentary* magazine:

> When I can undergo the deepest cosmic experience via some minuscule quantity of organic alkaloids or LSD, then the whole validity of my ontological assertions is in doubt.[52]

---

52. Yet the psychedelic experience, continued Rabbi Schachter-Shalomi, "can be not only a challenge but a support of my faith. After seeing what really happens at the point where all is One . . . I can also see Judaism in a new and amazing light. The questions to which the Torah is the answer are recovered in me." Reb Zalman, as he is known, is a Hasidic-trained rabbi. His explorations of psychedelic drugs, Eastern religious mysticism, the Esalen Institute's human potential trainings, and other aspects of New Age spirituality led to his excommunication from the Lubavitcher Hasidic movement (Chabad). Reb Zalman became a teacher to many Woodstocker Jews. In the 1980s, their activities coalesced into the Jewish Renewal movement, sometimes referred to as "neo-Hasidism," a mystically-oriented community that practices a fervent

Even while the fixing of God's location within the brain demands a religious reconsideration of theology, however, it also demands of skeptics that we reconsider our dismissive attitudes towards mysticism. After all, if the evolutionary process "wired" the human mind in ways that produced the capacity for mystical exaltation, then perhaps that exaltation — or, at least, the continuum of "unitary" experiences that peak with the mystical[53] — served a function in human survival. The thoughtful skeptic is challenged to ask: What is that survival value, and how might we harness it for positive social impact?

I am no evolutionary biologist, but it seems plausible, even for a layperson, to suggest that the capacity to connect strongly with other human beings, sexually as well as for purposes of hunting, gathering, child-rearing, protection and mutual aid, would have offered obvious survival advantages to our species as we developed. A brain that could be induced through such activities as singing and dancing (as well as sex, play and cuddling) to produce, in Newberg and D'Aquili's words, "a softening of the self" — along with a conviction that this merger experience is terribly important and more real than the strongly bounded sense of self — was a brain strongly susceptible to communal bonding and all the survival advantages it confers.

---

and joyous Judaism with a strong emphasis on egalitarianism and liberal social stances.

53. Newberg and D'Aquili see the unitive mystical experience as the peak of a "unitary continuum." "The most familiar point along the continuum," they write in *Why God Won't Go Away*, "is the baseline state of mind in which we experience most of our daily lives. We eat, we sleep, we work, we interact with others, and while we are consciously aware that we are, in some fashion, connected to the world around us (as part of a family, neighborhood, nation, and so on), we experience the world as something from which we are clearly set apart. . . . As we move up the unitary continuum, however, that separation becomes less and less distinct. We might be moved to a state of mild unitary absorption by art, or music, or walks in the autumn woods. We may reach deeper unitary states during periods of intense concentration or through the transforming intoxication of romantic love. . . . These activities, and the transcendent states they produce, are not religious in any formal sense, but in neurological terms they are similar to many unitary experiences produced by religious activity . . . . [Their] intensity is determined by the degree to which the orientation area [of the brain] is blocked from neural flow."

It therefore seems wrongheaded for humanists or atheists to dismiss mysticism as a mere boutique version of "the opiate of the people." By characterizing the mystical experience as pure escapism, or as a distraction from the hard work of creating social justice, we ignore the possibility that the mystical unity experience could actually play a catalytic role in that work. Since hopeful political change has so often been corrupted by power-hungry, paranoid or otherwise "unenlightened" leaders, it seems obvious that the creation of a more equitable, merciful and environmentally responsible social system requires not only the forceful reorganization of property ownership and power relations — the classic Marxist formula — but also the cultivation of compassion and higher consciousness in human beings. The maternal, loving, trusting sides of our nature need to be developed; the lustful, egotistical aspects of our nature need to be tamed and directed into socially constructive channels. Our perception of interconnection needs to be heightened and sustained; our perception of separateness, diminished and confined. Judging from centuries of testimony about the mystical experience, and from the limited testimonies of psychedelic research before it was proscribed in the late 1960s, it seems that the "unitive" experience may, indeed, help call forth those very aspects of self-awareness that make us into more loving, open-minded beings.

I am not making this argument on strictly utilitarian grounds ("mysticism fosters good character traits, therefore let's cultivate mysticism"), but in recognition of the fact that the mystical apprehension of "interconnection" is, indeed, the apprehension of a cosmic truth. Ecological science, genetics, astronomy, physics, and chemistry all testify to the shared origins of all matter and the ongoing symbiosis of all life systems. Human economies are certainly interdependent, and all activities that create wealth, from invention to production to distribution, are deeply collective. Our very bodies are collectivities that include once-independent organisms such as mitochondria and still-independent bacteria of all kinds. And our capacity for love and mutual support — which surely is as powerful, on a day-to-day basis, as our capacity for war and domination — is further testament to the existential reality of what we perceive most blissfully, and believe in most fervently, while in the mystical union state.

Spirituality might best be defined, in fact, as the *emotional surge we feel when our apprehension of the reality of interconnection is enhanced.* Perhaps such a specific and secular, baseline definition[54] can help non-believers perceive spirituality and spiritual practices as part of the tool kit for building a better world.[55]

MY OWN CAPACITY TO EVALUATE the transformative effects of psychedelic mysticism is obscured by my youthfulness at the time I actively took drugs. Who knows how many of the "awakenings" I had during those years were merely functions of my coming of age? In retrospect, I feel that much of the value of the psychedelic experience lay simply in my setting aside time for contemplative and sensual explorations.

---

54. I realize that my definition does not readily extend to the spirituality of the monastic experience, about which I have no first-hand knowledge. Can monastic isolation enhance the "apprehension of the reality of interconnection?" In terms of the functions of brain chemistry that Newberg and D'Aquili describe, I expect so.

55. "What moral is to be drawn from LSD mysticism?" asks humanist leader Paul Kurtz in *The Transcendental Temptation, A Critique of Religion and the Paranormal* (1986), in a passage that is the atheistic equivalent of Rabbi Schachter-Shalomi's confession about LSD's power to challenge his faith. Should we all "rush out and take mescaline, LSD and other drugs to bring about new forms of insight and truth?" Kurtz asks. "Or, do these new powers undermine the credibility of mysticism by pointing to a chemical basis of behavioral perception and consciousness and the possibility that such altered consciousness, rather than being extended, is distorted? . . . Is mysticism, at least in its exacerbated form, a kind of madness? And is this a form of truth? . . . It is all too simple to reject a point of view by questioning the character, motives, and in this case the sanity of those with whom one disagrees. Perhaps it is the skeptic who is blind and ignorant. I have wondered at times: Is it I who lacks a religious sense, and is this due to a defect of character? The tone-deaf are unable to fully appreciate the intensity of music, and the color-blind live in a world denuded of brightness and hue. Is mysticism, indeed psychosis — if these are parallels — a special kind of experience that enables a person to break out of a limited perceptual and conceptual world? Perhaps. One leaves the possibility open." Kurtz teaches philosophy at the State University of New York at Buffalo, and is author of the earlier-discussed "Humanist Manifesto 2000." and the founding chairman of the Committee for the Scientific Investigation of Claims of the Paranormal, which publishes *The Skeptical Inquirer* journal.

Perhaps if I had been raised in a culture or a family in which rapt concentration, intense social intimacy and existential contemplation were parts of daily life, the exaltation that I attribute to psychedelic drugs might have been mine without ever swallowing a pill.

Be that as it may, LSD was a teacher to me, and despite the unnerving quality of many of my trips, I have never regretted taking the journey. It distanced me, short-term, from my usual thought patterns and emotional habits, and from the ideologies and social structures of the society around me. It helped me to establish a lasting perception of myself and my society as constructs, assembled through choice over time rather than through some inevitable process. LSD therefore became fundamentally bound up with my identity as a bohemian and a social critic — an identity defined less by any particular political perspective than by a commitment to live with a creative, insurgent energy, to wriggle free of emotional deadness, to question authority, question ideology, question appearances. The fact that LSD and similar substances of tremendous consciousness-raising value are banned in America, and that seekers of that consciousness are liable, under law, to spend years in the most soul-deadening environment of all, the penitentiary, is testimony to the repressive spirit that currently haunts our ostensibly "free" society.

LSD also illuminated that part of my mind that is joyously alert to symbolism, metaphor and analogy — the kabbalist (Jewish mystic) within, who emerges in my fiction writing and artwork.

Finally, LSD mysticism granted me a perception of the natural world as so poignant in its sentience, complexity and unity that the entire paradigm of material progress through dominance over nature began to seem small-minded and fundamentally false to me. The difference to my drug-bewitched mind between what seemed "natural" (comforting, meant-to-be, life-giving) and what seemed "man-made" (anxiety-provoking, bizarre, death-dealing) was so pronounced as to earn rank as an empirical "perception" — a tremulous perception that I reconstruct with ease to this day, whenever I feel a bit of technophobic dread or recoil from the increasingly artificial and homogenized landscape of commercial America.

Years after my psychedelic journeys, as I became professionally immersed in Jewish religious idioms, the concept of "idolatry" struck me as the most apt description of that ideology of dominance-over-nature from which psychedelics first alienated me. Religious vocabulary thus joined with the vocabulary of the environmental movement in penetrating my consciousness during the 1970s and '80s. From this merger of idioms, I began to wonder if the humanistic value of mystical experience might be to help us transcend humanism itself.

Chapter Three

Biocentrism or Humanism?

"We are stardust,
We are golden,
And we've got to get ourselves
Back to the Garden."
— "Woodstock," Joni Mitchell

ACCORDING TO JEWISH LEGEND, the practice of idolatry began with the generation of Enosh, a grandson of Adam and Eve, who fashioned a *golem*, a humanoid figure, out of dust and clay. Louis Ginzberg tells the tale in Volume I of his *Legends of the Jews:* Enosh was trying to show "the people of his time . . . how God breathed the breath of life into the nostrils of Adam, but when [Enosh] began to blow his breath into the image . . . Satan entered it, and the figure walked, and the people . . . went astray after it."

Caught up in their excitement about their apparent ability to create life, the generation of Enosh next used magic, Ginzberg writes, to "set themselves as masters over the heavenly spheres" and force the sun, moon and stars to do human rather than Divine bidding. The people began to gather precious metals and jewels from all corners of the globe, from which they fashioned idols "a thousand parasangs high" (about four thousand miles).[56] They became, in short, too powerful and too rich — symptoms of imminent disaster in nearly every religious mythology.[57]

---

56. Quotes from Louis Ginzberg's *The Legends of the Jews*, Volume I, 1938. Ginzberg bases his book on the Talmud, Midrash, and other post-biblical texts.

57. In various *midrashim* (Bible-based rabbinic folktales), the sinful people of Sodom and Gomorrah are portrayed as having been perverted by overabundance. Their soil had gold flakes, their roadways were deeply shaded, their mines yielded gold, silver, and precious stones. As a result of their easy lifestyle, the people abandoned all pretense to hospitality and civic decency. Similarly, the sinful generation of Noah was portrayed as having the ability to raise

Subsequent generations lost "the likeness and image of God," Ginzberg recounts, and came to resemble "centaurs and apes," so that "the demons lost their fear of men." *Shekhinah,* God's intimate Presence, fled the earth from Her throne in the Garden of Eden — and Her brightness, which "makes all upon whom it falls exempt from disease," fled with Her, leaving people susceptible to illness. So it went on for eight more generations until Noah's time, when God lowered the boom, declared the entire human experiment corrupt and, as the Bible tells it (*Genesis* 6:13), "decided to put an end to all flesh" through a global flood.

Ancient though it is, this religious legend contains much of the content of a modern environmentalist's worst nightmare. Certainly, humankind has today set ourselves as "masters over the heavenly spheres" and forced the elements to do our bidding. Empowered by technological *golems,* we have lost our "fear of God," our ancient attitude of awe and terror towards nature, and have begun tampering with the fundamentals of creation itself — without a sense of sanctity or limit, without agreement from the great majority of the human race, and often for petty, selfish, commercial, and strictly human-centered purposes:

• We split the atom to keep our light bulbs glowing — meanwhile generating radioactive poisons for which we have no reliable storage technology, deadly poisons that will persist in the environment for thousands of generations after ours.

• We alter the eons-old genetic coding of seeds to enhance the durability and "marketability" of crops. We alter the genes of fish to grow them twice as fast to twice their natural size. We mess with species strictly on the basis of their utility for us, without even Food and Drug Administration standards to regulate our messing — and with only educated guesswork about the possible impact on the larger web of life.

---

enough food for forty years from the work of one planting, and benefiting from constantly beautiful weather. They could walk, according to *Genesis Rabbah,* "from world's end to world's end in no time at all, and while walking could uproot cedars of Lebanon." When women gave birth, the infants were immediately capable of running to fetch a flint with which to cut the umbilical cord! All these are signs, according to the ancient folklorist, of imminent comeuppance for an earth described by the Bible as "corrupt before God . . . for all flesh had corrupted its ways on earth" (*Genesis* 6: 11-12).

L a w r e n c e   B u s h

• We fetishize private property, grant our corporate *golems* the legal status and property rights of human beings, and allow them to change, and even desecrate, that which is entirely public — the earth, seas, air, climate, gene pool — without seeking approval from the collective multitude.

• We idolize wealth. We idolize technology. We idolize "progress." Our idols are more than a thousand parasangs high.

Now the boom seems to be lowering again. Global warming is melting the ice of the polar regions, changing the globe's weather systems and raising sea levels. New strains of disease are seeping through the protective net of antibiotics and public hygiene. Species extinction and habitat destruction promise a future in which vermin and parasitic species will predominate. Chemical pollution damages our water, our soil, our hormonal balance, our very cells. Radioactive and industrial wastelands dot the globe. The curses of the book of *Deuteronomy* (28:15-68), which God presents as the price of human disobedience, seem chillingly prescient:

> The Lord will strike you with consumption, fever, and inflammation, with scorching heat and drought, with blight and mildew; they shall hound you until you perish. The skies above your head will be copper and the earth under you iron. The Lord will make the rain of your land dust, and sand shall drop on you from the sky, until you are wiped out.

THE VISION OF ECOCIDE that I have been outlining above began spreading through baby-boomer population nearly thirty years ago as an apt replacement for the nuclear terror of our childhoods. Our generational turn towards spirituality was powerfully reinforced by new knowledge about our environment, knowledge that points to the interdependence and unity of all life on our planet. At the same time, the concept of a planetary environmental crisis brought us face-to-face with fundamental questions about how we should live our lives — questions about materialism and meaning, science and spirituality, capitalism and sustainability, self and community, the sanctity of nature and the heedlessness of human nature. Notwithstanding the cerebrations of philosophers and ethicists, such matters are most commonly addressed, in language that people can understand and with responses that people can implement, by religious traditions.

Environmentalism has thus functioned as a pathway to new theological excitement and to a renewed sense of taboo. Neither has been orthodox in spirit; instead, the Woodstockers have insisted on redefining theology and the religious lifestyle in accordance with insights garnered along the environmental path.

Existing religious institutions, for example, are themselves seen as "seriously deficient for not teaching more effectively that the natural world is our primary revelatory experience," writes environmental philosopher Thomas Berry in his book, *The Great Work: Our Way Into the Future.* Berry criticizes organized religion for placing "excessive emphasis . . . on redemption processes" (that is, schemes of soul-salvation) "to the neglect of creation processes." Because of this misplaced emphasis, our religious institutions, like our governments, corporations and universities, "are committed consciously or unconsciously to a radical discontinuity between the human and the nonhuman."[58]

The religious and social reinvention that Thomas Berry proposes as "the Great Work" requires us to shift from a homocentric (i.e., human-centered) to a "biocentric" perspective — to "appreciate the universe beyond ourselves as a revelatory experience of that numinous presence whence all things come into being. Indeed," Berry writes, "the universe is the primary sacred reality. We become sacred by our participation in this more sublime dimension of the world about us." He thus presents a religious naturalism that has become a major element of Woodstocker religion: a naturalism that views the natural world itself as sacred and as one of the major pathways by which God's presence is made mani-

---

58. All quotes taken from Thomas Berry, *The Great Work: Our Way Into the Future,* 1999. Berry, a priest of the Passionist order of the Roman Catholic Church, is the founder of the History of Religions Program at Fordham and the Riverdale Center of Religious Research. He is a pioneer of creation-centered religious thought and activism. For a compact and thoughtful discussion of his work, see *Thomas Berry and the New Cosmology,* with commentary by Gregory Baum, James Farris, Stephen Dunn, Margaret Brennan, Caroline Richards, Donald Senior and Brian Swimme, 1988.

fest to us.[59] Berry's emphasis is on human integration with the finely balanced ecology of our earth, an integration that goes way beyond the biblical principle of "stewardship" or the responsible humanism of Enlightenment thought. As he writes:

> In reality there is a single integral community of the Earth that includes all its component members whether human or other than human. In this community every being has its own role to fulfill, its own dignity, its inner spontaneity. . . . Every being enters into communion with other beings. This capacity for relatedness, for presence to other beings, for spontaneity in action, is a capacity possessed by every mode of being throughout the entire universe. . . . So too every being has rights to be recognized and revered. Trees have tree rights, insects have insect rights, rivers have river rights, mountains have mountain rights.

Now, AS AN ATHEIST and a critic of much religious thought, I approach all concepts of "sacred reality" cautiously, knowing that the perception of what is sacred is highly subjective, readily becomes ideological, and may provoke debate or even bloodshed. Nevertheless, when it comes to nature, a sense of the sacred is very active in me, as it seems to be in most human beings. I, for one, have never met people with all their senses functioning who were not charmed by the sparkle of sunshine, the color of flowers, the crackle of thunder, or the metaphoric allure of natural events. Notwithstanding the human independence from nature wrought by modern technology, and notwithstanding the "conquest of nature" ideology that has been dominant in the West for

---

59. Classic Jewish and Christian theologies, emphasizing a transcendent, miracle-working God, have historically been leery of religious naturalism, while religious naturalists have often used the phrase to preclude miracles and supernaturalism from their theologies. The baby-boomer spirituality with which I am grappling in this book, however, seems often to embrace the supernatural not as the antithesis of "natural" but as a "hidden" or "deep" aspect of the natural world.

centuries — at least since the 14th century's Great Plague, according to Thomas Berry[60] — we have not entirely transcended our rapturous relationship with nature as the unadorned crucible of life and death, the lone provider of sustenance, the true determinant of life's rhythms, the most "real" thing there is.

In any event, I know that the love of nature is powerful within me. I am one of those people who capture and release insects that have entered the house, or flinch with regret if I thoughtlessly kill them. My awe at the world's beauty and complexity, my sense of peace and blessing in natural surroundings, my responsiveness to domesticated animals, my fascination with the workings of evolution, and my pain and outrage at how the human race mindlessly and ruinously tramples the planet, are about as close as I get to what others might call religious feeling.

My atheism, I must add, blocks or compromises none of this feeling. To the contrary, it is Western theism (i.e., Christian, Jewish and Muslim), with its biased notion that the human animal was uniquely created "in God's image" and with all of the natural world devoted to our service, that I find peculiarly egotistical and sullying to my apprehension of the radical beauty, radical strangeness, and radical interconnectedness of our living world.

It seems that I would be a prime candidate to mix animal rights, biocentrism, and a bit of Buddhist compassion into a workable religious naturalism akin to Thomas Berry's. Essentially, I would be elaborating those sharp distinctions that I drew between the "natural" and the "man-made," while under the influence of psychedelic drugs, into a values system, a credo for living. This is exactly what many Woodstockers have done, in their devotion to organic foods, traditional healing methods, Eastern contemplative disciplines, and other aspects of the "alternative" lifestyle. What has given me pause, over the years, about taking the plunge and implementing my own perceptions about what is "sacred" or "profane," "real" or "idolatrous," is that I distrust these perceptions as ideologically driven. It is just too easy to arrogate the power of the term "natural" in order to serve a particular viewpoint or a particular aesthetic.

---

60. "The deep aversion to the natural world that resulted," Berry writes, "has profoundly conditioned the Western cultural tradition ever since."

Mathematician and social critic Norman Levitt puts it this way, in his very compelling book, *Prometheus Bedeviled: Science and the Contradictions of Contemporary Culture:* "'Nature' is a term that is hard to put into play without an implicit appeal to commonly received notions of transcendence. It invokes a hierarchy of values that equates virtue with a hypothetical (and often fictitious) 'natural' state of affairs. The impulse to prefer the 'natural' product to the 'artificial' without further investigation or analysis clearly illustrates this. . . . The great danger of such logic is that it short-circuits the empiricism, the attention to concrete and particular circumstance, on which accurate science [including environmental science] depends. In its way, it replicates the intellectual dangers of revealed religion."

Levitt notes how various philosophers and activists have used the power of the "natural" to bolster their viewpoints. "[D]efenders of capitalism," he writes, "have, since Herbert Spenser, proclaimed it the natural order of things for the strong to prosper and the weak to fall by the wayside. Against that, socialists and other anti-capitalists since Prince Peter Kropotkin have decried that same capitalism as a perversion of the natural propensity of human beings to live communally in mutual sympathy and solidarity. . . . Feminists see sexual egalitarianism as the state of nature, critics see male dominance deeply embedded in evolution and physiology." He continues:

> The root problem here is the attempt to divide the universe into the distinct spheres of the "natural" and the "unnatural.". . . The natural world is simply the world. One cannot conceptually prise away the complex phenomenon of humanity — what our species is and does — from the rest of the phenomenological cosmos. . . . The Interstate Highway System is just as natural as the body's network of blood vessels. The Grand Canyon of the Colorado is no more, if no less, a part of nature than the canyons of Manhattan. All are products of the unfolding of natural processes operating under uniform laws.[61]

---

61. All quotes are from Norman Levitt, *Prometheus Bedeviled: Science and the Contradictions of Contemporary Culture*, 1999. Levitt is co-author with Paul

Levitt would therefore probably dismiss as sheer idiosyncrasy those LSD visions of mine that distinguished between "natural" and "man-made," "sacred" and "profane." When I look at those psychedelic experiences through the lens of his rationalism, I see myself not actually perceiving a deeper pattern of reality but merely recruiting the power and virtues that attach to the concept of the "natural" to promote my own aesthetic preferences.

Levitt even fears that the sacralization of nature leads to an environmental stance that is anti-scientific and "essentially a call to worship which will be heard only by a small, eccentric minority." For that minority, "conformity to what is labeled 'natural' becomes the touchstone of all value judgments," and "any departure from this standard takes on the tincture of sin." He argues that environmentalism must be humanistic rather than biocentric, rational rather than theological, in order to be broadly based, effective, philosophically consistent, and prepared to harness science in the effort to salvage our planet from environmental disaster.

His is a classic humanistic vision of rationalism to the rescue. Standing next to Norman Levitt, I can easily perceive an environmental future that is fundamentally different from the ecocidal nightmare I described earlier:

• Atom-splitting research and technology will lead to clean fusion energy that will consume, rather than produce, radioactive wastes and help humanity move beyond the Petroleum Age.

• Genetic engineering of crops will make pesticides obsolete, resulting in the rejuvenation of our soil and waterways.

• Genetic engineering of fish will increase the farm stock so much as to permit wild species to be spared fishermen's nets and the oceans to replenish themselves.

• Increased food supplies, cheap energy, and intelligent population control will permit poorer countries to preserve their natural resources from slash-and-burn agriculture and other forms of exploitation and pollution that are driven by economic desperation. Advancing medical

R. Gross of *Higher Superstition: The Academic Left and Its Quarrels with Science*, 1994. Despite the intensity of his attacks upon left-wing critics of science in both of his books, Levitt describes himself in *Prometheus Bedeviled* as "a socialist in economics, a liberal in politics, and a conservative in culture."

Lawrence Bush

knowledge will erode the "folk medicine" customs and superstitions that have helped speed the near-extinction of the tiger, the rhinoceros, the elephant, the gorilla, and other species.

• Medical technology will double and triple our lifespans, changing our culture, our sexuality, our family and work lives.

• Brain science and psychology disciplines, including evolutionary psychology, will give us a much more profound understanding of our nature, our mental architecture, our motivations and behaviors — and how to channel them constructively.

• The only thing we will have to fear is fear itself — that classic religious fear of human power and prosperity expressed in the mythic legends of Pandora's Box, Prometheus' Fire, the fruit of the Edenic Tree of Knowledge of Good and Evil, and Enosh's *golem*. Putting these religious fears aside, we will recognize our capacity for mastery, and our grasping curiosity, as the only salvational forces available to us.

So which is it? Is our future essentially reliant upon a biocentric spiritual revolution and a "deep ecology" perspective, as Thomas Berry believes —

> We are now experiencing a moment of significance far beyond what any of us can imagine. . . . the foundations of a new historical period, the Ecozoic Era, have been established in every realm of human affairs. . . . The distorted dream of an industrial technological paradise is being replaced by the more viable dream of a mutually enhancing human presence within an ever-renewing organic-based Earth community.

— or does our well-being primarily depend upon heightening our scientific mastery, as Norman Levitt believes?

> That humanity is (as always) in serious trouble, and that technology has been directly instrumental in deepening our dilemma, is so clearly true that only obliviousness or insanity can question it. Yet it is equally true, if not quite so universally appreciated, that only through

technology do we stand a chance of climbing out of the abyss. . . .

Which is it? Are we dooming ourselves by stubbornly clinging to Western institutions, laws, religious beliefs and economic patterns that give no privilege to nature except as "property" —
Berry:

> The deepest cause of the present devastation is found in a mode of consciousness that has established a radical discontinuity between the human and other modes of being and the bestowal of all rights on the humans. The other-than-human modes of being are seen as having no rights. They have reality and value only through their use by the human.

— or is the greater danger the demonization of science as the problem rather than the cure, and the insistence upon a progressive "spiritual transformation" that is impossible to achieve on a mass scale?
Levitt:

> [E]nvironmentalism harbors a strong edenic strain, the desire for the whole of humanity to revert to a purportedly "natural" lifestyle. . . . The practical implications of this propensity are serious and unsettling. Consider . . . the changes necessary to meet the global-warming threat. It is unlikely that these will be accomplished if we insist at the same time that human values worldwide have to be made over in the image of the ecological ideal.

Which is it? Should we be reinventing compelling religious concepts such as "idolatry" and "taboo" in order to give pause to our materialistic drives and create a protective hedge around Mother Earth? Or is it the inflation of ecological consciousness into a religious sensibility and religious lifestyle that prevents us from finding effective compromise solutions?

Lawrence Bush

Obviously, the "either-or" choice that I am proposing here is unrealistically polarized. Most environmental activist groups, after all, seek to enhance environmental responsibility by discussing conservation and sustainable development, economic justice and human health far more than biocentric spirituality as their debating points — and most scientists are likewise restrained in their proclamations about wonder-working technology. Many environmental coalitions, in fact, have scientists and religious activists working together to bring much-needed ecological awareness into all corners of the culture.

Still, I suspect that many Woodstockers have been actively engaged in the debate I'm contriving here — and that Thomas Berry would be their champion, hands-down.[62] Berry offers a revolutionary view that links environmental salvation to systemic transformation: We must renounce the aggressive materialism and arrogant humanism of Western civilization if we are to survive. This argument has great appeal for the members of a subculture that has consistently conflated science with the evils of capitalism and mixed together political critique and spiritual conviction.

IN 2001, THE DEBATE about how to handle our environmental crisis was shaken by a bombshell of a book, *The Skeptical Environmentalist*, by Bjorn Lomborg, a Danish statistician who challenged the very idea that there *is* an environmental crisis. Lomborg took on the doomsday predictions of the environmental movement (he specifically targeted the literature of the Worldwatch Institute, Greenpeace, the World

---

62. One exception may be Woodstocker pioneer Stewart Brand, publisher of *The Whole Earth Catalogue* and a Merry Prankster in the 1960s. Brand "divides environmentalists into romantics and scientists," according to a profile in the *New York Times* (February 27, 2007) by John Tierney. According to Tierney, Brand "is now promoting environmental heresies," meaning "heresies" from the perspective of Woodstocker culture. Brand "sees genetic engineering as a tool for environmental protection . . . He thinks the fear of genetically engineered bugs causing disaster are as overstated as the counterculture's fears of computers turning into Big Brother." He increasingly favors the scientific approach to environmental salvation. "My trend," Brand told Tierney, "has been more toward rational and less romantic as the decades go by. I keep seeing the harm done by religious romanticism, the terrible conservatism of romanticism, the ingrained pessimism of romanticism. It builds in a certain immunity to the scientific frame of mind."

Wide Fund for Nature, and several well-known environmental activist-experts) and argued, with an abundance of statistics, that "our usual conception of the collapse of ecosystems . . . is simply not keeping with reality." His findings include that air and water are getting cleaner around the world; that biodiversity is *not* being radically assaulted, notwithstanding habitat destruction; that there are more forested areas on the earth than ever before; that the supplies of food and oil are ample to sustain generations to come; that "the majority of indicators show that [hu]mankind's lot has *vastly improved.*"

> During the course of the past century we have more than doubled our life expectancy, to 67 years. . . . Infants no longer die like flies . . . We are no longer almost chronically ill . . . We have far more food to eat — despite the fact that the Earth is home to far more people: the average inhabitant in the Third World now has 38 percent more calories. . . . We have experienced unprecedented growth in human prosperity. In the course of the last 40 years, everyone — in the developed as well as the developing world — has become more than three times richer. . . . We have gained access to far more amenities, from clean drinking water to telephones, computers and cars. . . . *We have more leisure time, greater security and fewer accidents, more education, more amenities, higher incomes, fewer starving, more food and a healthier and longer life.* . . . This is the real state of the world.[63]

What?! my own internal Woodstocker cried when I read this. *Is he nuts? Or is he simply on the Exxon-Mobil payroll?*

In fact, Lomborg writes that he "had never really questioned [his] own belief in an ever-deteriorating environment" before researching his book. That research led him to believe, however, that the "doomsday" perspective on environmental degradation is way off, and that the key global issue that needs solving is poverty, because environmental

---

63. Bjorn Lomborg, *The Skeptical Environmentalist*, published originally in Danish in 1998.

preservation never becomes a social priority until populations have transcended economic desperation. Even if our environmental problems do reach crisis proportions, Lomborg believes, this should not be interpreted as a testament to the spiritual bankruptcy or core corruption of Western civilization, but as the outcome of that civilization's remarkable success at improving the lives of the planet's billions of resource-consuming human beings.

Since its publication, *The Skeptical Environmentalist* has been widely scrutinized, critiqued and condemned by many scientists and politicians (and defended by others). My purpose in citing it here is not to evaluate Lomborg's information or interpretations — which is beyond my powers to do — but to ask why his optimistic assessments seemed so counterintuitive to me, even downright heretical, *before* I had learned of the controversies surrounding his book. Why does the argument that humanity, under the guidance of Western science, is actually making great progress, seem outrageous and unlikely? Why am I reflexively wedded to the view expressed in a classic graffiti that occupied an entire wall in New York's East Village, a cradle of Woodstocker culture, when I lived there in the 1960s: "What do you think of Western Civilization, Mr. Gandhi?" it said, in large block letters. Gandhi's purported reply: "I think it would be a good idea."

Lomborg attributes such negativism, particularly in the environmental arena, to a variety of factors: media culture ("A good story is usually bad news"); the funding of research ("If a scientist says that she has investigated her field and not found any general problems, we as a society need do no more"); the vested interests of organizations seeking support for their environmental advocacy ("since we tend to treat environmental organizations with [little] skepticism, this might cause a grave bias in our understanding of the state of the world"); and human psychology ("our knowledge of things close to us, which is derived from our own experiences, is not the primary source of our fears for the environment. On the contrary, we seem more worried about conditions *the further away from us they are,* both physically and mentally"). Perhaps our attachment to doomsday beliefs, he speculates, also constitute "a nemesis, to punish our overconsumption, a penalty for our playing the Sorcerer's Apprentice."

Whatever its causes, Lomborg believes there to be a virtual "clash of two religions" in the environmental debate. His own belief system is quite similar to Norman Levitt's: that we can, in Lomborg's words, "deal with the basic problem[s]" and "identify the best possible policy to deal with [them]" without requiring solutions that "also help fundamentally change the fabric of society." The other side of the debate, according to him, is represented by Al Gore, whose film about global warming, *An Inconvenient Truth*, did not exist when *The Skeptical Environmentalist* was published, but whose 1992 book, *Earth in the Balance, Ecology and the Human Spirit*, Lomborg cites as "an excellent example of the mood." Gore insists, writes Lomborg,

> that the loss is not only in the environment but also within ourselves. We have lost our natural contact with the Earth and become strangers to our own existence . . . concentrating on [here Lomborg quotes Gore] "the consumption of an endless stream of shiny new products." We have constructed "a false world of plastic flowers and Astroturf, air-conditioning and fluorescent lights, windows that don't open and background music that never stops" . . . We have forgotten our "direct experience with real life.". . . Gore sees this civilization as the new antagonist . . .[64]

While it is hard to imagine that a lifetime politician and former vice-president of the United States shares the anti-establishment fervor that has marked Woodstocker culture, it nevertheless seems to me that Lomborg has put his finger on the reason why the counterculturalists of our generation, with or without Al Gore, would be particularly attracted to the kind of transformational environmentalism that Thomas Berry champions.

---

64. Lomborg argues further that Gore's perception of "a dysfunctional civilization" and our loss of "direct experience with real life" reveals "both a scary idealization of our past and an abysmal arrogance toward the developing countries of the world. . . . The fact is . . . that this civilization has over the last 400 years brought us fantastic and continued progress."

THE KEY IS WHAT SOCIAL CRITIC Gerhart Niemeyer has called "oppositional-salvational ideology," a worldview that involves the "total critique of society" and the "indictment . . . not [of] this or that concrete choice or a pattern of evil actions but [of] the entire historical condition of human existence."[65] Our self-awareness as the Woodstock Nation was in large part founded on such an ideology, and given what we were up against — the horrors of the Vietnam War, the moral bankruptcy and physical brutality of racial segregation, and the repressive qualities of conformist America — it is no surprise that a "total critique of society" would become our byword.

The oppositional piece of our message was loud and clear: We were opposed to racism, violence, conformity, injustice, and the predations that emerge from the logic of capitalism — the stoking of consumer lust, the homogenization of culture worldwide through military and economic imperialism, the marginalization or cooptation of liberationist lifestyles, the continued refusal to share the wealth with the poor, etc. All of this comprised what we Woodstockers called "the system," "the Establishment," the "beast" in whose belly we lived.

The salvational piece of our "oppositional-salvational ideology" was equally compelling: a youth culture of unpossessive love, shared material wealth, uninhibited expression, and "natural" living — with "the bombers," as Joni Mitchell put it, ". . . turning into butterflies above our Nation." Her hymn to the 1969 Woodstock Festival, which appears as a frontispiece for this chapter,[66] captured our salvational yearnings most hauntingly: "We are stardust, we are golden, and we've got to get ourselves back to the Garden." Recognizing our generation's continuity with other generations ("We are stardust, million-year-old carbon," Mitchell sings in the final chorus), the song nevertheless affirms our perception of ourselves as uniquely positioned to end, for once and for all, the painful alienation of life.

Our efforts to achieve that salvation involved genuine heroism, as we became involved in some of the most effective peaceful social movements in history. Eventually, however, we ended up with "million-year-

---

65. Gerhart Niemeyer, quoted in Aileen Kraditor's *"Jimmy Higgins"— The Mental World of the American Rank and File Communist, 1930-1958*, 1988.

66. "Woodstock," on her 1970 album, *Ladies of the Canyon*.

old carbon" on our faces: Our radical political movements imploded, our social experiments went commercial or ran out of steam, our sexual liberation was hijacked by AIDS, our "human potential" movements were overrun by the biochemical school of mental health. By 1980, while Ronald Reagan used "The Age of Aquarius"[67] as his inaugural theme song, we were falling hard from our heights of self-aggrandizement.

Our deepening embrace of spirituality, particularly of Eastern spirituality (untainted by the fundamental flaws of "Western Civilization"), produced a "bounce" from that fall — a bounce for our self-esteem, our sense of generational identity and drama, and most especially our oppositional values and salvational dreams. Social historian Todd Gitlin describes this turn to spirituality as less of a willful *escape* from political engagement than a *transference* of thwarted transformational energies. He likens it to the Ghost Dance that swept the defeated Plains Indians in the final decade of the 19th century: "The impulse to collective action," Gitlin concludes, "blocked on the plane of human action, gets diverted towards the spiritual," which he generously terms "the continuation of expressive politics by other means."[68]

Rennie Davis, a long-time anti-war activist who became best known as a defendant with Abbie Hoffman, Jerry Rubin, Bobby Seale and others at the Chicago Eight conspiracy trial for their protests at the 1968 Democratic Convention in Chicago, helped sanctify the turn from oppositional politics to a spiritual lifestyle in the Spring of 1973, when he announced his new allegiance to Guru Maharaj Ji, the "14-year-old perfect master" from India. For Davis, this did not signal renunciation of social concern; rather, the guru's Divine Light Mission, Davis told

---

67. From the musical *Hair*, which both caricatured and captured the spirit of Woodstocker dissidence.

68. Todd Gitlin, *The Sixties: Years of Hope, Days of Rage*, 1987. The Ghost Dance was the central ritual of a messianic religion led by a Paiute named Wokova. He prophesied that the whites would leave the land and that the Native American ways would be restored. The defeated and humiliated tribes of the West embraced the religion with a fervor that white authorities interpreted as insurrectionary, resulting in a massacre by U.S. soldiers of hundreds of Lakota (Sioux) at Wounded Knee, South Dakota.

the *New York Times*, offered a "practical way to fulfill all the dreams of the movement . . . to end poverty, racism, sexism, imperialism." Within two decades, the trend had fully matured: Woodstockers found themselves satisfied to live within their booming subculture, to develop the organic food market and pursue alternatives to "allopathic" medicine, and to meditate and track the tingling of their chakras, rather than trying any longer to bring about structural political change.

One issue that formed a bridge between political beliefs and a "spiritual" lifestyle was environmental protection, which sprang to life as an concern in the middle of the 1970s, while the anti-Vietnam War movement networks were still intact.[69] The environmental issue had tremendous import for the Woodstock generation, as the human capacity to wreak havoc upon the planet was being highlighted by the Worldwatch Institute, Greenpeace, and numerous other environmental watchdog groups (most of whose dire predictions, as both Bjorn Lomborg and our lived experience show, proved to be considerably off the mark). Rainforest devastation, the mass extinction of species, global warming, major fisheries becoming barren, waterways and groundwaters polluted by chemical dumping — as these conditions hit the headlines throughout the 1980s and '90s, it all seemed symptomatic of a civilization gone terribly wrong, a civilization deeply deserving of meltdown.

But was it all really happening? Our ideology said *yes*, but the scientific evidence was usually less than clear. Because of today's scientific consensus, for example, about the reality of global warming and its connection to human-made greenhouse gases, it is easy to forget that only a few years ago, atmospheric scientists were doing a fair amount of guesswork. As Elizabeth Royte wrote in the February, 2001 issue of *Discover* magazine, "the study of climate change" is "remarkably young. . . . Twenty-five years ago, atmospheric scientists fretted about global cooling. Today scientists agree that Earth's surface is warming, but

---

69. Environmentalism hit its early stride with the growth of the anti-nuclear power movement. Ralph Nader's 1974 "Critical Mass" anti-nuclear conference in Washington, D.C. was attended by more than 1,000 activists and helped meld disparate local anti-nuclear power groups into a national movement. Five years later, a nuclear reactor accident at Three Mile Island in Pennsylvania turned public opinion strongly against nuclear power.

they can't reach a consensus on exactly how much and why. The more scientists study the atmosphere, the more complicated it appears."[70]

Understanding such complexities was beyond the ken of the vast majority of us who are, for all intents and purposes, scientifically illiterate. Environmental doomsday therefore became a phenomenon in which we "believed" or "disbelieved," based less on true knowledge than on our general feelings about Western civilization and on our judgments about which informants to trust. In other words, our perspectives on the environment were very much influenced by ideology. Once nuclear power was stymied,[71] this left us with little to do in the activist realm short of a total overhaul of the Western lifestyle and a total overthrow of corporate power. Daunted by such impossibilities,

---

70. See Elizabeth Royte, "The Gospel According to John," *Discover*, February, 2001. Royte's article is a portrait of John Christy, an atmospheric scientist and leading skeptic about global warming. Christy opposes measures to curb greenhouse-gas emissions, especially those that advise taxing fossil fuels, because "he believes the tax would wreak havoc on poor areas [of the world] by indirectly raising the prices of goods and services.'" A former missionary in Kenya, Christy views environmental activism, particularly the "deep ecology" movement, as "people in the Northeast and the West trying to control how others live . . . Some extreme environmentalists . . . say that a whale is more important than your child," he tells Royte. "These people, they want us to live in the Stone Age." Christy's opposition is rooted, however, in Christianity, not a secular humanism: "All [that] God created is precious," he says, "and humans are the most precious part of creation."

71. According to *Public Citizen News* ("The Nuclear Genie," by Wenonah Hauter, Vol. 21, No. 1, 2001), "no new reactors have been ordered and subsequently completed in the U.S. since 1973," and "93 reactors have been canceled over the past three decades." Nevertheless, "the nuclear industry continues to operate more than 100 plants in the U.S. and is building dozens of new plants overseas." Despite the significant impact on public opinion made by the anti-nuclear protests and mass arrests of the late 1970s, it was the fundamental problems with nuclear safety (those that made the technology unprofitable) — and *not* political action — that ultimately shut down the industry. The shutdown proved only temporary: The new concern over global warming threatens to make nuclear power seem like a "clean energy" alternative, or at least the lesser of two evils, despite the still unsolved (and virtually unsolvable) problem of designing waste storage facilities for nuclear fission's deadly plutonium by-product, which endures as a poison in the environment for hundreds of thousands of years.

we mostly claimed innocence of the "taint" of Western civilization by virtue of our green lifestyles and our holistic spirituality, and left the actual work of environmental protection to legislators, scientists, environmental lobbyists and corporations.

Now, ADMITTEDLY, AS THE SON of Communists, I am probably exaggerating the role of the oppositional-salvational ideology in cultivating the radical environmental perspective and the alternative spiritualities of the Woodstock generation. My own escape from the grip of ideology in the 1960s and '70s was a slow and torturous process, very much like breaking with a religion in which one is raised, and just as the recovering alcoholic must be vigilant against moods and circumstances that can lead back to the bottle, so am I, as a recovering ideologue, oversensitive to all traces of it.

Revolutionary Marxism was essentially that, a classic oppositional-salvational religion, with theories about history and society elevated to "scientific" gospel and promoted with evangelical zeal, notwithstanding the constant disproofs offered by Communist dictatorships themselves. Correlative to this stubborn gospel were sweeping vilifications of the "damned" capitalist world and sweet if vague promises of a salvational future, the "historically inevitable" advent of a harmonious, class-free society. Yet it was not really my parents and their generation who bred me as a little ideologue; rather, it was during my college years that I aspired to master Marxism and "explain the world" — and in this, I was hardly alone. Throughout the 1960s and '70s, SDS, the Weather Underground, the October League, the Workers World Party, the Black Panthers, and numerous other Marxist, Marxian or pseudo-Marxist organizations and sects were active on every major college campus, infecting the opinion-shapers of our generation with their own strains of oppositional-salvational ideology. As a young adult, I wrestled with the various "political lines" presented by these groups just as intensely as I wrestled with the mystical teachings of Carlos Castaneda and his ilk — in hope of finding an ineradicable Truth that would determine my life decisions.

Was the Weather Underground, for example, correct that African Americans constitute an oppressed nation, that surrendering "white-skin privilege" and submitting to the leadership of black revolutionaries are the main tasks of white radicals, and that the goal of revolution should be the dismemberment of the imperialist U.S.A. (with the Southwest being returned to Mexico, the Deep South reserved for the black nation, etc.)? In which case, I should, at the very least, stop performing Woody Guthrie's "This Land Is Your Land" during my stints as an amateur musician, since the song was, as one above-ground Weatherwoman pointed out to me, a celebration of white-skin privilege.

Was China's Cultural Revolution, as lauded by the October League, an incubator for the "new socialist man" — whose sense of ambition, responsibility, community and personal well-being would likely be incomprehensible to, and far in advance of, personalities such as mine, which were deformed by the class system? In which case, I should cease my intellectual strivings and my efforts to develop as a writer and find a job that would bring me into contact with "the people."

Was fascism an inevitable outgrowth of the inevitable crisis of capitalism, as I learned from literature of the Communist Party and many other leftwing groups? In which case, I should regard reformers of capitalism such as Ralph Nader, and defenders of "bourgeois liberties" such as the American Civil Liberties Union, as "running dogs of the ruling class" rather than as allies (and prospective employers).

Was marriage inherently oppressive to women, and lesbianism more natural and liberating for women than heterosexuality, as preached by certain feminist separatist groups? In which case, rather than moving on from living together to getting married, my girlfriend and I should at least experiment with bisexuality within the context of an "open" relationship.

Was Zionism a form of racism, as contended by nearly *every* leftwing group? In which case, despite its astonishingly tenacious liberalism, the Jewish community deserved only my scorn.

Which of these realities were real — and how should my life choices reflect that reality? The question tormented me, for even while I was desirous of making an ideological commitment, even while I yearned to understand it all, there was a large measure of skepticism always standing watch in my mind. The ideologue in me was at war with this skeptic, vilifying him as a weak, petty-bourgeois character who was clinging to his male, heterosexual and white-skin privilege by fence-sitting, yet my skeptical critic hung on — and was strengthened, to an enormous degree, by my growing familiarity with Jewish philosophy.

Jewish teachings about society and social relations, at least according to my interpretations, seemed to emphasize moderation, restraint, conscience, and both individual and collective responsibility — hardly the stuff of revolutionary fervor. This was encapsulated for me by the famous story of the Hillel, the great sage of the 1st century, who was asked to summarize Judaism while his interlocutor balanced on one foot. "Do not do unto others what you would not want done unto you," Hillel said. "That is the whole Torah. The rest is commentary. Now go study it!"[72] I found it impressive that Hillel had stressed a *negative* golden rule, a rule of live-and-let-live restraint — which felt strikingly different than the Christian, Stalinist or Maoist zeal for "doing *unto* others."

The complex nature of Jewish identity also seemed to defy ideological cubbyholing: It was neither a wholly religious identity, nor a wholly national one, nor a wholly ethnic one, but rather a weird, hard-to-analyze hybrid identity that had nevertheless played a dramatic role in human history for centuries.

Jewish economic philosophy seemed to blend marketplace and distributive economics, capitalist and socialist features, in search of a balanced and just state of affairs. Judaism urged a communal response to poverty that went far beyond the individualism of capitalist thought — yet Judaism also accepted the idea that "there will never cease to be needy people in your land" (*Deuteronomy* 15: 11), which was a far cry from the "classless society" eschatology of Marxism.

Judaism also eschewed asceticism and urged us to emulate the God of *Genesis*, who declares the world to be not corrupt, not tainted, but "very good." (People will be "called to account in the hereafter," teaches Rav in the Palestinian Talmud, for each pleasure they deny themselves without sufficient cause.)[73]

---

72. Babylonian Talmud, *Shabbat* 31a.

73. Palestinan Talmud, *Kiddushin* 4:12. Rav (Abbar bar Aivu) was a 2nd to 3rd-century rabbi based in southern Babylon. He is referenced more than 1,500 times in the Babylonian Talmud and hundreds of times in the Jerusalem Talmud.

Ultimately, Jewish philosophy encouraged me to believe that "heal" rather than "smash" was the byword of true political change, and that compassion (*rakhmones,* from the Hebrew root for "womb"), not rage, was the passion best to be mobilized on behalf of progress. ("Anger is a fool," says a Yiddish proverb.) There seemed to be little place for a "total critique of society," to use Gerhart Niemeyer's phrase again, in such a philosophical tradition.

Even the salvational element of Woodstocker ideology was made less powerful for me by Judaism, especially by the Talmudic disparagements of messianism that I came to discover — such as the striking declaration, attributed also to Rav, that "all the calculated dates of redemption have passed, and now the matter depends upon repentance and good deeds."[74] Repentance and good deeds! As a political mandate, this was

74. Babylonian Talmud, *Sanhedrin* 97b. One of the many fascinating aspects of Talmudic literature is the effort on the part of the rabbis to dampen the messianic expectations of the Jewish community. Messianic fervor had helped motivate the disastrous wars against Rome in the first and second centuries, C.E. The Mishnah, for example, makes no demands concerning belief in a forthcoming messiah or messianic age, and the Palestinian Talmud fails to record messianic speculations. Only the Babylonian Talmud indulges the subject — and often with a firm hand of restraint, typified by Rabbi Samuel bar Nahman's outburst (*Sanhedrin* 97b): "Blast the very existence of those who calculate the time of redemption!"

My favorite statement on the subject is attributed to Rav: "All the calculated dates of redemption have passed, and now the matter depends upon repentance and good deeds." This dictum constitutes a strong statement against ideology. Rav seems to express the understanding that belief in the calculability of redemption implies belief in its inevitability — "It's coming, we just need to figure out when!" A belief in inevitable outcomes (because "history is on our side" or "God is on our side") lends an extraordinary arrogance to salvational enterprises. It renders non-believers, especially those who oppose our version of salvation or propose alternative solutions, into arch-enemies. They become opponents not only of *our* designs, but of Goodness itself. The "knowledge" of the inevitable also serves to lend to each true believer an awesome, uplifting sense of responsibility and power. The ideologue thus gains, according to Aileen Kraditor (in *"Jimmy Higgins"— The Mental World of the American Rank and File Communist, 1930-1958,* as previously cited), "the promise of intellectual control of reality . . . Belief in inevitable outcomes is really belief in the infallibility of the theory that predicts them."

Yet the Talmud is not content to simply dispose of the ideological style of thinking by dampening messianic beliefs. After declaring the calculated

a far cry from the revolutionary, "back-to-the-Garden" dreams of the Woodstock Nation.

Yet even while I journeyed into Judaism, God remained only a myth and a metaphor to me. To believe otherwise, to allow my admiration for Jewish thought to make me receptive to Jewish supernaturalism (God is an all-knowing, all-powerful being; the Torah is His communication given to the Jews as a blueprint for ethical living; miracles have happened and can again; etc.) would have seemed like backsliding into an ideological worldview. My goal was the opposite: to wed myself to skepticism and shed the very idea that the workings of the universe and the human race can be explained within a single, comprehensible framework. It would not have felt like progress, for example, to switch from belief in the central historical role of the proletariat to the classic Jewish belief in chosenness — or from belief in the historical inevitability of socialism to that belief that the messiah will someday come. The Judaism that I embraced was simply a humanistic philosophical and folk tradition that acknowledged the enormous complexity of the world, not a theology and faith system that read the Torah as a map of the world.

THERE YOU HAVE A BRIEF SUMMARY of my escape from the "oppositional-salvational" ideology that seemed to shape Woodstocker consciousness in the 1960s and '70s.[75] Between my struggles with

---

dates of redemption to have passed, Rav calls upon us nevertheless to participate in the redemption of the world through repentance and good deeds. This, too, presents a bold challenge to the ideological style of thinking, on two fronts. First, by calling for universal repentance, Rav is withholding from the ideologue a claim to innocence and exceptionalism. He poses not an "either-or" political paradigm ("If you're not part of the solution, you're part of the problem"), but an "and-therefore" paradigm: "We're all part of the problem and the solution, therefore let's get to work." By issuing a call for good deeds, Rav denies what Kraditor calls the "Grand Negation" — the vilification of the world as a "fallen" place. A world that can be improved by good deeds is a world not systematically flawed, but rather in need of care. Rav thus affirms the kind of 'reformism' that has been the bane of every ideological sect I've ever encountered.

75. For more details, see my "Babel and Political Sectarianism" in the Spring, 1996 edition of *The Reconstructionist* (Vol. 61, No. 1).

psychedelic mysticism and my struggles with leftwing ideology, I was a tormented, indecisive basket case in my young adult years! — and those intense struggles have probably led me, as noted, to exaggerate about the ideological nature of Woodstocker culture and Woodstocker spirituality.

While I am out on a limb, however, I might as well test its bearing capacity by offering some specific observations:

• The overwrought devotion of many Woodstockers to "natural" food, "alternative" healing, and traditional or neo-traditional teachings about bodily "energy," divination, extrasensory perception, and so on strikes me as classically ideological: Each choice, deed and belief constitutes an implicit critique of "the system," of Western rationalism as a whole, and therefore amounts to an indispensable part of the calculus of salvation and a badge of membership among the "chosen." Suspicion of "Western medicine," in particular, has come to be viewed as an essential part of the culture of dissent. Even public health inoculation campaigns and the fluoridation of public water supplies, which were opposed as "creeping socialism" by the far-right John Birch Society during my own childhood, have been revived as objects of paranoia among ultra-orthodox Woodstockers.

• Science and technology, industrialized agriculture, the American military machine, the unethical behavior of pharmaceutical corporations — it's all viewed by Woodstockers as part of a single fabric of villainy or, at best, soullessness. Accompanying and helping to cultivate this worldview is the invention of a utopian past — whether the lost civilization of Atlantis or the goddess-worshipping civilizations posited by Riane Eisler[76] — that denies the reality of human suffering as the norm of history and therefore undermines all sense that our contemporary system, for all of its failings, might be relatively progressive.

• The embrace of teachers who claim to transcend the laws of physics strangely resembles communist "cults of the individual" and the reality-

---

76. Eisler is author of the best-selling *The Chalice and the Blade*, which uses archaeological evidence to argue that a "cooperator" civilization with a creation-centered goddess religion existed in pre-history, before warring, patriarchal "dominator" cultures brought it down. It may be so — but her work has been embraced far more by feminists eager to write women back into history than by archaeologists and scholars of antiquity.

defying bravado of isolated political sects. Carlos Castaneda insists that his teacher, Don Juan, can fly; Dr. Larry Dossey suggests that prayers for the sick, out of their presence and without their knowledge, help facilitate their healing;[77] Rudolph Steiner claims that reading readiness and children's dental development are interrelated[78] — and such claims are met not with skepticism and demands for proof but with a will to believe that indicates a deep yearning for transcendence and a deep suspicion of reality.

• The cultural pretensions of baby-boom spirituality, the sense of belonging to a more advanced and innocent community representing the next stage of human evolution, seems like a spiritual version of Marxist-Leninist vanguardism. At the same time, the scorn with which true believers greet skeptical argument, and the depth of passion expressed in defense of the unproved, the unlikely, and the irrational, testify to beliefs that are powerfully bound up with group identity.

NEVERTHELESS, "just because I'm paranoid," as the old joke says, "doesn't mean that everyone *isn't* out to get me." Just because the Woodstock generation was prone to oppositional-salvational ideology doesn't mean the Earth as an ecosystem *isn't* being assaulted by the grasping needs of human society — or that the Woodstocker critique of Western materialism is altogether irrelevant to environmental policy-making.

Even hardcore skeptics like Bjorn Lomborg perceive that the demands of the ever-growing global population have produced a worldwide commitment to economic development and human longevity that present a real challenge to the planet's limited carrying capacity. Science continues to postpone the collision by increasing that carrying capacity: The Green Revolution and genetic engineering are among the best-known examples of the many scientific ventures that seek to augment our planet's ability to deal with human demand. Each scientific innovation, however, brings in its wake a new set of liabilities

---

77. Dossey is executive editor of *Alternative Therapies* and author of *Healing Words: The Power of Prayer and the Practice of Medicine* (1993). A critique about the therapeutic benefits of intercessory prayer can be found in *The Skeptical Inquirer*, March/April 2000.

78. Steiner's philosophy is embodied in the Waldorf educational system, a popular alternative to the public school system for many Woodstocker families.

that require their own fine-tuned scientific responses, so that our Earth becomes more and more dependent upon technological prostheses and life-support systems. More than thirty years ago, the "underground" political cartoonist, R. Cobb, portrayed the nightmare version of these prostheses in a drawing of an ennervated human being sitting inside a wheeled bubble with a grossly polluted landscape as his backdrop. The caption was: "Man triumphant over nature."

Even if this grim vision remains in the realm of science fiction, and even if Lomborg's optimistic hope that economic development will yield a higher level of environmental stewardship comes true, scientific and technological innovations are going to continue to have enormous and enduring impact upon our planet and all of its living creatures. This impact deserves much more broad-ranging discussion and evaluation than it is usually receives, for absent that, corporate profitability becomes the only serious measurement of value and worth, greed goes unleashed, and the "triumph over nature" — including the triumph over the more spiritual and caring parts of *human* nature — inches closer to reality.

To what extent, for example, is the industrialization of the food system, made possible by innovations in chemistry, transportation and farm technology, a blessing for humankind — and to what extent does it degrade local economies, destroy water supplies, disintegrate communities and alienate us further from nature?

How will the cultivation of "perfection" in our foods through genetic engineering (no more midget grapes on the cluster, no more insipid-tasting ears of corn) affect human powers of discernment? How does the "instant gratification" of modern computers and communication technology influence our capacity for patience, commitment, sustained effort, and responsible citizenship? How far should we let technological innovation go towards shielding people from the heat of summer, the cold of winter, the darkness of the night? At what point do we become too "soft" for our own good?

How will the development of human cloning, or prenatal genetic engineering, affect social relations? Will the human species remain one species for long?

How much should we actually pay heed to the folk fear about scientific "overreaching"? Should it be credited with having any genetically-encoded survival value? Should we respect any widespread sense of "taboo" at all?

And who shall lead these discussions? Shall it be the massively powerful corporations, which are responsible for developing many and marketing nearly all major scientific and technological innovations — whether needed or not? In fact, most corporations resist efforts to be held accountable to any community beyond their stockholders, and are empowered in that resistance by their increasing control of information flow, the absence of meaningful international environmental law and law enforcement, and their status as legal "individuals" with full property rights and full protection from criminal or civil prosecution for their managers and shareholders.

Governments? They are variously distrusted by their populations, neutered or controlled by business or military interests, led by domineering males who are incapable of exercising effective communal leadership, or caught up in ethnic, religious, economic and political competition with one another.

The United Nations? The UN lacks an effective international environmental policing and cleanup role — despite Mikhail Gorbachev's innovative 1987 proposal to establish such a UN role as part of the "peace dividend" of U.S.-Soviet détente.[79]

The mass media? They certainly create some dialogue and amplify some voices of conscience, but tend to be muzzled by the pressures of corporate or government ownership and by the public's preference for entertainment over serious information.

Universities? They haven't the unity of vision or the amplitude of voice, the financial independence or the grassroots authority, to take an important leadership role.

---

79. Gorbachev's proposal eventually led to the creation of Green Cross International, an international environmental rescue and activist organization of which Gorbachev is president. In *The Great Work*, Thomas Berry calls particular attention to the "World Charter for Nature passed in the United Nations Assembly in 1982," which "states quite clearly that 'Every form of life is unique, warranting respect regardless of its worth to man, and, to accord other organisms such recognition, man must be guided by a moral code of action.' A similar attitude," Berry continues, "is expressed in the Earth Charter . . . prepared for presentation to the United Nations in the year 2002." The Earth Charter is a project of Green Cross International.

Non-governmental organizations? NGOs are of crucial importance in their research and activism, but are dwarfed by the abusing corporations and governments that they monitor, and sometimes lack a clear and inspiring set of fundamental values or social vision, beyond oppositional passion, that might convert the unconverted.

Even scientists themselves — whose knowledge base is increasingly exclusive and privileged, and whose powers to manipulate reality seem increasingly magical to the rest of us — are in no position to claim a leadership role on questions about the social or ethical impact of their achievements. Scientists tend to be committed specialists, with little interest in engaging in a major way in public dialogue, and "citizen-scientists" of Albert Einstein's stature are not likely to appear soon, particularly as the sciences grow in complexity and scope beyond the highly publicized "genius" of individuals. Scientists also lack organizational clout and leadership, or sufficient ownership of the fruits of their labor, to command real political power — and the history of those scientists who nevertheless express opinions in opposition to the policies of the "military-industrial complex" (J. Robert Oppenheimer is the best-known example) is not encouraging.

PERHAPS THE LACK OF A VITAL CENTER for ethical discussion and decision-making in our globalized world has also helped fuel the revival and renewal of religious traditions internationally. Religious institutions, after all, are among the few places in which ethical inquiries are made about the way we live our lives, and religious leaders represent, for better or worse, among the few coherent voices speaking about the ethical or moral values that directly bear upon "environmentalism" in its very broadest sense.

Religion commodified as dogma, however, is as useless to the environmental cause as any other unrecyclable product. A Catholicism that opposes contraception, based on a particular view of sexuality and sin, cannot be taken very seriously as an advocate of environmental protection in today's highly populated world. Neither can a Judaism that shuns nature-oriented worship for fear of engaging in Biblically forbidden "idolatry," or that separates the human being from the web of life by pretending we are uniquely "created in God's image." To fulfill their real potential as "guardians of the earth," religious traditions and institutions require reinvention, not mere revival.

Thomas Berry even suggests that the very idea of a transcendent God may be disempowering to the environmental cause. "Our traditional spiritual values," he writes in *The Great Work,* insist "on the unsatisfactory nature of the existing order of things and the need for relief by reference to some transearthly experience." This orientation "has made us vulnerable to superficial attitudes towards the difficulties we experience. When in a position of great danger we are prone to believe we will be saved by some transearthly intervention within the functioning of the planet." Attachment to the concept of a transcendent God may thus help deter us from recognizing our own immense power and the immense consequence of our own actions. Although humanity has become, as Berry puts it, "a macrophase power, something on the level of the glaciations or the forces that caused the great extinctions of the past," we as yet have only "a microphase sense of responsibility or ethical judgment."

Interestingly, Norman Levitt shares this critique. The traditional religious struggle to "come to terms with difficult and intimidating ways of understanding the world is obsolete," he writes in *Prometheus Bedeviled.* What reigns now in religious life is "a much-cheapened notion of transcendence — transcendence as pure anodyne . . . demanding nothing of us." However, unlike Thomas Berry, who seeks to shift theology towards religious naturalism, elevating nature to a plane of holiness and revelation while perhaps diminishing God to a plane of metaphor and human consciousness, Norman Levitt believes that religion has altogether surrendered its claim to being a serious forum for the kind of deliberation and decision-making needed to take us safely into the future. He would prefer to empower that sector of society best versed in those "difficult and intimidating ways of understanding the world" — namely, scientists!

Only by granting science a "social authority commensurate with its astonishing success in living up to its own ambitions," Levitt argues, will society start to measure environmental impact realistically, motivated not by the possibility of profit, nor by political or spiritual ideology, nor by religious dogma, but by objective, expert opinion. As a model of this kind of authority, he points to the Federal Reserve

Board, a regulatory organ of government that has evolved into "an extra-constitutional 'fourth' branch of government" that is "in some ways the most powerful one. . . . A modest step in that direction with respect to the policy organs concerned with science would actually be beneficial." Participating scientists would, of course, have to renounce political ambitions, limit their advisory role to their scientific fields of competence, and credibly distance their judgments from any financial or institutional self-interest. The goal is to develop greater freedom for scientific opinion by insulating it from both the anti-scientific and pseudoscientific prejudices of the majority and from the profit-motivated sponsorship and manipulation of corporations.

I am sure that Levitt's advocacy for the elite authority of science would give the heebie-jeebies to the great majority of Woodstockers, for reasons that I have enumerated. Even as a critic of Woodstocker biases, however, I have serious problems with Levitt's concept, which is stewed in his own ideological sectarianism. In the course of making his spirited defense of scientific authority, Levitt has lost respect for the broad range of humanistic disciplines that must be involved in making human beings aware of the power of their deeds and the profundity of their decision-making.[80] His humanistic commitment is too shallow, his reliance upon science too narrow, for the fact is that the environmental questions of our time include not only "Can we?" but "Should we?" — moral and ethical questions that scientists will not necessarily ask on their own.

The work of the Federal Reserve Board, to which Levitt points to as an example of effective, extra-constitutional authority, exemplifies the narrowness of perspective that I am criticizing. The Fed bases its decision-making upon the assumption that the U.S. economy must grow in order to be healthy. It does not actively explore the idea that zero-growth or even "planned shrinkage" might be alternative routes to economic health; it does not encourage research about the economic

---

80. "Whatever might be said for the special talents of humanistic thinkers and social philosophers, in practice the outside world pretty much shrugs them off," Levitt dismissively writes. "Even worse, the spirit that has governed their disciplines has tended to look at the question of 'truth' with a resigned shrug. Grace of expression and moral passion have traditionally counted for more than the evidentiary protocols that the sciences relentlessly apply. At some level, these disciplines have implicitly abdicated."

restructuring that would be needed were low-impact living somehow to replace ostentatious wealth as an American "status symbol." As our society evolves more and more towards a "post-scarcity" status, however, with the production of goods and services incredibly cheap yet the fragility of the environment terribly real, the concept of a viable, no-growth economy becomes more and more deserving of scrutiny. Federal Reserve Board economists are not necessarily the most likely to venture "outside the box" this way — the ideas might just as likely come from an environmental activist, a hippie capitalist, a renunciate Buddhist monk, or an expert on the economic philosophy of Judaism!

Similarly, Levitt considers nuclear power to be a viable clean-energy source that is broadly opposed only because of "factors that go far beyond scientific skepticism," including "its mere association with nuclear weapons" and "a widespread feeling that atom splitting in its own right constitutes a primordial crime against the natural order." Yet my own earnest opposition to nuclear power is based far less on techno-phobia than on the half-life of plutonium, the most deadly by-product of nuclear fission, which persists in the environment for hundreds of thousands of years — an eternity, as far as human society is concerned. The very fact that fission produces such a powerful poison does, indeed, give me pause and make my sense of taboo tingle — but even if I don't permit myself to make a metaphor out of "unnatural" plutonium, the idea that we, in the 21st century, should feel entitled to do *anything* that will burden thousands of future generations with large amounts of poison seems morally unconscionable to me. However assured the arrogant scientist may be of his or her capacity to safeguard plutonium technologically, that sheer span of time makes all predictions about the maintenance of that technology ridiculously hubristic. Who knows what hundreds of thousands of years might produce in terms of war, political and environmental change, and social stability?

So perhaps there are, indeed, limits to where human beings should permit themselves to trespass. Perhaps the biblical injunction about blessings and curses — that we, like God, should "extend kindness to the thousandth generation" while visiting "the iniquity of parents" only "upon children and children's children, upon the third and fourth generation" (*Exodus* 34: 7) — deserves to be heeded as an enduring formula of survival wrought by our collective wisdom. Would Levitt's "scientific Fed" include such fundamentally *religious* considerations in its deliberations on nuclear power?

Many other issues of science, technology and the environment beg for "outside-the-box" thinking and non-scientific expertise that can help define values and priorities beyond the pages of corporate cost-benefit analyses. Yes, we will soon have the capacity to extend the lifespan of human beings to 200 years or more — but *should* we? In a world in which thousands still die of highly preventable diseases every hour, should we permit the development of man-made evolutionary enhancements that will be available only to a privileged sector? What would be the cost to our species-consciousness, our empathy, our capacity for global cooperation? Anthropologists, gerontologists, medical ethicists, psychologists, international relief workers, ethnic and tribal leaders, and numerous other experts might all have important perspectives to bring to such a discussion — along with the genetic and evolutionary biologists whom Levitt would, presumably, assign as chairpersons!

Yes, we can design a house like the one Bill Gates made famous in his book, *The Road Ahead* — a computerized abode programmed to know the residents' tastes and anticipate their desires — but *should* we? What forces of cultural evolution do we set in motion by having an utterly domesticated environment that serves us hand and foot? What, if anything, is lost to the imagination and the artistic impulse if we never have the experience of groping to find a light switch in a dark room? A roundtable on this question might include chairs for architects, futurists, theologians, and artists — as well as computer scientists and designers of artificial intelligence.

I realize that the very idea of hammering out a new environmentally-conscious moral consensus — or, at least, of evaluating the environmental impact of new innovations before they are permitted to come to market — raises vexing issues about democracy, church-state separation, pluralism, and more. While the "free market" often comes into conflict with the health of the planet, we know, too, that over-regulation can lead to the dissolution of freedom and to bureaucratic abuses that are just as hazardous to the environment. The fact is that neither Thomas Berry's call for a cultural and spiritual shift towards biocentrism, nor Norman Levitt's call for the privileging of science and scientists to a rank of special authority, adequately addresses the fundamental challenge to democracy and individual freedom that would accompany the development of a society-wide commitment to "social responsibility." Still, the need for a far-ranging discussion about what we *can* do and what we *should* do on this frail planet of ours is essential, and we should not shy away from it for fear of giving too much power to some ethical commissars or back-room powerbrokers. Surely there must be effective ways to honor, organize and ensure the dispassionate service of diverse people who combine expertise and wisdom — Nobel laureates come to mind as one highly respected pool of talent — in order to shape an objective world advisory board that could serve as a counterweight to the self-interested, unaccountable forces of political and economic power that currently dominate our planet. And surely, on such a board, both the radical spirituality of Thomas Berry and the radical humanism of Norman Levitt would deserve representation.[81]

THOMAS BERRY's *The Great Work* calls to the deeply spiritual, interconnected sensibility of human beings; Norman Levitt's *Prometheus Bedeviled* calls to our intellectual vibrancy. Berry's writing is motivational, subject to ideological bias; Levitt's is problem-solving, subject to humanistic arrogance. If the symbol of Levitt's faith in science is, indeed, to be Prometheus, the mythic bearer of fire and enlightener of humanity,[82] perhaps the symbol of biocentric transformation, as suggested by the resemblance between Thomas Berry's and Native

---

81. Nelson Mandela's 89th birthday on July 18, 2007, was marked by the formation of an international advisory group called "The Elders." Members include Mandela, Jimmy Carter, Kofi Anan, Archbishop Desmond Tutu, and Mary Robinson, the former president of Ireland. "This group can speak freely and boldly, working both publicly and behind the scenes on whatever actions need to be taken," said Mandela, according to the *International Herald Tribune.* "Together we will work to support courage where there is fear, foster agreement where there is conflict, and inspire hope where there is despair." "The Elders," Jimmy Carter said, "won't get involved in delivering bed nets for malaria prevention. The issue is to fill vacuums — to address major issues that aren't being adequately addressed."

82. In Greek mythology, Prometheus is variously described as the creator, benefactor or savior of humanity for giving mankind the gift of Fire. He was punished by Zeus in a fit of jealousy over the human race's enhanced status. Prometheus was bound by Force and Violence to a mountain in the Caucasus,

American spirituality, might be the Sacred Eagle.[83]

Must the Eagle occupy itself with gnawing at Prometheus' liver? Must our instinct to sacralize nature lead to the binding of science as the scapegoat for our alienation?

Must Prometheus' liberation depend, in turn, on killing the Eagle? Must science clip the inspirational wings of our religious instincts, making them useless for flight, in order to be unfettered in its mission?

I would prefer for the Eagle and Prometheus to unite against their master — the amoral, predatory and vastly powerful Zeus, Inc., who currently stands

> ". . . omnipotent.
> All else [has] been subdued to me; alone
> The soul of man, like unextinguished fire,
> Yet burns towards heaven with fierce reproach, and doubt,
> And lamentation, and reluctant prayer,
> Hurling up insurrection . . ."
> Percy Bysshe Shelley, "Prometheus Unbound"

Our quest for the "should" and the "why" of scientific innovation is today a fundamental element of that "insurrection." Whether our questioning follows the path of biocentric spirituality or scientific humanism is less important than that it lead away from the deep pockets, deep cynicism, and deep emptiness, of corporate culture.

---

to which an eagle flew daily to tear out his liver. Eventually he was freed by Hercules, who killed the predatory bird.

83. For details about the role of the eagle in Native American religion and culture, see: http://www.snowwowl.com/swolfeaglefeathers.html.

Lawrence Bush

Chapter Four

Cosmic Coincidence

"Jacob awoke from his sleep and said, 'Surely the Lord
is present in this place, and I did not know it!'
Shaken, he said, 'How awesome is this place!'"
Genesis 28: 16-17

THE PHONE RINGS as you're thinking about a long-lost friend — and it's the long-lost friend calling. A stranger's passing comment resonates profoundly with your thoughts and leads you to a life-altering decision. A bird crashes into your window pane and snaps you out of an angry tirade against your child. A rainbow appears just as you step out of your house on a first date.

Synchronicity — those richly meaningful coincidences in which your psyche and the outer world seem mysteriously synchronized — is probably the most common form of religious revelation in the world. "God is watching over us," "Nothing happens by accident" — these ubiquitous sentiments are given powerful credence by real-life episodes of synchronicity, particularly since they seemingly happen *to* us, without any qualifying acts of religious devotion or even conscious desire on our parts. Suddenly the material world seems attuned to our psyches, the flow of events seems shaped by our developmental needs, the creatures crossing our path are not only neighbors but angels. Our everyday perception of cause-and-effect becomes inadequate to explain what has happened, and the whole panoply of spiritual possibilities — karma, reincarnation, a responsive God, disease as metaphor, spiritual healing, dimensions before birth and beyond death, and so on — gain in credibility.

For the Woodstock generation, the impact of synchronicity experiences has been strengthened during the past two decades by the religious interpretation of modern physics, that most prestigious and philosophical of the sciences. The mysterious oddities of quantum physics, in particular, have been invoked in films and books to suggest that "anything is possible" — and explicable in scientific terms. Transformed from mathematics into metaphor, from physics into metaphysics, quantum dilemmas are invoked as "scientific evidence" that there is a spiritual reality beyond the materialism of our minds and the boundaries of our senses. The interpretation of coincidence as revelation then requires no leap of faith — for if subatomic particles that are gazillions of miles apart from one another can, as quantum physics suggests, be "entangled" so that what happens to one happens simultaneously to the other, and if at the subatomic level all of reality seems interdependent and relational, without discrete separations, why think that synchronicity, here at the macro level of existence, isn't also about the entanglement of meaning and event, reflecting the interdependent and relational nature of *all* reality?

THIS DISCUSSION ABOUT SYNCHRONICITY and science has intrigued me whenever it pokes its head into the popular culture because, atheist or not, I have had a number of mind-blowing synchronicity events of my own — experiences that spoke powerfully to my inner life, opened doors to life-changing opportunities, and felt very much like communications from some cosmic source. Let me tell a few stories.

EVENT #1: In 1981, I had my first breakthrough as a fiction writer when the *Village Voice* accepted a sci-fi vignette I'd written about human cloning, titled "Designer Genes." The story was framed as a letter written to an attorney by a man whose son was custom-designed by the genetic engineering division of Pierre Cardin, Inc. The man has spotted his son's exact double — industrial theft! — and wants to know if he can sue the offending family and the company.

I was overjoyed by the prospect of seeing my byline, "Larry Bush," in a major publication for the first time, which brought a sense of exuberant relief from the ambition and anxiety that often drove my writing. Before the story was even published, however, my respite was ended by a call from my *Village Voice* editor: A gay writer, also named Larry Bush, had suddenly emerged with an article about anti-gay backlash under the new Reagan administration. Did I want to alter my byline on "Designer Genes," perhaps add a middle initial, to differentiate me from my real-life clone?

In good conscience, I couldn't disavow my namesake and his struggle that way; I would have felt ashamed for allowing homophobia, my own or the public's, to call the shots. Instead, after both pieces were published — and after I'd fielded several phone calls intended for the "other" Larry Bush — I interviewed him in the *Village Voice* offices and learned some profound lessons about the deeper meaning of a byline.

A one-time presidential speechwriter in the Nixon administration, Larry had been stripped of his job after publishing a letter to the editor under his own name on a gay-rights issue. The son of a Mormon family, he faced ostracism and excommunication for "coming out" this way — a letter, nothing more! — and his parents were under pressure to disown him. There I was, all atwitter at the excitement of seeing my name in print, — and the other Larry had been severely sanctioned for exactly that experience.

I wrote up the interview as a meditation on names and identity, "To Be Or Not To Be Larry Bush," published in the *Village Voice*.[84] In the piece, I confessed that for years my homophobia had helped to shape my image (*cut your hair!*), my wardrobe (*ditch the drawstring pants!*), and my behavior (*don't cross your legs that way!*). In the process, I had seriously curbed my freedom to be myself. Reacting to my fear of being mistaken for gay, I had forced my gender identity into narrow channels of expression — an experience not so different, I reflected, than that of my name-changing Jewish relatives, who, in the 1920s, switched from "Babushkin" to "Bush" for fear of anti-Semitism. There were parallels between the gay experience and the Jewish experience, and bonds of solidarity between Larry Bush and me. I vowed, henceforth, to honor these bonds by trying to be more attuned to the social value of my writing than to the social status of my byline.[85]

---

84. The piece was anthologized in Harry Brod's *A Mensch Among Men: Explorations in Jewish Masculinity*, 1988.

85. After making this commitment, I did relaunch my byline as "Lawrence Bush," but so did the "other" Larry Bush, who appeared with gay-themed articles in the *Atlantic Monthly* and *The New York Times*. His byline seemed to disappear, however, at the height of the AIDS crisis, and I now fear that our "competition" may have been resolved tragically.

EVENT #2: In 1984, after spending our entire lives in New York City, my wife Susan and I decided to move to the country, for a number of reasons: We were sick of the endless concrete, the lack of sky, the architectural winter winds, and other aspects of the urban environment; the expense of city living was becoming ridiculous; we were coping with infertility and imagined that the slower pace of country life might reduce our stress and help us achieve a pregnancy. So I gave notice at the small Jewish magazine for which I served as assistant editor, and we rented a summer cabin with the plan of searching out a permanent home.

Driving north to take occupancy, Susan and I spoke of nothing but my employment prospects. What should I do next with my writing skills? What kind of status in the job market had my few years of magazine work earned? It was a nerve-wracking conversation, and as we stopped for coffee at a diner in the middle of nowhere along the parkway, I begged that we change the topic. The very notion of networking had me intimidated, I explained — if only I could simply be *discovered*, instead of having to call upon strangers!

Susan agreed to wind down the conversation, but first summed up her view that I should leave the world of Jewish publishing and seek a position on a more mainstream magazine. Perhaps so, I replied, yet I had already invested effort in developing my Jewish knowledge and contacts, and I found the many issues of Jewish identity intriguing, so if I could get a job, let's say, working with Al Vorspan . . .

Vorspan was the social-action spark plug of the Reform synagogue movement, America's largest Jewish denomination. I knew him from his writings and reputation as an outspoken liberal activist. If I could work with Al Vorspan, I trumpeted to Susan, it would broaden my influence, preserve my principles, make use of my expertise, and spare me from having to undergo a job search!

As I concluded this little declaration, the only other customer in the diner rose from the counter, paid his bill, and then strolled back towards us. "I hear you talking about Al Vorspan," he said. "I'm his brother-in-law. I was just about to call my sister, his wife . . ."

A minute later, I was on the phone with Mr. Vorspan. A week after that, we met. Soon we were co-authoring a book. Ultimately, Al passed me on to the president of the Reform movement, Rabbi Alexander M.

Schindler — who settled my career dilemma by retaining me as his speechwriter for the next dozen years!

EVENT #3: Our successful move to the country, and the phenomenal blessing of my work-at-home job, did nothing to alter our infertility. In 1986, we inaugurated a private adoption process, and soon made contact with our birth mother, who was only two months pregnant. In her third month, we learned that a new sonogram showed that she was carrying twins.[86] Joyously committed to going through with the adoption, we nevertheless wondered how we would handle what so many people commonly describe as "double trouble."

The next month we took a vacation trip to Nova Scotia. In only ten days of travel by car and boat, we met eight sets of twins! — whose parents, without exception, told us how wonderful their experiences were.

Weeks later, as we exited the New York State Thruway to meet our children's birth mother for the first time, the odometer in our rental car read: 222.2.

EVENT #4: My baby son's middle name became "Morrie," in honor of my father, deceased five years earlier. Dad was buried in a labor union sector of a cemetery that was halfway between our country home and New York City, and one Sunday I decided to visit the cemetery en route to an appointment in the city.

I had not been a frequent visitor to the grave and had no written travel instructions. The trip took much longer than I'd expected, and I was near to calling off the visit, for fear of being late for my appointment. Dad the atheist would certainly not be turning over in his grave if I failed to show! Still, I wanted to fulfill the impulse. I was a new father and needed to make a connection to my own. . . .

At last I found the cemetery and rushed into the office to be re-

---

86. Earlier, at Passover — at which time, our birth mother was pregnant but had not yet contacted us — Susan found a double yolk in the hard-boiled egg, the symbol of fertility, on her ritual seder plate. With our infertility weighing heavily on us, she'd described the omen as a "bad joke." Eighteen years later, on the morning of our children's high school graduation, Susan broke an egg for breakfast— and again came up with a double yolk! Bookend omens!

minded of the location of my father's site. There in the office behind the reception desk hung a 12-foot banner on continuous-feed computer paper that said: WELCOME, LARRY!!!

Now, EACH OF THESE EVENTS might be dismissed as simple coincidence by hard-core rationalists (in #4, the most spooky of the lot, the sign turned out to be a greeting for a computer repairman named Larry who had been summoned to the cemetery office for some emergency repairs). Yet each stands out from the usual rush of good luck/bad luck coincidences because of its portentous nature and its direct bearing upon my psychological development.

All four incidents occurred during a four-year period, as I was gaining my first accomplishments as a writer, building my capacity to earn a living, and preparing to become a father. These quests seemed to me at the time to be interrelated, dependent for their success upon my inner struggle for maturity. The side of my personality that was driven to achievement and hungry for notice and admiration seemed more and more to be a false construct, which I had cultivated as a young child in response to my parents' needs, and which I now needed to strip away in order to advance into my adulthood. In this self-analysis — which reads like a page from Alice Miller's *The Drama of the Gifted Child*[87] — I saw myself cast as my parents' savior, the grace note of their unrelenting marital squabble. My mother, deeply dependent and narcissistic, relied on me for love and appreciation, which her emotionally stingy husband denied her; my father, a restless, thwarted intellectual, held himself aloof and made his love and respect seem like prizes for others to win. By being a sunny lad, full of talent and accomplishment, I could fulfill their needs and serve as the glue binding their relationship. My failure, on the other hand, could bring disaster, the dissolution of my family.

I viewed these childhood dynamics as crucially linked to my career

---

87. Alice Miller's central contention is that children have "an amazing ability to perceive and respond intuitively, that is, unconsciously" to the emotional needs of their parents "and to shape their personalities to meet those needs" — at great cost to the children's inner peace and self-esteem. See *The Drama of the Gifted Child: The Search for the True Self*, 1979.

fears and perhaps even to my infertility.[88] My need, I believed, was to cultivate a more authentic and compassionate self, motivated less by the teeth-gnashing need for individual glory than by the recognition of connection and mutuality as the underlying reality of life. It was this emergent self to whom the "messages" of my synchronicity omens seemed directed, almost as a summoning.

CARL JUNG WOULD HAVE LOVED this stuff. The Swiss psychiatrist was particularly fascinated by the role of coincidence in our psychological development, and gave a name and a description to this "emergent self" phenomenon. He called it "individuation," a process of psychological maturation in which

> . . . the ego is ousted from its central role and dominating position and thus finds itself in the role of a passive observer who lacks the power to assert his will under all circumstances, not so much because it has been weakened in any way, as because certain considerations give it pause. That is, the ego cannot help discovering that the afflux of unconscious contents has vitalized the personality, enriched it and created a figure that somehow dwarfs the ego in scope and intensity. This experience . . . convinces the ego that in spite of all difficulties it is better to be taken down a peg than to get involved in a hopeless struggle in which one is invariably handed the wrong end of the stick.[89]

---

88. As I resigned myself to our infertility, I even began to value it as the termination of my (dysfunctional) family curse and as a chastening of my egotism. This kind of psychologically interpretive or magical thinking about disease or unexpected impairment was described by the late Susan Sontag in her books, *Illness as Metaphor* (1988) and *AIDS and Its Metaphors* (1990).

89. Carl Jung, "On the Nature of the Psyche," from *The Basic Writings of C. G. Jung*, edited by Violet Staub De Laszlo, 1959. Jung proposed a four-step process of individuation consisting of: 1) becoming aware of "the shadow," the dark side of our psyches that is filled with repressed materials; 2) becoming aware of the anima and animus, the inner femininity of every man and the inner masculinity of every woman; 3) becoming conscious of our "archetypal

This concept of "individuation" is vividly conveyed in the archetypal biblical story of Jacob — a story worth discussing here because of the links it illustrates between the process of individuation and synchronicity. Early in his saga (*Genesis* 27), Jacob is a classic egotist, self-serving and ambitious, whose name is a play on a Hebrew verb meaning "to overreach." He usurps his twin brother Esau's place as first-born and steals their father Isaac's blessing through disguise and deception. Jacob pretends to be someone he is not, to please his scheming mother and fool his weak-willed father.[90]

Fleeing Esau's vengeance, the young man has a revelation at a place he names Bethel (the House of God), where he dreams of a stairway ("Jacob's ladder") filled with angels going up and down. In Jungian terms, the image suggests permeability between the unconscious mind and the ego: Jacob's unconscious mind has offered what Jung called a "compensation" for his ego's shortcomings.[91]

Awake, Jacob takes a first step toward "individuation" by vowing to worship the God who has spoken to him in the dream. At this stage, however, his ego is not so ready to stand aside: Jacob's vow is contingent on God's guaranteeing his safety and daily bread during this period of exile. It is not until 20 years later — after Jacob has been cheated the way he cheated his brother and has undergone 14 years of penitential labor, as well as becoming a father many times over — that he is ready to be truly transformed by another moment of synchronicity. Facing a reckoning with Esau, Jacob encounters a "divine being," with whom he strives all night. As a result of this mysterious experience, the over-

---

spirit," which Jung conceived of as some eternal representation of the unity of spirit and matter; and finally 4) self-realization, arriving at the "transformed self."

90. Many biblical commentators have noted that Isaac seems to participate in his own deception. Perhaps Isaac is subconsciously aware of Jacob's identity and believes Jacob a worthier spiritual heir than Esau. In this scenario, Jacob is playing a charade to fulfil the needs of both his parents.

91. "The unconscious processes that compensate the conscious ego contain all those elements that are necessary for the self-regulation of the psyche as a whole." Carl Jung, "The Relations Between the Ego and the Unconscious," in *The Basic Writings of C.G. Jung*, 1959.

reacher is renamed "Israel," meaning "God-wrestler" — and his hip socket is wrenched so that he will have a permanent limp. Humbled both physically and spiritually, Jacob is now capable of discovering and expressing his authentic self.

To Jung, this unfolding of the authentic self was the motor force of human psychology and the actual purpose of life. As his interpreter Marie-Louise von Franz expresses it, "individuation and realization of the meaning of life are identical — since individuation means to find *one's own* meaning, which is nothing other than *one's own* connection with the universal Meaning."[92]

AH, BUT THERE IT IS! — the leap from meaning to "universal Meaning," from psychological insight to mystical sensibility, from Jacob's dream to Jacob's God — a leap that synchronicity events so easily tempt us to make. Carl Jung obviously made this leap, viewing the process of individuation as nothing less than a wrestling match with Divinity. "Since psyche and matter are contained in one and the same world," he wrote, "and moreover are in continuous contact with one another . . . it is not only possible but *fairly probable, even, that psyche and matter are two different aspects of one and the same thing. The* synchronicity phenomena point, it seems to me, in this direction . . ."[93] (italics added).

This leap of faith was precisely what I have been unwilling — and perhaps am constitutionally unable — to make, notwithstanding the power of my own synchronicity experiences. While it was my pleasure to *welcome* these experiences as bounties of good luck, and to handle their metaphoric contents *as if* they embodied messages from some Hidden Messenger, I have clung to my belief that synchronicity equals meaningful coincidence, nothing more — and that the meaning is purely subjective, not a "message" from a sentient universe.

Affirming otherwise would require me to accept the existence of unknown forces of interconnection (let's call them UFIs) between

---

92. Marie-Louise von Franz, *Psyche and Matter*, 1992, as quoted in Victor Mansfield's *Synchronicity, Science and Soul-Making*, 1995.

93. Carl Jung, "On the Nature of the Psyche," quoted in Victor Mansfield's *Synchronicity, Science and Soul-Making*, 1995.

my consciousness and the material world — forces that defy our rational and everyday understanding of that world. Such belief in UFIs seems to pervade every mystical charting of reality that exists, from the many-worlds view of the Jewish *kabbalah* to the Buddhist notion of karmic consequence. Unidentified Forces of Interconnection are invoked in defense of astrology: How otherwise could the infinitesmal gravitational pull of the other planets upon the earth, or the faint glow of stars that are gazillions of miles apart from each another, billions of years older than their visible glow, and patterned into zodiacal "signs" (constellations) only by human design, have any shaping influence upon our personalities? UFIs lend credibility to telekinesis and extrasensory perception: How else could the human brain, notwithstanding its variety of weak "waves" and electrical impulses, overcome the law of inertia and move a stationary object, or project "thoughts" across state lines? UFIs are used to explain homeopathic medicine: How else can solutions with active ingredients that have been diluted beyond the dilution limit, so that the active ingredient no longer has a molecular presence, nevertheless affect bodily health?

UFIs, in short, are invoked to hush the barking dog of rationality whenever and wherever the irrational trespasses.

I should add that the notion of a cosmic "aether" that pervades creation and makes non-material "transmissions" plausible predates the ancient Greeks and has a long history within the scientific community itself. Even Isaac Newton, a father of modern science, explained the force of gravity as the working of an invisible "luminiferous aether," which, he suggested, might also be responsible for light, heat, magnetism and electricity — and might be susceptible to human thought. (Such observations, along with Newton's sustained interest in astrology and the occult, led John Maynard Keyes, a collector of Newton manuscripts, to observe that ""Newton was not the first of the age of reason; he was the last of the magicians.")

But astrology, telepathy, telekinesis, homeopathy, and even Sir Isaac's theorizing offered no real challenge to my stubborn materialist skepticism about UFIs — skepticism that has been borne out by scientific testing of all kinds over the decades. Skeptic and stage magician James Randi ("The Amazing Randi"), for example, has since 1964 offered prize money (now $1 million) to anyone who

Lawrence Bush

can show evidence of any UFI event ("paranormal, supernatural or occult power or event" is how the website of the James Randi Educational Foundation describes it at www.randi.org) under observing conditions designed by both Randi and the one claiming to exercise such power. In most cases, preliminary tests occur at the site where the claimant lives, *not* in a scientific laboratory. Everything from water dowsing to psychic healing has been tested this way, and no one has ever passed even the preliminary tests.

NOW ALONG COMES QUANTUM METAPHYSICS — a field of spiritual scientific theorizing pioneered by Fritjof Capra, whose *The Tao of Physics* (1975) was an international bestseller.[94] Victor J. Stenger, a physicist at the University of Hawaii who coined that phrase, "quantum metaphysics" and is one of its sharpest critics, nevertheless offers a fair summary of its principles:[95]

"*The notion of a holistic universe, with everything instantaneously connected to everything else,* occurs in a number of interpretations of quantum mechanics," Stenger explains. "In one class of interpretations, still-undetected sub-quantum forces operate on particles . . . instantaneously over any distance" — an interpretation that contradicts the well-established theory that the speed of light is an uppermost limit for all forms of energy transmission, and suggests a universe of simultaneity and interconnection in which all separateness dissolves.

Then there is the quantum uncertainty principle — the bewildering fact that the position and momentum of subatomic particles cannot

---

94. Deepak Chopra's is the other best-known and best-selling advocate of quantum metaphysics. He emphasizes the promotion of good physical and mental health based on the notion that "the physical world, including our bodies, [are] a response of the observer. We create our bodies as we create the experience of our world." Amit Goswami's book, *The Self-Aware Universe: How Consciousness Creates the Material World*, likewise argues that "psychic phenomena, such as distant viewing and out-of-body experiences, are examples of the nonlocal operation of consciousness," a theory undergirded, he says, by quantum physics.

95. See Victor J. Stenger, "The Myth of Quantum Consciousness," in *The Humanist*, May/June, 1992. Stenger is the author of *The Unconscious Quantum: Metaphysics in Modern Physics and Cosmology*, 1995, and *God: The Failed Hypothesis, How Science Shows that God Does Not Exist*, 2007.

be simultaneously known with complete precision, and that the act of observation itself affects the particles' behavior — which has led quantum metaphysicians, says Stenger, to infer that "[human] consciousness controls the course of events throughout all of space and time. In these interpretations," he adds, with a note of contempt, "the universe is one and we are one with it."[96]

Quantum metaphysicians have used scientific theory and terminology to make the mystical seem highly plausible to modern minds. That grossly dishonest 2004 film, *What the #$@! Do We Know?*, depended upon this technique for its success, as it beguiled viewers into believing that the interpretation of quantum physics as an explanation of synchronicity and psychic phenomena is widely embraced in the scientific community.[97] This general trend of seeking scientific authentication for spiritual belief is especially widespread in Woodstocker circles and literature. A glance at a recent catalogue of the Omega Institute for Holistic Studies in Rhinebeck, New York, the best-established spiritual retreat center on the East Coast, is revealing in this regard: Yoga is described as the "science of happiness," and reflexology as an "ancient art and science"; astrophysicist Fiorella Terenzi explores "feminine forces and phenomena in the universe, the interconnection between space and cyberspace, and the concept of cosmic time and its influences over our earth-bound experience;" Deepak Chopra of-

---

96. See Victor J. Stenger's "Quantum Quackery," in *Skeptical Inquirer*, January, 1997 and "Mystical Physics: Has Science Found the Path to the Ultimate?" in *Free Inquiry*, Winter 1995-96.

97. The film has been sharply criticized by David Albert, a Columbia University physicist who appears on camera, as follows (reported in *Popular Science*, October, 2004, and at several online sites that critique the film): "I was edited in such a way as to completely suppress my actual views about the matters the movie discusses. I am, indeed, profoundly unsympathetic to attempts at linking quantum mechanics with consciousness. Moreover, I explained all that, at great length, on camera, to the producers of the film . . . Had I known that I would have been so radically misrepresented . . . I would certainly not have agreed to be filmed." Other "experts" presented in *What the #$@! Do We Know?* include John Hagelin, a leader of the "Natural Law Party" affiliated with the Transcendental Meditation movement (though he is not so identified) and Jeffrey Satinover, a medical doctor involved in "curing" homosexuals and who has written that "liberalism causes brain damage."

fers "spiritual wisdom and technology" that "teaches you . . . how your biological responses determine which level of reality you are able to access" — and so forth.

These and other Woodstocker leaders all think it worthwhile to their marketing effort to couch their teachings in quasi-scientific language. Quantum metaphysics, particularly when championed by professional physicists, is simply the brightest star in their firmament of "scientific" endorsements.

But I do find that star winking at me (WELCOME, LARRY!!!)....

So I TURN TO ANOTHER PHYSICIST named Victor: Dr. Victor Mansfield, a proud quantum metaphysicist who specializes in synchronicity. In his book, *Synchronicity, Science and Soul-Making*, Mansfield blends quantum theory, Jungian psychology, Buddhist wisdom and personal anecdote to open his readers' minds to the possibility that synchronicity is, indeed, a real-world phenomenon with metaphysical significance, not merely a human projection of meaning onto moments of coincidence. Particularly because of his status as a professional astrophysicist (at Colgate University) and his overt claims about the scientific underpinnings of the synchronicity experience, Mansfield's line of argument can seem very impressive, and is worth following a short distance.

First, he harnesses some startling outcomes of Einsteinian relativity — the fact, for example, that objects accelerated to near-light speed take on dramatically different physical sizes, relative to a given observer, than when at rest — to confound our "absolutist" notions about physical reality and thereby open our minds to the possibility that our inner world and the outer world might be, as he puts it, "related through meaning." "[S]pace and time are not the rigid absolutes we unreflectively believe them to be," Mansfield writes. "Many properties we believe are intrinsic to objects have only a relational being, one that depends for its value upon the reference frame in which it's observed."[98]

Next, Mansfield mobilizes that befuddling quantum uncertainty principle to "strike at the heart of our unreflective belief in a world populated by independent or separately existing entities" and to suggest that human consciousness is a primal force of nature. "[P]articles and

98. This and all other statements by Victor Mansfield are taken from his *Synchronicity, Science and Soul-Making*, 1995.

waves do not exist simultaneously [in an experimental beam of light] in some definite way . . . ," he writes. "Prior to measurement [that is, the interjection of consciousness], the system is truly indefinite, lacking in independent existence."

Mansfield hones his assault on our everyday perceptions of reality through an examination of the "entanglement" paradox of quantum physics, which was posed by Albert Einstein, Boris Podolsky and Nathan Rosen. This paradox notes that two photons resulting from a quantum reaction (for example, an ultraviolet laser beam passing through a crystal, which converts the beam from a single photon into two photons of lower energy) can fly off to opposite ends of the universe and yet maintain an identity of behavior, a "knowledge" of one another that seems to defy the fact that no energy or information can travel faster than the speed of light. Einstein described this as "spooky action at a distance" and believed that it proved quantum theory to be incomplete. He insisted on separability: "things claim an existence independent of one another," Einstein said, "insofar as these things 'lie in different parts of space.'" His great peer Niels Bohr believed, however, that "the possibility of speaking about phenomena as existing objectively" finds limits in the "formulation of quantum mechanics."[99]

Notwithstanding Einstein's skepticism, the phenomenon of "entanglement" has been generally accepted and implemented technologically; interpretation of the paradox is what has been debated throughout the century. For Victor Mansfield, this fact gives tremendous credence to a view of synchronicity that emphasizes the unity of mental and material reality. "[Q]uantum correlations," he writes, "reveal that nature is *noncausally* unified in ways we only dimly understand. We are so used to conceiving of a world of isolated and independently existing objects that it's very difficult for us to understand what the experiments are telling us about nature. They are truly confronting us with the demand for a major paradigm shift at the foundations of science and philosophy — one with enormous implications for fields well beyond the boundaries of science and philosophy."

---

99. Einstein, "Dialectica," 1948, translated by Donald Howard, and Niels Bohr, *Atomic Theory and the Description of Nature*, 1934, both quoted by Mansfield.

By this point, the majority of readers who have only a dim understanding of quantum theory might be likely to shrug and surrender to Mansfield's enthusiasm and expertise. He is not content with that, however, and instead bludgeons us with an analogy between the classical scientific belief in the independent existence and integrity of things and a so-called "ideology of separateness." This "ideology," Mansfield writes, "can lead to difficulties ranging from an inability to appreciate synchronicity . . . to rampant racism and nationalism with all the bloodletting that usually follows in its wake."

What a bullying comment! I would not argue with the idea that "ideologies of separateness" have given license to the worst of human nature through the ages, but to identify scientific belief in the discrete existence of things as a prime source of such an ideology requires, at the very least, ignoring all the racism, nationalism and bloodletting that *preceded* the advent of scientific reasoning, as well as the rich insights about the interconnection of life that has emerged from "classical" sciences.

Still, I find myself easily enthralled by Mansfield, for I share my generation's tendency to associate "separateness" with the dissecting and atom-splitting habits of science. "Separateness" is, for us, the great illusion of dualism, which "higher" consciousness resolves; "separateness" is the lonely alienation of atheism, which religion surmounts. "Separateness" also seems an apt term for the habits of egotism that my synchronicity experiences had moved me to try to abandon. Mansfield is thus using the same dynamics of compulsion and conversion that numerous gurus exercised upon Woodstockers during our years of immaturity. He plays upon our social conscience, our conflation of science and capitalism, and our misperception of the scientific enterprise as being "anti-holistic," to win a kind of guilty assent.[100]

Throughout the remainder of his book, Mansfield displays deep affinity for Jung's theories of the collective unconscious and "the ultimate

---

100. "[I]f one is predisposed to regard [the] Western position of privilege as wicked, for its prejudices and for its history of conquest, then one will inevitably regard Western science with suspicion and perhaps with contempt. Sooner or later any critique of Western values aspiring to be comprehensive must offer an analysis of natural science, preferably scathing." Paul R. Gross and Norman Levitt, *Higher Superstition, The Academic Left and Its Quarrels with Science*, 1994.

nature of mind," as well as for the "emptiness" concept of Middle Way Buddhism ("inherent existence, what we erroneously consider the core reality of an object, is simply non-existent," he writes, while our ongoing belief in "inherent existence" is "the primary cause of our suffering"). In the end, Mansfield posits a purely idealist view of the world as "a construction within our mind." He therefore leaves the great majority of rationalists, and even religious believers, standing on the docks as he sails to the edges of our "illusory" world.[101] Nevertheless, he seems to have given the synchronicity phenomenon some cutting-edge scientific support and to have removed the "Unidentified" label from our Unidentified Forces of Interconnection.

NOT SO, REPLIES the skeptical Victor, Dr. Stenger, who might say that UFIs become BFIs — Bogus Forces of Interconnection — when scientists like Mansfield are at work. Stenger points out that it was quantum theory, in league with relativity, that "established discreteness, rather than continuity" as the unifying principle of physics. To "turn this around," Stenger argues, "and say that 20th-century physics initiated some new holistic view of the universe is a complete misrepresentation of what actually took place."

> Einstein's principle that no signals can move faster
> than light implies that separated events in the universe,
> even those an atomic diameter apart, cannot be simul-
> taneously connected. This fundamentally contradicts
> the holistic view of an instantaneous interconnected-
> ness among all things. . . . A universal cosmic field
> like the aether, providing a mechanism for intercon-
> nectedness, requires a violation of Einstein's relativity.
> But relativity has passed every experimental test that

---

101. Mansfield fails entirely to discuss the nature of evil, suffering, and terrible coincidence within the context of his "mentalist" view of reality. Perhaps this failure is a mercy, as it seems that any mind-over-matter perspective must yield to powerlessness or resort to racism, sexism and other forms of prejudice when confronted by the concentration of suffering in certain human communities.

has been put to it since being introduced in 1905, so it cannot be casually discarded.[102]

Stenger stresses that "the quantum world only appears paradoxical when we force macroscopic principles upon it that do not apply at that [subatomic] level" — principles of time and causality, for example. It is quite a stretch, in other words, to assume that "as above, so below" — that mathematical equations concerned with behavior of subatomic particles can necessarily shed light on our waking reality.[103]

Mansfield's "reply" to this point is really quite weak. The "personal experience of interrelatedness in synchronicity," he admits "clearly differs" from examples of interconnectedness in physics: "One is a psychological experience while the other is a property of photons and particles investigated in the laboratory. Nevertheless," he continues, "it's accurate to say that we are examining the same principle from within two different disciplines," both of which deny "the fundamental commitment to isolated and independently existing entities."

To which Stenger would essentially reply: *Sez you!* "Not all interpretations of quantum mechanics are equally economical, or equally useful," he argues. "For example, those interpretations which claim that human consciousness determines the nature of reality are not parsimonious since this bizarre notion is not required by a scrap of reliable data." In fact, Stenger continues, since non-mystical explanations of quantum paradoxes *do* exist, the principle of Occam's Razor — "What can be

---

102. Victor J. Stenger, "The Myth of Quantum Consciousness," in *The Humanist*, May/June, 1992.

103. Stenger in *Free Inquiry*, Winter 1995-96. "The apparent paradoxes of quantum mechanics in fact disappear," he writes, "once we recognize that elementary processes do not distinguish between past and future or cause and effect. Experiments that seem to require superluminal connections when viewed in our familiar time direction are perfectly subluminal when the arrow of time is reversed. While this violates our common intuitions, those intuitions are based on our experiences in a world of many particles where phenomena that are fundamentally statistical nevertheless behave very predictably . . . In our lives, time flows one way, for all practical purposes. . . . At the quantum scale, however, no such consensus can be formed as particles interact without regard for an arrow of time."

done with fewer assumptions is done in vain with more"[104] — can be invoked to be rid of the very notion of UFIs.

Victor Stenger thus fortifies my rational (and exhausted!) mind — or, more honestly, my rationalist bias, since for the majority of us who are without training in physics or mathematics, this imaginary debate can be refereed only on the basis of our biases. After all, is Einstein's long-accepted theory that light speed is an absolute limit for the universe any *more* comprehensible or *less* mind-boggling to most of us than the theory of the instantaneous interconnection of all matter and energy? We who lack the tools to evaluate such abstruse theoretical material are likely to respond and judge based on its metaphorical appeal, and on that basis, even the most widely accepted scientific theories, as popularized in the culture, are likely to feed our spiritual impulses.

Doesn't Big Bang cosmology, for example — the theory that the whole shebang emerged from a cosmic egg in a microsecond some 15 billion years ago — make it seem likely that the universe, spawned from that single point of reality, would be interconnected, perhaps even a single, sentient organism?

Doesn't modern knowledge about the evolutionary tenacity of DNA — the fact that we are all living packets of DNA with replicating messages that are millions of years old — give rise to the feeling that the whole universe is bristling not only with shared physical and evolutionary laws but with profound meaning?

Human beings seem simply unable to resist rendering the world's patterns into symbols of significance. The "redness" of the planet Mars leads us to assign to it a bellicose persona; the resemblance to the human form of the ginseng root "explains" its energizing power; the ubiquity of male-female sexuality in nature leads us to posit the existence of "yin and yang energies" in the universe. This homeopathic inclination to interpret similarity as highly significant underlies many religious customs, from the "sympathetic magic" of indigenous pagan peoples to the occult beliefs of urbane New Agers. It seems hardwired into our natures, and we simply can't shake its grip for long.

My hardwiring must be on the fritz, however, for I remain stub-

---

104. Occam's Razor was formulated by William of Occam, a 14th-century English philosopher who urged parsimony or economy in the explanation of phenomena.

Lawrence Bush

bornly loyal to my rationalist family faith — WELCOME, LARRY! — as I continue searching for an Occam's Razor-stroke of my own: a simple, rational explanation of the extraordinary and auspicious events of my life.

ENTER RICHARD DAWKINS, the Charles Simonyi Professor of Public Understanding of Science at Oxford University. In his *Unweaving the Rainbow: Science, Delusion and the Appetite for Wonder*,[105] Dawkins provides the tools for demolishing the uncanny power of synchronicity: statistics and probability. He tells of how his wife once bought for her mother an antique watch, only to find when she peeled off the price label that the gift was already engraved with her mother's own initials, M.A.B.! Had Dawkins' wife been ruminating heavily about her relationship with M.A.B., the event would surely have enough "meaning" content to qualify as a synchronicity event, a step towards "individuation," a "spooky action at a distance."

But how remarkable *was* the coincidence? Dawkins considers the number of letters in the alphabet and the population of Britain (55 million) to calculate that "If every one of them bought an antique engraved watch we'd expect more than 3,000 . . . to gasp with amazement when they discovered that the watch already bore their mother's initials." Factoring in the actual probability of M.A.B. appearing as *British* citizen's initials (Dawkins uses a telephone directory for sampling), he further calculates that more than nineteen thousand Britons could have bought that particular watch and had their rationalism challenged by the experience.

Seen in the context of large populations with shared human traits, Dawkins argues, most coincidences readily reveal their true, non-mystical nature. Within any group of at least twenty-three people, for example, the mathematical chances are slightly greater than 50 percent that two of them will share the same birthday. Similarly, "quite a

---

105. Richard Dawkins, *Unweaving the Rainbow: Science, Delusion and the Appetite for Wonder*, Houghton Mifflin, 1998. The phrase, "Unweaving the Rainbow," is derived from John Keats, who expressed the opinion that Isaac Newton had "destroyed the poetry of the rainbow by reducing it to a prism." Dawkins' best-known work is *The Selfish Gene* (1976), and his most recent is *The God Delusion* (2006).

few people die every night, masses of people dream every night, they quite often dream that people die, and coincidences like this [troubled dreams that seem to predict actual deaths] are probably happening to several hundred people in the world every night."

Even viewed apart from large populations, our individual lives present endless opportunities for coincidence, Dawkins points out. We are constantly seeing, hearing, sensing phenomena; we are constantly flitting from one thought to the next, and we are genetically inclined "to see significance and pattern in coincidence" as "part of a more general tendency to seek patterns." He concludes: "There are so many minutes in every individual's lifetime that it would be quite surprising to find an individual who had *never* experienced a startling coincidence."

Seen through this lens, each of my personal synchronicity events can be rationalized. The concentration of writers and gay men in New York made it not-so-improbable that a gay writer with my rather common name would emerge. The concentration of approximately 1.5 million Jews in the New York metropolitan area, and the relative wealth of the Reform Jewish community, made it likely that several thousand Reform Jews could have provided me with a connection to Al Vorspan, one of their most visible leaders, had I bumped into them en route to their vacation homes north of the city in the early summer season. Spotting eight sets of twins when looking for them in the course of ten days at camping grounds and other family-friendly sites is not mathematically unlikely. Et cetera. Mysteries solved!

EVEN AS I BOW to Richard Dawkins' logic and knowledge, however, I find myself strangely *resistant* to his demystification of some of my most meaningful memories. When Dawkins plaintively asks, "What is so threatening about reason? Mysteries do not lose their poetry when solved" — I am tempted to reply: "Speak for yourself!"

Certainly, scientific insight can enhance our poetic sense of awe about the natural world; modern astronomy has especially unveiled a far more wondrous portrait of the physical universe than our pre-Copernican ancestors could ever have conceived. In the realm of personal experience, however, the rationalism of science somehow seems less enriching. How much more flattering to believe that the cosmos speaks to me through synchronicity — that the particulars of my career and my fatherhood are the workings of destiny! — than to reduce synchronicity to coincidence and destiny to dumb luck.

And so I sputter with inept arguments as I read Dawkins' explanation of his wife's engraved watch coincidence ("But 55 million Britons were *not* purchasing watches on that given day!"). I feel frustrated by his mathematically authoritative assertion about birthday coincidences — and, in desperation, I become skeptical that mathematics are actually predictive of reality. Leaving poor Dawkins aside, I have to explain to myself, again and again, the commonplace facts about chance and odds: that each successive flip of a coin, for example, has the same odds of coming up heads or tails. Five heads in a row make it no more likely that the next flip of the coin will yield tails — but those five-in-a-row *feel* significant, they *feel* as if they've shifted the odds!

My "intuitive" wrong-headedness is by no means my unique problem, but an indication of how we are all, by nature, inclined towards expecting an attuned and responsive world. We also find the magical interpretation of life experiences to be highly motivational, as in *God made me do it!* — or *the devil made me do it!* As Dawkins implies, however, the alternative to magical interpretations of reality need not be a lack of passion. Even while I remained agnostic, for example, about the metaphysical significance of my synchronicity experiences, I nevertheless did learn the lessons of my encounter with Larry Bush, did go to work as a writer for Rabbi Schindler, and did proceed, with delight, to become an adoptive parent. I was exercising moral, aesthetic, and emotional choice, and managed to steer myself towards the maturity I sought, with no less energy than had I believed that it was "God" who had delivered these opportunities to my feet.

SO WHAT IS IT ABOUT, this tenacious attraction to viewing the universe as enchanted, a fount of "messages," even for modern, scientifically-minded people? Why does that sixth coin flip, after five heads in a row, feel weighted with different odds — even when we know, rationally, that it is not?

Richard Dawkins attributes this "willing[ness] . . . to see pattern where there is none" to brain evolution. Due to the small populations of our evolutionary ancestors' communities and the limited range of their everyday experience, he writes, "our brains became calibrated to detect pattern and gasp with astonishment at a level of coincidence which would actually be quite modest if our catchment area of friends and acquaintances had been large." Numerous other scientists have added similar observations to the brew: that human beings were shaped by evolution to think magically and assign agency to unfamiliar events (it is far less risky to mistakenly interpret the shivering of a bush as the sign of lurking predator than to ignore its pattern-breaking movement); to systematize these perceptions; to create ritual behaviors and infuse them with symbolic power; to imitate one another; to form "in groups" and "out groups." These and other mental inclinations help to make popular certain worldwide patterns of religious belief.[106]

Investigations of the evolutionary roots of religion can, indeed, produce conclusions, quite thrilling for atheists, that seem to explain the miracles of synchronicity as simple misapprehension and to make unnecessary such explanations as UFIs or Divine Intervention. At the same time, however, the theories of evolutionary biologists, neuropsychologists and other scientists who are trying to map human nature have been disheartening for people of the political left, who have historically championed developmental theories that stress the impact of "nurture" over "nature" and the possibilities of human change over the seeming fixity of human "hardwiring." More importantly, the new sciences of evolutionary biology, evolutionary psychology, and neuropsychology seem to be based largely on the subjective interpretation of scant and fragmentary fossil evidence, infant and animal testing, and new brain-mapping technologies that yield results wide open to interpretation. These sciences are in their infancy and should be viewed with skepticism, for all of their compelling logic and "common sense" appeal.

The explanation of religious intuition that I grew up favoring draws its strength from psychology more than from evolutionary science. Sigmund Freud, in his tidy little classic, *The Future of an Illusion*, suggested that perceptions of a meaningful and nurturing universe arise

---

106. See especially Pascal Boyer's fascinating study, *Religion Explained: The Evolutionary Origins of Religious Thought*, 2001, which identifies the specific kinds of religious concepts that are especially credible to the mental architecture of human beings.

"from the necessity of defending oneself against the crushingly superior force of nature," in particular, the "terrifying impression of helplessness in childhood," which gives rise to "the need for protection" that we project onto a god-figure."[107] Ernest Becker, in his 1973 Pulitzer Prize-winning work, *The Denial of Death,* unpacked and updated Freud's explanation: The survival instinct displayed by virtually all life forms, says Becker, becomes a complicated matter in the human being, who must contend with death not only by striving to live but by symbolically overcoming it. We do so through a quest for "heroism" — "a feeling of primary value, of cosmic specialness, of ultimate usefulness to creation, of unshakable meaning," which enables us to repress the otherwise paralyzing awareness of our mortality. This "heroism," Becker concludes, is the "vital lie" that is "first and foremost a reflex of terror of death."[108]

Whether I am quoting Freud or Becker, however, I realize that I am dealing here with speculations that have even less verification than the new sciences can claim from their fossils and brain scans! What psychoanalyst has reliably charted the so-called "unconscious mind"? What researcher has glimpsed the real workings of infant consciousness beyond facial recognition and a few other elementary features? What clinical psychologist has proved that it is the terror of death that shapes our character and belief systems?

And what about my own fears? If religion is essentially a denial of death, why do I prefer the consolations of atheism to the supposed consolations of religion? Why do I prefer the prospect of leading a life

---

107. Sigmund Freud, *The Future of an Illusion,* 1964 (originally published in 1927).

108. Ernest Becker, *The Denial of Death,* 1973. Our sense of "heroism" is presumably not dependent on our being gifted or self-admiring: The majority that is either too downtrodden or mediocre to bask in a sense of personal heroism can rely on self-delusion as well as the vicarism of Hollywood, professional sports, political parties and other hierarchies and ideologies that provide heroic role models and salvational promises. Religion is obviously not least among these "heroic" institutions, with its fantasies of almighty beings and/or discernible meaning in the cosmos, its ubiquitous mythologies of rebirth or life-after-death — and its real-life heroic acts of charity, sacrifice, discipline, and community-building.

unjudged by any but my intimates to the prospect of Divine Judgment? Why do I feel, like the biblical Jacob, "shaken" by the idea that my own moments of synchronicity might be anything more than coincidence — that "God is present in this place, and I did not know it!"? Why does the idea of a universe of accountability and consequence terrify me more than the idea of a universe of happenstance?

"There is no psychology," wrote one of its most dogged and controversial critics, Thomas Szasz, "there is only biography and autobiography."[109] To the extent that I share this view, I cannot "trump" religious-minded arguments with psychological insight any more than I can disprove quantum mysticism with evidence from the physical sciences.

WHY, THEN, HAVE I continued to distrust the enthralling evidence of my own experience when it comes to synchronicity? The reason is straightforward: I have learned from science that the evidence of our own experience is not fully trustworthy. Eyewitness accounts are often inaccurate; intuitions are often misleading; our senses are easily fooled; our minds run in patterns that can be manipulated. Objectivity can be achieved only by double-blind testing and other techniques that make certain we are not being beguiled by what seems "obvious." No such tests have ever established the reality of UFIs, or Divine Intervention, despite our most fervent, intuitive conviction of their reality.

Given the shallowness of my scientific knowledge, however, I do recognize my atheism to be essentially an exercise not in proof or disproof, but in interpretation, bias, or aesthetic preference. "Coincidence" rather than "omen" simply makes more sense to me — despite my heart-stopping experiences. Likewise does the metaphor of "accident" appeal to me more than the metaphor of "design," the metaphors of death and temporality more than the metaphors of reincarnation and transcendence of the soul. I prefer the feelings of intelligence and exceptionalism that skepticism affords me to the feelings of humility and accountability that faith provokes. I am making a choice, in other words, to disbelieve — despite the evidence of my

---

109. Thomas Szasz, *Second Sin*, 1974.

Lawrence Bush

own experience, the biases of my own generation, and the murmurings of my own heart.

Part Two

Shaving Off God's Beard

Chapter Five

Original Sin

"God is a concept
By which we measure our pain.
I'll say it again:
God is a concept
By which we measure our pain."
—John Lennon, "God"

RUSS, MY OLDER BROTHER, is a Christian. His conversion some 30 years ago was a classic baby-boomer experience of spiritual awakening that led from psychedelic mysticism to yoga and meditation to a home-grown Christian sect to mainstream Orthodox Christianity — all this from the son of left wing, secular Jews.

The groundbed of Russ' conversionary process seemed to be psychological pain. He had always been a sensitive and afflicted soul, prone to shyness and depression, envy and rage, and beset by allergies, adolescent acne, poor vision, and other physical annoyances that made his boyhood difficult. The drugs, sex and rock 'n' roll culture of the 1960s seemed to deepen, rather than alleviate, his inner turmoil, and by the time he graduated from college in 1970, Russ seemed pretty much a lost soul. His days were spent working at the post office, living with our parents (whose domain I had left the year before), and generally despising his life.

Why did my brother suffer so — and how had I managed to avoid his afflictions, though we shared many fraternal similarities? In later life, as I familiarized myself with Bible lore, I came to think of our relationship as a Cain and Abel story: Cain, the elder brother, a tiller of the soil, struggles with the earth to win its bounty, while Abel, the younger brother, is a shepherd who wanders happily with his flock. Cain's offering is inexplicably ignored by God, while "the Lord paid heed to Abel and his offering" (*Genesis* 4:4). Interestingly, it is Cain who actually converses face-to-face with God more than any biblical character but Abraham and Moses:

> And the Lord said to Cain:
> "Why are you distressed,
> And why is your face fallen?
> . . . Sin couches at the door;
> Its urge is toward you,
> Yet you can be its master." (*Genesis* 4: 6-7)

While I never feared physical violence from "Cain" beyond the occasional poke or punch, I did feel guilt over his suffering. Although his junior by nearly three years, I had been the first to ride a bike, the first to kiss a girl, and the first to move out of our family home. I was the worldly, happy one — or so it seemed in my contentious and depressed family. While Russ was actually a real mentor to me, a much-adored older brother who turned me on to folk music, rock 'n' roll, *Mad* magazine, late-night talk radio, and everything else that seemed cool, smart or worthwhile in American culture, my precocity must have been, for him, a constant prod and irritant. In a sense, by converting to Christianity, Russ managed to opt out of our fraternal competition, and out of our family dynamics altogether.

Russ's JOURNEY BEGAN with a sudden decision to attend a ten-day Integral Yoga silent retreat — a last-minute move that cost him his post office job. At a subsequent summer yoga institute, Russ became friendly with a few guys who were interested in forming an "ashram," a collective house committed to yogic disciplines. They rented a place on the Long Island Sound, but their experiment faced dissolution after only nine months, when the returning summer season drove their rent sky high.

After those nine months of meditation, careful eating, a disciplined schedule, and a drug-and-alcohol-free environment, Russ felt very certain that he did not want to return to his unhappy routine in New York, but no alternative had presented itself. Then synchronicity hit. One day he found himself in the parking lot of a mall at a traveling carnival. Here's how Russ told his own story, in a videotaped interview some years ago:

> There was a nickel toss game, and this magnificent goblet that you could win — carnival glass, actually, it was a fake, but I wanted that goblet. I kept missing and missing, and then with one last nickel, I said, "This is it." Bing! I had my goblet.
>
> As I was leaving the carnival, this hawker pulled me over to his ring-toss game. I gave him a buck, started playing, but he kept changing the rules and taking my money while dancing me around. Finally, I said, "Listen, Sir, have you been ripping me off? I'm not angry about it, I just need to know for my own sanity: You've been ripping me off, haven't you?"
>
> He got very angry. "Listen, kid," he said, "if you want to learn the rules of the road, you gotta *live* on the road. Now, get out of here!" And he pointed to the exit gate.
>
> I'm walking to my car and suddenly I'm facing this moment of decision. "You know," I say to myself, "you've been wondering what to do . . . you *could* join that carnival."
>
> "*Me?* Join a carnival? With criminals and low-lifes?"
>
> "Yeah, *you.* The man said it: 'If you want to learn the rules of the road . . .' You *could* join that carnival."

So Russ headed back into the fairgrounds, found the hiring office, and spent much of 1972-'73 living on the road, sleeping in trucks, pitching the big-top tent, caring for a baby elephant, and so on. His decision to interpret the carny's outburst as though the man were a fateful messenger helped my brother to avoid returning to New York and eventually led him on a life-changing odyssey. In Denver, Colorado, Russ had a chance encounter on a bus with a woman from a small Christian sect called the Holy Order of MANS[110] (an acronym for the Greek words *mysterion*, mystery, *agape*, love, *nous*, mind, and *sofia*, wisdom). She conversed with him for a while and then brought tears to his eyes by saying, "You've had a hard life." Russ was invited to attend some study and prayer classes, and soon thereafter he joined the Order as a "renunciate brother," living under vows of poverty, chastity, obedience, and more. "I felt as though a spiritual structure, like a pyramid, had been constructed by the yoga," Russ reports, "and by all these points of decision at which I moved away from darkness and self-destruction. The final piece at the top, the piece that completed the pyramid, was Jesus Christ."

Russ's CONVERSION came at the height of the cult craze, when the Moonies, the Hare Krishna movement, the Divine Light Mission and assorted others were recruiting heavily among the lost souls of the baby-boom generation, "love-bombing" them into a sense of group loyalty and exhausting their rational resistance with sleep deprivation, isolation from family and familiars, indoctrination, endless chanting, poor diet, and other mind-control techniques. None of these supposed signs of cultism were in evidence to me, however, when I visited Russ — now living as "Brother Tim" — in various group homes maintained by the Holy Order of MANS in small cities around the country. There seemed to be no adored guru, only a typical religious hierarchy of bishops, priests, monks, nuns and novitiates. Russ was not isolated from the world or exhausted by meaningless drudgery, but spent his days employed at Goodwill Industries or other charitable institutions and his evenings in study, prayer, contemplation and group-home chores.

---

110. The Holy Order of MANS was founded in 1968 in San Francisco by Earl Blighton, a former electrical engineer. By 1974 it had approximately 3,000 members in "mission centers" in 60 cities and 48 states. Among its activities was the establishment of homeless shelters called Raphael House, which still exist in several locations today. Blighton died in 1974, and the Order began to split into several groups. For an overview, see: http://religiousmovements. lib.virginia.edu/nrms/holymans.html.

He did not accost me with proselytizing or paranoia, and did not seem to have undergone a major personality alteration.

What *was* different about my brother was his sudden rejection of the countercultural pleasures to which he had introduced me throughout our lives together. Russ would not listen to or discuss rock 'n' roll or folk music. He would not read *Mad* magazine or Paul Krassner's *The Realist* or any other culturally insurgent literature. He would not talk politics. He would not drink or smoke pot, tell jokes or laugh uproariously. He would not show even mild interest in cute women on the street. Russ had determined the "sin couch(ing) at the door" to be the very energies of the 1960s that I considered to be most creative and insurgent. Once a "freak," Russ was now a "straight."

Although he did not articulate it as such, I sensed that Russ perceived all of that '60s stuff as egotism, self-indulgence, flirtation with the devil. *Oh, aren't we precious?* he might have said. *Aren't we an enlightened generation? Aren't we sexy and free? Bullshit! We are, like all human beings, tainted by original sin.* That was the Christian concept that seemed to have grabbed him most powerfully: original sin, the fallen nature of humankind, which represented a 180-degree turn away from the leftwing presumptions of human progress and perfectability that had been our intellectual inheritance.

But did my brother really believe that Adam and Eve and the Garden of Eden once existed? Did he really believe that a virgin named Mary was impregnated by the Lord and gave birth to a God-made-flesh, Jesus the Christ? Did Russ really believe that this Man healed the sick, raised the dead, and fed thousands from a few loaves of bread? Did he really believe that Jesus was crucified, done to death, and then walked in the world alive, resurrected? In the course of my visits, I used these literalist questions to defend my faithlessness from Russ's influence, and to draw him away from the kind of religiosity that would seem completely alien to me. If only I could get Russ to examine his Christian metaphors from a Freudian perspective, I believed, the true motives of his conversion would become clear to him and the need to persist in this monastic life would dissipate.

Look at the symbolism of Jesus on the cross, I wanted to say to him — *Jesus, spread-eagled, with a slit in his abdomen. The castrated man with the displaced wound . . . the mother who is a virgin . . . the father who is all-powerful . . . It's the Oedipal complex, resolved! Think about it: how we always submitted to Dad, saw him as the attractive parent, yearned for him and were, in turn, betrayed — "Father, father, why hast thou forsaken me?" — by his moodiness, his inattention, his stinginess. And how we despised Mom, as Dad wished for us to do — "Who is my mother . . . ? Whoever does the will of my Father in heaven . . ."*[111]

YEP, I KNEW a few things about the symbolism of Jesus the Christ, for only two years before Russ' conversion, I'd undergone an LSD trip, the last of my psychedelic career, in which I *became* Jesus for one night. It was during a cross-country, hitchhiking summer pilgrimage. I was 19 years old, newly arrived in Los Angeles, without money and eventually without clothing as I ran about the streets of Venice Beach, stark naked and proclaiming the glories of creation to startled pass-ersby. The acid was the strongest I'd ever swallowed, and I had lost the awareness that I was under its influence and that other humans were not actively sharing my reality. Instead, I believed that I had discovered a Perfect System of Communication — a sort of instant intimacy based on making presumptuous remarks to people after peering into their inner souls. I believed that through this system the gap between human beings could be bridged, all alienation could be overcome, and we would somehow merge and find peace.

I believed, moreover, in the slogan of Chicago, 1968: "The whole world is watching." I believed that all activity on the globe had paused and that all human consciousness was focused on me and my endeavor that night. If I succeeded in "perfecting" myself, the New Age would be ushered in. If I failed, we were *kaput* — the Bomb would fall.

So I ran out naked to the streets, preaching to people. When the police came and handcuffed me, I preached to them. When I was put into a small padded cell in the Venice County jail, I preached to myself. I prayed to the world's leaders, chanting, "Nixon, Mao, Kosygin. Nixon, Mao, Kosygin, God. Nixon, Mao, Martians, God! *Je parle seulement français et anglais* and a *bisl Yiddish*. Let there be peace, oh, please."

Outside my cell the toilets of the jail flushed automatically every few minutes. I believed these sounds to be roar of the Bomb, coming

---

111. *Matthew* 12:48-50

closer to ground zero and growling its terrible warning. I was failing, failing utterly!

Then finally — mercifully — I passed out.

Twenty-four hours later, this very messy and embarrassing psyche-delic psychosis ended with a transcontinental call to my parents and a transcontinental flight by a very disapproving father, to get me out of my fix and return me to the East Coast. During the months that fol-lowed, however, I continued to engage with the experience in a kind of self-analysis of writing and reflection. I came to see my messian-ism as a conditioned response to my parents' marital wars. I had been cast from a very young age, it seemed, as a golden boy able to fetch a rare smile from Dad and bring a little love to Mom — or, failing that, as the crucified one whose suffering could motivate them to call temporary truces (hence I was an accident-prone child and teenager). Based on this supposed self-understanding, I viewed Russ' embrace of Christianity as a similar "acting out," and I was intent on helping him escape the "padded cell" of his religious conversion by bringing him to psychological terms with it.

It didn't work out that way.

My campaign to reclaim Russ was quickly halted by the realiza-tion that I had little to offer him as an alternative to his new salvational beliefs. This was especially confirmed for me when my father, angry and disappointed that one of his sons could have "fallen for that non-sense," sent Russ a copy of Bertrand Russell's *Why I Am Not a Christian* and then cut off the relationship. Yikes! Did Dad really think Bertrand Russell's philosophy was going to save Russ from his near suicidal depressions? Or that a Marxist analysis of class society would alleviate his debilitating feelings of envy? Or that a Freudian understanding of religious infantilism would deter him from being self-destructive with food and drugs? Or that a skeptical view of miracles and pseudosci-ence would grant him a feeling of community and security? Or that my father's own *conditional* paternal love could win its contest with the *unconditional* love of Jesus? It struck me hard that the humanism our family offered promised neither healing nor hope to my tormented brother.

Russ' conversionary process, on the other hand, was having a compelling influence *on me*. I had never before loved and admired a person who actively believed in a religious system and used that belief to build his inner character. During his eight years as a novitiate monk in the Holy Order, Russ' ongoing display of discipline, humility, and courage in pursuing his faith, despite the bewilderment of all his closest friends and the ostracism that emanated from my father, made me sharply aware of my own condescension and ignorance when it came to religion. I had never even read the Bible! I knew less about my own Jewish heritage than I knew about Christianity, and my head was filled with special disdain for observant Jews. I had discounted the religiosity of my most admired historical heroes — Martin Luther King, Jr. and Mahatma Gandhi — as though they had only opportunistically expressed their quests for justice in the idioms of faith. I was blind to the community-building, celebratory, inspirational, and morally uplifting potential of religious practice, and had simply scorned it all as a system of deceit, ignorance, sexual repression and escapism. Now my arrogance was giving way to fear — fear that I was constitutionally incapable of belief of any kind, and could serve no cause in life greater than my own glory.

None of this youthful soul-searching made the actual Christian mythology that Russ was embracing any more credible or savory to me, but with an open mind I began to explore Judaism, to explore modern theologies, and to engage with the career that I have now pursued for more some 30 years. As the baby boomers embraced spirituality, I came to realize that there were a large number of my peers who were blending their politics and their spirituality without turning to fundamentalism. Abandoning my desire to reclaim Russ as a rationalist, I began to wonder if we might journey together in the direction of this progressive religious camp.

So BEGAN SEVERAL YEARS of political and religious dialogue between brothers. I would challenge Russ to remain openhearted and liberal about social issues that were being demonized by the Christian Right, and to remain creative and interpretive in his engagement with the Bible stories, parables and symbols of his faith. He, in turn, would challenge me about my loyalty to the values of the Woodstock Nation

— as when I asked him why he always dressed unfashionably, rather like a refugee from KMart, and he replied, "Why would I want to be all involved in sexual stuff when I'm walking down the street?" His question forced me to distinguish between vanity and self-esteem, and to dig more deeply into questions of marital commitment, sexual monogamy, sexism, aging, and my own fear of mortality.

Russ and I were careful not to go too far in the direction of disagreement. I stopped asking, for example, if he believed that all Muslims, Hindus, Buddhists, animists, and Jews, including little ol' me, were bound for hell. We had plenty to share as brothers besides religious dialogue, particularly as our relationship normalized once Russ was barred from taking permanent vows by his higher-ups in the Holy Order of MANS (vows, they said, were meant to reflect and support a spiritual state, not impose one, and he was having a very hard time with chastity and obedience). My brother's time as a monk thus ended, and he reemerged into the world — just in time for my father's funeral, in 1981. Russ returned to my geographic area, married, had children, and actively participated in a Holy Order church community. Ultimately, the Order split into several factions, the main body of which merged with the Orthodox Church of America in 1988. This merger resulted in the defrocking of all their women priests and the adoption of a very different and elaborate liturgy, but my brother stuck with his community and is now a practicing Orthodox Christian (what most of us know as "Russian Orthodox"). When we get together as a pair or in our families, "God talk" is usually only a minor part of our chit-chat.

Throughout this evolution, Russ continued to serve as the only intimate friend with whom I consistently spoke about religious and moral matters. As I plugged into the writings of liberation theologians who were incorporating feminist, environmentalist, and non-authoritarian wisdom into their theologies, I thought to share some of my discoveries with him, with the goal of finding common ground. Therefore, in the late 1980s, I mailed Russ a copy of *The Cosmic Christ,* a book by Matthew Fox that I'd received for review. Although I had never read Fox — I was too busy enough trying to catch up on my Jewish studies! — I knew him as a progressive and controversial Catholic activist and theologian, much-admired in liberation theology circles, so I figured

The Cosmic Christ would be a challenging, engrossing book for my brother and me to talk about.

To my chagrin, Russ mailed it right back, informing me that Fox's writings were "forbidden literature," proscribed by the leadership of his church. Our "common ground," it seemed, was to be fenced off by edict. I decided to read Matthew Fox to find out why.

FOX IS AN EX-ROMAN CATHOLIC PRIEST, author of more than 27 books on theology, spirituality and culture, who was silenced for a year (1988) by the Vatican and dismissed from the Dominican order five years later, after efforts to prove him a heretic and have him excommunicated failed. Today, he is an Episcopal priest and resides in Oakland, California. As a radical innovator in the fields of worship and education, he became best known for incorporating dance and trance music in religious services that he called "techno-masses." Of the reasons for his persecution by the Church, Fox, in 1993, said the following: "Their first [charge] is that I'm a feminist theologian, although I didn't know it was heresy to be a feminist. Secondly, I call God 'mother'; well, I proved that medieval mystics do [that] and even the Bible does. Thirdly, I call God 'child.' Well, mystics do this too. Number four, I don't condemn homosexuals. Number five, I believe in Original Blessing more than Original Sin. Number six, I'm not depressed as they are."[112]

Flippancy aside, Fox's list reveals several elements that make his theology attractive to liberal-minded people who want their religious practice to empower their real-life desire to transform the world. Fox envisions a Creation-centered Christianity that takes a salvational view of life, not of the after-life. As practiced in the mainstream today, he says, Christianity is too introspective and otherworldly, denying not only the power of death but the power of life. It represses the feminine and the erotic, devalues our sense of awe and blessing, and emphasizes "original sin," the sinful nature of our humanness, rather than our enormous potential as "royal personages," created, as the Bible tells us, in God's own image. Mainstream Christianity hasn't the capacity,

---

112. These comments by Matthew Fox are contained in a 1993 interview to be found at www.levity.com/mavericks/fox.htm. Other quotes are from Fox's *Original Blessing*, originally published in 1983, re-released in 2000.

therefore, to awaken us to our planetary crisis and give us a real stake in our worldly salvation. "We have everything to lose," Fox declares,

> . . . and that's why the only resolution is an awakening of gratitude and reverence for the planet, and falling in love in more than an anthropocentric fashion. In that experience there is an [abundance] of gratitudinal energy, and that's what we need to change our destiny.

In the best-known of his books, the dense and poetic *Original Blessing*, Fox reveals his celebration of diversity and syncretism[113] by bringing together voices from dozens of faiths, artistic traditions, cultures and historical eras, all in the name of a Creation-centered spirituality that will serve planetary survival. "When creation becomes the starting point of spirituality once again," he writes, "then hope will return also. We will see everything differently, including Divinity itself. . . . The issue at stake is nothing less than *biophilia vs. necrophilia.*"

Specifically, Fox promotes "our moving from theism to panentheism," which he carefully differentiates from the classic heresy of pantheism: "Pantheism . . . states that 'everything is God and God is everything.' Panentheism, on the other hand, is altogether orthodox and very fit for orthopraxis . . . for it slips in the little Greek word *en* and thus means, 'God is *in* everything and everything is *in* God.' . . . *Panentheism is a*

---

113. Fox's syncretism has personal roots: "I grew up in Wisconsin," he explains in his online interview, "and I was certainly influenced . . . by the presence of the Native American spirit . . . from the time I was very little I had Indian dreams. It was a university town and the whole issue of ideas became very important to me. I was Catholic and my best friends were Jewish and agnostic, and we'd get into these philosophical debates which were a lot of fun. . . . My father was Irish-Catholic, my mother was half Jewish and half Anglican and although she became a Catholic, she always kept her freedom. So it was a very ecumenical household. When I was a teenager we lived in a large house with my six brothers and sisters. As they went out to college my parents would rent out their rooms to foreign graduate students. So I spent my high school years next door to a Sikh from India who wore a turban at three in the morning, a man from Venezuela who would pull his shirt up to show his bullfighting scars, a communist from Yugoslavia, and an atheist from Norway. It was a very broad education."

way of seeing the world sacramentally" (italics added).

Our human task, Fox continues, is "to develop our powers as images of God." He favors the beautiful definition of sin offered by Rabbi Abraham Joshua Heschel: sin as our refusal to become who we are, to become fully human and to acknowledge our interconnection. "Take any sin: war, burglary, rape, thievery," Fox writes. "Every such action is treating another as an object outside oneself." This "dualism," he continues, "accounts for the sin of putting the egological ahead of the ecological. It is, when one thinks of it, a rather substantial sin of omission to omit the cosmos itself." Yet thanks to the "profoundly introspective" fall/redemption tradition of Christianity, Fox writes, we are doing precisely that:

> We are without cosmos, without myth, without ritual worthy of the name. No wonder we are cosmically sad, cosmically lonely, cosmically destructive in our military plans to rain death on the rest of the creation we know. It is time that religious believers of all creation-centered traditions unite forces to wake themselves, other believers, and the culture up. . . . The earth can no longer tolerate the sin of introspective religion.

Whereas introspective Christianity emphasizes "righteousness," Creation-centered Christianity emphasizes "justice." Whereas the introspective emphasizes "duty," the Creation-centered emphasizes "beauty." "Guilt and redemption" become secondary to "thanks and praise," and "purity from the world" secondary to "hospitality to all of being." The "struggle to clean one's conscience" is subordinated to the "struggle to make justice of injustice and to balance the cosmos," and the view of human beings as sinners is subordinated to the view of human beings as "royal persons who can choose to create or destroy." The concept that "eternal life is after death" translates into "eternal life is now," ascetic practice becomes aesthetic practice, sexual passion is celebrated as a blessing rather than a curse — and so on.

MUCH OF THIS HAS TREMENDOUS APPEAL for me in my search for religious metaphors that are more or less free of irrationality and offer humanistic (or even better, biocentric) inspiration for constructive behavior. Even most atheists would not argue with the need to cultivate in the human race a "sacramental" view of our living world — a conserving, loving, filial view of Mother Earth that might provoke us to pause in our greed, take heed of our future, and restrain the destructive power of our collective egotism. And what progressive critic of modern capitalist society would not hop at the chance to reshape our social institutions based on a recognition of interconnection and shared blessing instead of competition and "dualism"? And what ex-hippie would not be attracted to a spirituality that emphasizes creativity, community, diversity and eros?

Yet I lose my sense of solidarity with Matthew Fox whenever he reiterates his attachment to the fundamental stories and texts of Christianity — as he does throughout *Original Blessing*. His book maps out four, interconnected paths of Creation spirituality, and for each, Fox presents Jesus Christ as the embodiment:

• The *Via Positiva*, a path of "cosmic blessing and our own royal personhood": "The Good News that Jesus brings is news that all are considered royal persons by God, all have rights, all have divine dignity."

• The *Via Negativa*, a path of "darkness, silence, and emptiness": ". . . Jesus knew that the only way to live life fully was to let go of it radically. . . . Fear of death is the cause of so much sin . . . Jesus' liberation, then, is of the most radical and the most universal kind."

• The *Via Creativa*, a path that expresses the "full meaning of humanity's being an 'image of God'": "Jesus was a poet, a storyteller, an artist. . . . Fall/redemption theologies have reduced Christianity to the cross alone . . . and have forgotten . . . Jesus' choice of action as an artist."

• The *Via Transformativa*, a path of "creation renewed, seen anew, and righted from its state of sinful or unjust relationships": "The death of Jesus on the cross was meant to be the last instance of human violence toward the beauty of creation and toward justice-making, compassionate persons. . . . Jesus calls all persons to be compassionate prophets, transformers of society and of pain and suffering."

Why should I be repelled by any of this? Why not set aside my scorn for literalism and simply embrace the teachings, if not the divinity or even the historicity, of Jesus of Nazareth as interpreted by Matthew

Fox? I have, after all, lit Sabbath candles without believing that God rested on the seventh day after creating the universe in six; I have embraced and written about much of Judaism's economic philosophy without believing it was divinely ordained at Mt. Sinai; I have been willing to make my living as a writer who regularly translates religious philosophy into humanistic terms. So why do anything but cheer Matthew Fox's efforts to restore to Christianity what he calls "the Jesus energy, the prophetic energy, the anger to change things"?

In truth, mostly my response is one of prejudice. Even the basic story-line of Christianity — God offering redemption from sin to humanity by sacrificing his "only begotten son" in a torturous death — has always seemed far more grim and repellent than redemptive to me, while the notion that this world of ours has ever known a messiah/ redeemer seems ludicrous in the face of the painful reality I perceive around me. Such judgments are further inflamed by a scabrous feeling of Jewish injury at Christian hands and by my ongoing distress at the repressive, Republican spirituality of the "born again" movement that now looms so large in American culture. At bottom, there seems to me to be a fundamental moral defect in Christianity — its salvational, and therefore condemnatory, triumphalism — that makes it impossible for me to embrace even Matthew Fox's humanistic perspective on Jesus. All of Christianity's historical crimes were given license by this triumphalism, in such passages of the New Testament as *John* 3:18, which proclaims: "He who believe in [the Son] is not condemned; he who does not believe is condemned already."

Then there is the related critique offered by my father's shining knight, Sir Bertrand Russell, who wrote, in 1929, in *Why I Am Not a Christian*: "There is one very serious defect to my mind in Christ's moral character, and that is that He believed in hell. . . . "

> I do not myself feel that any person that is really pro-
> foundly humane can believe in everlasting punishment.
> . . . all this doctrine, that hell-fire is a punishment for
> sin, is a doctrine of cruelty. It is a doctrine that put
> cruelty into the world, and gave the world genera-
> tions of cruel torture; and the Christ of the Gospels,
> if you could take Him as his chroniclers represent

Him, would certainly have to be considered partly responsible for that.

The idea "that we should all be wicked if we did not hold to the Christian religion," Russell continues, has made Christianity into "the principal enemy of moral progress in the world. . . ."

> [E]very single bit of progress of humane feeling, every improvement in the criminal law, every step toward the diminution of war, every step toward better treatment of the colored races, or every mitigation of slavery, every moral progress that there has been in the world, has been consistently opposed by the organized churches . . .[114]

Matthew Fox might counter that these crimes stem from sixteen centuries of monstrous distortion of Jesus' teachings. It was Augustine, in the 4th century, he argues, who established the "hegemony of salvation as deliverance over salvation as blessing," which was seized upon by the Church just as it was inheriting the Roman Empire. "[A]n exaggerated doctrine of original sin," Fox explains, "one that is employed as a starting point for spirituality, plays kindly into the hands of empire-builders, slavemasters, and patriarchal society in general." Fox maintains that prior to Augustine, and during a resurgence of the Goddess during the 11th and 12th centuries, Christianity was a force for progress and human exaltation — for building heaven on earth, not for threatening hell in the afterlife.

One could make a parallel argument about communism — it was the practice, not the theory! — but I have learned to be wary of apologias that separate ideologies from their alleged hijackers. Stalin, Mao, Pol Pot *et alia* could not have developed strangleholds on their peoples without such Marxist concepts to justify their crimes as the "dictatorship of the proletariat," "scientific socialism" and the communist vision

---

114. "Why I Am Not a Christian," by Bertrand Russell, 1929. The pamphlet is a reprint of a lecture given by Russell to the South London Branch of the National Secular Society.

of a classless, creative, conflict-free future. Likewise Christianity, empowered as a political force for twenty times longer than any Marxist state, could not have pursued the Crusades, the Inquisition, the forcible conversion of pagan peoples, the mass burning of "witches" and countless other crimes, without the justifying faith in God's personhood, in Jesus' unique divinity and unique salvational power, and in Divine judgment, reward and punishment.

While Bertrand Russell identified the belief in hell as Christianity's great moral failing, I would argue that the very embrace of the idea of a *knowable* God, a God with personality and biography, is what opens the door to religious fundamentalism and triumphalism — just as the embrace of the Marxist conceit of there being sure-fire evolutionary form and meaning to history's flow opens the door to political totalitarianism. The human will to dominate others receives tremendous license and energy from messianic dogmas of any sort, or from any conviction that "God is this way and not that" — for once *belief* is established, it will give license to reality-shaping crimes, all in the name of salvation. Perhaps that is why the Talmudic rabbis, contemporaries of the early Church fathers, viewed the very concept of a divine "Son of God" as idolatrous mysticism. The messiah of their eschatology was not a knowable God but a redeeming human king, and they understood the social value of portraying redemption as a future event to which we might all aspire rather than a *fait accompli* in which we do or do not participate.

I should note here that I am not here trying to argue that Judaism is somehow less driven by superstitious doctrine than Christianity. Jewish doctrines of "chosenness," the Divine Revelation at Mt. Sinai and the Divine authorship of the Torah are hardly less salvational in character than many Christian dogmas,[115] and kabbalistic mysticism, in particular, has been feverishly devoted to trying to assign knowable features to God. Judaism, however, was never politically empowered on

---

115. The Jewish path to salvation, however, is communal. The entire community (including future generations, according to the Talmud) receives and affirms the Torah at Mt. Sinai, the entire community's behavior will summon the messiah, a quorum of 10 is required for the utterance of certain prayers, et cetera. Christianity, in seeking to become a "universal" religion, broke down this emphasis on the communal over the individual by turning salvation into a matter of individual faith (accessible to all) rather than collective works.

Lawrence Bush

a scale approaching Christianity's partnership with the Roman Empire, so Jewish triumphalism could never really work up a head of steam. To the contrary, the Talmudic rabbis were extremely wary of bloody repression by Rome and seemed actively to have suppressed messianism within their community and their texts, for they were well aware of its role in empowering zealotry and rebellion.[116] For Christianity, however, messianic speculation was the launching pad and remains the core belief: that Jesus of Nazareth was the Christ, the "Anointed One," and that human salvation is uniquely linked to him.

Now, Matthew Fox is often fuzzy in his writings about the line between metaphor and reality, but he does seem to believe in Jesus as an historical person who was something more than human — an incarnation of humanity perfected, immaculate conception and all.[117] "Jesus' birth comes about not through an ordinary father but through the Holy Spirit," he writes in the concluding chapter of *Original Blessing*. "This makes his birth a cosmic event, as was the original birth of creation. This makes Jesus not only a prophet of the New Creation but the New Creation itself. . . . Jesus, who is a new creation, calls all persons to reconciliation with themselves, with one another, and with creation." This is no secularized perspective on Jesus as a Jewish firebrand! Rather, Fox is making the leap of faith that Christianity demands, affirming the fateful meaning of Jesus' life for all humanity, his miraculous conquest of death, the Gospels as truth-telling documents, etcetera. Fox may be heretical and a whole lot less depressed than the Church authorities who abuse him, but he remains enthralled by the concept of God-made-flesh.

---

116. See footnote 74.

117. Fox posits that the Virgin Birth represents "the recovery of motherhood in a patriarchal society." He quotes Otto Rank ("one of the greatest prophets of the 20th Century," according to Fox) saying that Christianity represents "a revival and reinterpretation of the original mother-concept which had given way to the masculinization of Eastern civilization." Fox continues: "The fear of motherhood, the suspicion of creativity, the displeasure with birthing processes that characterize patriarchal cultures are exposed. And with this exposure comes the salvific power of rebirth, of motherhood for everyone."

FROM A PLANETARY PERSPECTIVE, of course, my atheistic reservations about Matthew Fox's christology are a whole lot less significant — even to me! — than the attitudes of the Christian world towards his life-affirming interpretations. Given my faithless and pragmatic approach to religion, Fox's Christian spirituality is certainly one I would like to see ascendant. "I would like to see Christianity move from being a religion to being a way of life and spirituality again," he says.[118] "It doesn't have to be a religion any more. The empires are over." Amen!

I'm afraid, however, that "original sin" will prove to have tremendous staying power as a religious precept in our tortured world, while the concepts of "royal personhood" and "original blessing" that Fox advocates can only be undermined, in the long run, by human suffering and human nature. For too, too many people, our world is, indeed, a fallen place and the *"Via Negativa"* is a much broader experiential path than the *"Via Positiva."* Belief in original sin provides what I would call a *"Via Comfortiva"* — a cosmological context, or at least a sense of fatalistic comfort, to suffering Christians, who can then turn to Jesus for individual salvation through individual piety. I imagine this spiritual cycle to be particularly powerful, if not empowering, for people who have little control over the material circumstances of their lives — which may help explain why both Roman Catholicism and evangelical Christianity are growing most rapidly in impoverished zones of the world.

"Original sin," in other words, may be an irreplaceable active ingredient of the "opiate of the people." Fox hopes to transform that opiate into an aphrodisiac, and his prescription may well work for the Woodstock generation, whose main experience of pain is *ennui* and whose inner selves have not been brutalized by greed, cruelty, injustice, or alienating labor. Such people, already "saved" by their good fortune, will happily add to their spiritual repertory whichever techniques are capable of sparking the "interconnection" or "God" portion of our brains — and dogma be damned.

Sadly, however, John Lennon's poignant rendering of God as "a concept by which we measure our pain" has enduring truth for more human beings than Matthew Fox's rendering of God as a concept by

118. From "Dr. Matthew Fox — Some Frequently Asked Questions on His Theology," at: http://nineoclockservice.tripod.com/mattiefx.htm.

Lawrence Bush

which we measure our blessing. For my brother Russ, after all, the conversionary trigger was not "Count your blessings" but "You've had a hard life." Without original sin, that hard life would have had no cosmological context, no explanation besides bad luck and personal failure, and no salvational escape clause.

RUSS STILL HAS NOT READ Matthew Fox, but he has shared with me an old critique of *Original Blessing* in the Holy Order of MANS's *Epiphany Journal* that would probably approximate his point of view. In this critique, Stephen Muratore, a staff writer, accuses Matthew Fox of trying to harness Christian concepts to serve a worldly political agenda. Muratore argues that Fox "takes as the 'creation' only the corporeal realm and makes the maintenance and enjoyment of it the goals of human life. This is Christianity upside-down. Traditional [Christian] spirituality," Muratore continues, "sees union with the Creator as the goal and transformation of the visible creation through sacramental knowledge and action . . . as the path. " Fox's "creation-centered spirituality," he concludes:

> does not lead beyond human potential to the well of
> theological being and love. It does not open the person
> to communication with higher dimensions of nature but,
> instead, attaches him [sic] to the corporeal mode. It calls
> one to political action because this is the only effective
> action visible to those who live in a one-dimensional
> universe. Unlike traditional spirituality, which aims at
> restoring to man his sacerdotal powers of knowledge
> and virtue whereby he can redeem the creation, Fox
> . . . confines us to face-lifting operations on the "old
> man" and urban renewal projects for Babylon.[119]

It is ironic the Holy Order of MANS and I seem to share mirror-image critiques of Fox's theology of worldly hope and worldly accountability. Muratore fears that Fox's spirituality is "a decoy: a lure away from the truly cosmic spirituality which is traditional Christianity." I

---

119. Review of *Original Blessing* by Stephen Muratore in *Epiphany Journal,* Spring, 1985.

also fear that Fox's spirituality is a decoy, indulging the escapism of traditional Christian lore to lure people away from secular answers to our collective questions. At this juncture, therefore, my brother and I stand like wallflowers on opposite walls at a techno-mass. We both ridicule and resent the ecstatic dance of the worshippers while complaining about the chill in the air. In encountering Matthew Fox, Russ the devout Christian and Larry the devout atheist have, at last, found common ground: the hardscrabble of our father's pessimism, which views religion as Marx's "sigh of the afflicted creature, soul of a heartless world" — not, as Fox would have it, as the *Via Positiva*, the path of "cosmic blessing."

IN READING ABOUT MY BROTHER'S conversionary journey, most of my Woodstocker friends, I imagine, would demur from my description of it, at the start of this chapter, as "a classic baby-boomer experience of spiritual awakening." *What has Russ's Christianity to do with us?* they might say. *We don't buy the Jesus thing, the Virgin Birth, the miraculous healings, any more than you do! Christianity is the stuff of reactionary, authoritarian Americans and downtrodden Third World peasants. Had your brother stuck with yoga, or become a Hare Krishna devotee or a follower of Baba Ram Dass — now, there's a conversion we can relate to!*

In fact, Russ has told me more than once that he nearly joined the Hare Krishna movement in the weeks before joining the Holy Order of MANS. Had he met a Hasidic Jew on that bus in Denver, he says, he might have become a Hasid; had he met a Buddhist monk, he might have joined the monastery. It was not the repressive comforts of authoritarian religion that he was seeking, but the assurance that we live in a meaningful and fate-filled universe. That "message" came to him garbed in biblical language, but it could easily have come from a dozen other sources in that spiritually besotted decade.

Only rarely do my fellow Woodstockers recognize the kinship between Western religious miracle tales, which we scorn as provincial and reactionary, and the Eastern religious miracle tales that excited our fancies and underwrote many conversionary experiences decades ago. This was driven home to me during a recent viewing of a film, *Ram Dass: Fierce Grace*, about the man formerly known as Richard Alpert, who is most famous as the author of *Be Here Now*. Ram Dass (the name means "god-servant") was expelled with Timothy Leary from Harvard's psychology department in 1965 for psychedelic experimentation and advocacy. He went on to become a major figure in the religious awakening of the baby-boom generation. In recent years, Ram Dass has been struggling to recover from a stroke (or from "being stroked," as he puts it). Just as he was once a generational pioneer in the realm of consciousness expansion, he now describes himself as a pioneer in the realm of meaningful aging. I saw *Ram Dass: Fierce Grace*[120] in an art cinema in the Mid-Hudson Valley of New York, where I live, among an audience of baby boomers who, judging from their gasps and chuckles as viewers, seemed well acquainted with the Eastern spiritual path and countercultural scene of the '60s and '70s.

Midway into the film, Ram Dass tells of his central conversionary experience: his first encounter with his life-long guru, Maharaj Ji (Neem Karoli Baba),[121] in the Himalayas. The night before arriving at the guru's encampment, Ram Dass recounts, he had a rapturous time gazing at the amazingly starry sky, which evoked thoughts about his mother, who had recently died of an enlarged spleen. The next day, he continues, the Maharaj Ji's first words upon meeting him were something like: *You were out under the stars last night, you were thinking about your mother.* The guru then described her death — "she got very big in the belly" — and, after closing his eyes and rocking back and forth a bit, he spoke the word, "spleen."

Well, I concluded, perhaps the Maharaj Ji knew in advance that his guest had lost his mother and was simply being sympathetic — or perhaps he was being manipulative and seeking to impress Richard Alpert with his "all-knowing" nature. Perhaps the guru knew about the spleen — or perhaps he said something else in his accented English that Ram Dass interpreted as "spleen." Whatever the answer, I was stunned to learn that it had been this simple magic trick that had apparently precipitated Alpert's "ego-death" and readied him to "be here now!" But as Ram Dass described on screen his awe at the guru's mind-reading

---

120. Directed by Micky Lemle, 2001.

121. Not to be confused with the "perfect 14-year-old master," Guru Maharaj Ji — see footnote 47.

abilities, the stirring of the movie audience indicated a shared sense of faithful wonder that left me feeling quite alone in my skepticism.

Of course Ram Dass had looked at the stars!, I thought. *What foreign traveler (apart from a blind person) would not look at the Himalayan night sky and be stunned by the profusion of stars? And stargazing evokes in all of us those thoughts about mortality, humility, love, meaning, regret . . . and mothers! Especially if you're a young Western man not yet entwined with a partner or children of your own, when you're going through changes or feeling exhilarated or thinking deeply about your past, present and future, it's a safe bet that your thoughts will include your mother!*

Whether tipped off in advance or not to the fact and nature of Alpert's mother's death, Maharaj Ji, it seemed to me, had read his visitor like a book, gambled against excellent odds and hit the jackpot, gaining a wealthy Harvard psychologist as his follower. The guru had risked nothing: Even if Ram Dass had gone to sleep early the night before without seeing the stars or thinking about his mother, or even if the mother had died of a heart attack, without a swollen torso, the mind-reading comments might easily have been "spun" to seem profound, or at least profoundly cryptic.

Call me a cynic, but I expect that if you look beneath the veneer of sainthood of all miracle-working religious leaders, you will witness the close observation and canny manipulation of human psychology. No matter if they wear gauzy cotton robes or polyester suits, no matter if they use their abilities to amass material fortunes or renounce all that and lead the simple life in the mountains: Any spiritual leader who resorts to the paranormal or magical to blow minds and win converts has marked himself, to me, as a professional magician, out to make a living — or, worse, a carny, just like my brother's ring-toss "angel." I see only superficial differences, therefore, among the Christian faith-healer who gets the lame to walk, the television spiritualist who contacts the dead through careful questioning of the living relatives, and the Hindu avatar who gazes into your eyes and tells you your innermost thoughts. All of them are plying tricks to make a living, tricks that take advantage of our powerful will to believe and belong, our lack of criteria for making skeptical assessments, and the tremendous psychic release that people gain from surrendering their "no" and giving in to "yes."

For many Woodstockers, however, such an analogy is sacrilegious, even traitorous. Eastern spirituality entered our lives at a time when we viewed American society in vastly polarized terms — with the Eastern gurus counted on "our side," the side of peace, enlightenment and liberated consciousness, versus the forces of authoritarianism, repression, and status quo. Eastern religions appeared so non-theological (Buddhism) or fluid in their theology (Hinduism) as to be viewed more as "technologies" for consciousness exploration than as religions. We knew little about their historical baggage — for example, about the feudal social relations that empowered the Dalai Lama as head theocrat of Tibet, or about the grim inequities of the Hindu caste system — while we were well acquainted with the outrageous historical crimes of Christianity. As a result, I can naysay the Pope, Billy Graham, Jim and Tammy Bakker, Pat Robertson, and the like: Hypocrisy, sex scandal, power-mongering and money-grubbing are seen as par for the course for Western religious leaders. But despite the steady stream of sex, money and power scandals that have washed ashore with the gurus of the East, the benefit of the doubt clings to them like the scent of incense — and the burden of disproof lands on my shoulders.

WELL, I AM NOT OUT TO "DISPROVE" the reality of their teachings about *chakras*, the multiple levels of consciousness, the wheel of reincarnation, whatever — any more than I am out to disprove Christianity's teachings about Jesus' divinity or the existence of heaven and hell. To me, these are simply metaphors that express the hopes, fears and perceptions of human beings and the ineffable feelings that result from shifting brain chemistry; to others, they are mappings of the hidden but objectively real structure of the universe. How can we debate our differing conclusions when religious faith is not really subject to empirical observation or rational investigation? As Benjamin Franklin put it in *Poor Richard's Almanac,* in 1743: "Many a long dispute among divines may be thus abridg'd: It is so; It is not so; It is so; It is not so."

But if rationalism cannot *disprove* religious dogmas, neither should it be discredited through tricks that startle people into a state of suggestibility. Spirituality, the enhancement of our sense of "interconnection," especially when wrought by years of meditation or other disciplined activities, may indeed yield heightened compassion, self-awareness, self-control, sensory acuity and other strengths. It cannot, however, yield powers that defy the laws of physics and biology: the capacity for telepathy, levitation, telekinesis, to go indefinitely without food or water, to cure cancer through touch, and so on. Any religious leaders who claim or imply otherwise should be subjected to sharp skepticism, not awe.

This is my only agenda of disproof: to draw the curtain open and reveal the "Great and Powerful Oz" at his console. That Oz was a trickster does not deny him his most important spiritual assets: his hot-air balloon, capable of taking Dorothy back to Kansas, which is all she really wanted; and his homey wisdom, capable of bringing peace of mind and self-esteem to the Scarecrow, the Tin Man and the Cowardly Lion.

Or as Jesus of Nazareth put it (*John* 6:26) for my brother Russ to hear: "Most assuredly, I say to you, you seek me, not because you saw the signs, but because you ate of the loaves and were filled."

Chapter Six

"There Is No God, and Mordecai Kaplan is His Prophet"

Pray for me
all of you
who
bend your knees,
move
side to side
daven up
daven down
cover your heads
mumble and chant
in beautiful
ancient languages
on weekends
when you're tired
of unholy activities
wash in holy waters
eat foods
with a purpose
light candles
when the occasion
is appropriate

Pray for me.
Pray for me.

— Esther Cohen, "Pray for Me"[122]

---

122. Published in *Jews.* #2, Autumn, 1999. Used by permission of the author.

OF ALL MODERN THEOLOGIANS, Rabbi Mordecai Kaplan (1881-1983), the founder of Reconstructionist Judaism, offers the one and only invitation to faith to which I feel compelled to RSVP. Other religious renovators who similarly hedge their religious affirmations with concessions to rationalism, humanism and scientific knowledge simply arouse a 'why?' in me: Why, if they have shaved off God's beard and left superstition behind, do they cling to theism at all? But Kaplan somehow arouses a 'why not?' that demands my answer.

He achieves this by disembodying God altogether. For Mordecai Kaplan, there is no divine being who hears prayer — there is only the reality of human prayerfulness and its related feelings of awe, hope, love, blessing and righteousness. The very existence of these feelings implies, to Kaplan, "the existence of conditions that favor abundant life, or salvation. . . . [T]aking for granted that such conditions exist is the basis of the religious conception of God." As he wrote in 1948:

> When we think at all about the world and arrive at
> conclusions that justify our right to feel at home in it,
> or that warrant our striving after perfection and self-
> fulfillment, those conclusions constitute a conception
> of God. . . . Every experience of success in overcoming
> the misery of cowardice, envy, hate and greed is an
> experience of God. Faith in God is faith in the pos-
> sibility of such achievements.[123]

Kaplan, in short, sees God as an organizing principle of the universe by which "the world of inner and outer being, the world of society and of nature . . . is so constituted as to enable man [sic] to achieve salvation"[124] — by which he means not some otherworldly bliss but "the good life," fulfillment here on earth. Kaplan considers humanness at its best to constitute both a proof and a reflection of this organizing principle: The fact that we are capable of generating and experiencing

---

123. Mordecai Kaplan, *The Future of the American Jew*, 1948.

124. Mordecai Kaplan, *The Meaning of God in Modern Jewish Religion*, 1937. All of the rest of the passages from Kaplan, except when otherwise indicated, come from this book.

Lawrence Bush

our most buoyant, optimistic and loving feelings is testament to the force of God in the universe, or the godliness of the universe. "We have to identify as godhood, or as the divine quality of universal being," he writes, "all relationships, tendencies and agencies which in their totality go to make human life worthwhile in the deepest and most abiding sense. The divine is no less real," he adds, "no less dependable for our personal salvation or self-realization, if we think of it as a quality than if we think of it as an entity or being."

Indeed, for people made skeptical by modernity, Kaplan understands that conceptualizing and describing God as a being can cultivate atheism. "Religion can no longer be a matter of entering into relationship with the supernatural," he writes. Rather than seeking "communion with God . . . as the source of power," we should identify God "as the source of goodness," and "invoke His [sic] aid to acquire control not over the external forces but over those of human nature in the individual and in the mass."

> [I]t is only as the sum of everything in the world that renders life significant and worthwhile — or holy — that God can be worshiped . . . Godhood can have no meaning for us apart from human ideals of truth, goodness, and beauty, interwoven in a pattern of holiness.

For such teachings, Kaplan was excommunicated by a *beyt din* (rabbinical court) of the Union of Orthodox Rabbis in 1945. Happily, such writs of excommunication are not universally honored in Jewish life, and Kaplan, who lived to be 102, maintained a half-century career of teaching at the Jewish Theological Seminary in New York and achieved broad respect as one of the great Jewish theologians of the 20th century.

HIS IS A HUMANISTIC AND NATURALISTIC THEOLOGY, designed to preserve Judaism from the skepticism that will surely be provoked among modern Jews, Kaplan believed, by outmoded, supernatural conceptions of God. It is an intimate theology: Kaplan does not spend time speculating about the God of Creation portrayed in the first chapter of *Genesis*, or about whether a universe without human beings would still be a God-infused universe. He seems more interested in the human origins of what he calls the "God idea" than in the actual nature of God, which he considers to be "beyond our understanding . . . just as our conception of life does not begin to give us the faintest idea of what life means to the infinite variety of living creatures . . ." In fact, his writings about the "God idea" often read like secular anthropology:

> [The] standards, norms and mores [of a people] require some sanction to validate them. . . . Resort is had to the God idea, for that idea inherently endorses the rightness of that which we regard as right. . . . [L]iterature that reflects the mind of the group . . . [is] ascribed to God . . . for the pragmatic significance of the God idea is the recognition of certain elements in life as supremely important. . . . Epoch-making events in the national history . . . become holy days, when the people seek communion with God for renewing their faith in those ideals . . . associated with the day.

Kaplan makes his theology uniquely palatable for atheists by emphasizing its utilitarian virtues. I often respond by thinking, *Why not? If sanctifying human goodness by calling it "God" helps us to be good, why not? If we are helped in sustaining our quest for "salvation" by viewing it as evidence of a sympathetic or "enabling" universe, what harm is there? Lord knows, we need all the help we can get!*

Besides, he portrays atheism in such bleak terms — as the belief that "consciousness is a disease, civilization a transient sickness, and all our efforts to lift ourselves above the brute only a vain pretense" — that none but the heavily sedated could bear to carry the banner!

There is a great deal about Kaplan's philosophy that I just plain love. He is deeply committed to a view of religion as a pathway to social justice. "*The real purpose of religion,*" he writes, with italics for emphasis, "*is to direct attention to the problem of salvation and to the means of its attainment.*" (Again, by "salvation" he means worldly fulfillment, both personal and communal.) This approach to religion has far more in common with the outer-directed humanism of Felix Adler, the founder of Ethical Culture, who was Kaplan's mentor at Columbia University, than with the inner-directed psychedelic and Eastern mysticism of the Woodstockers. To Kaplan, a commitment to improving the world is the ultimate proof of one's religiosity: "[T]hose who, at great danger and cost to themselves, are identified with some cause of social reform or humanitarian benefit . . . must be classified with religious believers. They act as witnesses of God, regardless of what they say. In their desire to break with the limited traditional conception of God, they may proclaim themselves atheists, yet they are the first to accord genuinely divine honors and adoration to persons, texts and events through which the world promises to come . . . nearer to their hearts' desire."

He is also deeply committed to cultivating the communal consciousness of human beings and dampening our hierarchical antagonisms. Religion is, to him, the seedbed of that communal consciousness, which occupies a higher rung than individualism on the ladder of cosmic reality, at least within Jewish religious philosophy.[125] "*What differentiates man from the beast*," Kaplan writes, in a formulation that beautifully blends religious and socialist idealism with evolutionary theory (italics in the original), "*is that his nature not only makes for the survival of the fittest, but aims to make the greatest possible number fit to survive.*"[126] Humans alone "hear not only nature calling . . . but also God." Therefore, humanity is "exempt from the law of natural selection, and becomes subject to the law of spiritual selection."

Kaplan is also an internationalist: "If the issue of one world or none is to be met realistically, every people, church and civilization must henceforth foster the kind of religion which will enable the individual to discover in every human being of whatever race or creed or nation a kinsman whose well-being and salvation are bound up with his own." And he is optimistic about science: "[B]y revealing to us the laws behind forces that once seemed arbitrary interferences with human life, [science] has enabled us to turn even those forces to human needs" and to create "the daily miracles by which we live. . ."[127]

---

125. See footnote 115.

126. Kaplan, *The Future of the American Jew*.

127. *Ibid*.

For Kaplan, it is religion that serves the people, not the other way around. He warns against identifying Jewishness exclusively with Judaism, for "this would leave the majority of Jews without status because the majority of Jews . . . if pressed by questioning . . . will admit that they are Jews by virtue of indefinable sentiment rather than of affirmative religious conviction." Towards this end, Kaplan is happy to jettison problematic dogmas such as Jewish "chosenness" and to critique Jewish Orthodoxy's role in enforcing the religion's most alienating and irrelevant customs, particularly its insistence on second-class status for women. "Orthodoxy's insistence upon the supernatural origin and the immutability of Jewish law," he writes, ". . . actually contributes to the further dissolution of Judaism."[128]

GIVEN MY IDENTIFICATION with much of this, I often call myself a Reconstructionist and happily embrace Kaplan as my teacher. From 1993 to 2006, in fact, I served the Reconstructionist synagogue movement as founding editor of its quarterly magazine, *Reconstructionism Today,* and felt no identity crisis or ideological compromise in doing so. I can even say, depending on my mood, that I believe in Kaplan's God — since, by his definition of atheism, only a blackguard could not! If by using the word "God" we mean to acknowledge that the universe has a system that makes life possible — well, obviously, here we are. If by using the word we mean to acknowledge that human beings have some wonderfully creative and loving potentialities — sure, I'm a husband and a parent and I know what love means and does. If by thanking "God" we mean to say that our planet is astoundingly beneficent in what it provides for living creatures — hey, I thank my stars for the bounty on my plate every day.

For the same 13 years, however, I have wondered: If the blessings and exaltations of life are what we mean by "God," why not name them for what they are? If God equals Goodness, why not simply say so? Why use the same idiom, and often the same prayer language, as those for whom "God" means the Judge of humankind, the Warrior who urges *jihad,* the Autocrat who legislates inexplicable laws, the Son who is the sole path to eternal life, and so on?

---

128. *Ibid.*

L a w r e n c e   B u s h

Applying Kaplan's theology to prayer especially confounds me, for whenever I attempt to recite Jewish liturgy, even in a reconstructed form, I find it impossible to avoid envisioning the God in whom I don't believe. This atavistic response makes me feel snappish and argumentative — and ashamed of myself for having so little control over my thoughts — and takes me out of the stream of yearning and appreciation and generous feeling that prayer is meant to cultivate. Is the problem mine alone, bred of my lifelong atheism and my lack of familiarity with the dynamics of prayer? I thought as much, thought of myself as a "special needs" person in the realm of spiritual practice, until I read an article by Mordecai Kaplan's own granddaughter, psychotherapist Ann Eisenstein, in which she admitted to experiencing "a conflict between the pull to the familiar, personal God imagery and rational beliefs" when she attempts to "relate personally to a nonsupernatural God" through prayer.[129] Eisenstein's reflections made me realize that I am not alone in experiencing the "call of the wild" from the magical thinking center of my brain whenever I surrender my skeptical silence and try to pray to "the force that makes for salvation."

I suspect, in fact, that even the most minimalist and humanistic theology, especially when animated through prayer and other ritual activities, becomes a slippery slope. Kaplan himself feared this to be so, conceding that the human mind is inclined to remystify his demystified God idea:

> In our thinking about God we must avoid all those mental habits which issue in logical fallacies. The most common of these is the habit of hypostasis, or assuming the separate identifiable existence of anything for which language has a name. There is a considerable difference, for example, between the way a scientist thinks of gravity and the way most laymen think of it. A scientist regards it as a property or quality of matter, a descriptive term for the way masses of matter behave in relation to one another. The average layman, however, thinks of it as a force, an invisible something that acts upon masses of matter pulling them together. Ac-

---

129. Ann Eisenstein in *The Reconstructionist,* Vol. 70, No. 1, Fall, 2005.

cording to both conceptions, gravity is real and must undeniably be reckoned with, but the layman finds it difficult to regard gravity as real without at the same time thinking of it as a thing, an object, a self-existent being or entity.

When we study the historical development of the God idea, we realize to what extent the mental habit of hypostasis . . . has been responsible for the contradictions and ambiguities that have discredited the conception of God and driven many to atheism.

And hypostasis seems just the half of it! As I have noted several times, numerous evolutionary biologists and other practitioners of brand-new scientific disciplines have been arguing in recent years that the human mind's hardwiring inclines us towards the embrace of religion — that is, classically superstitious religion. "Human minds," argues Pascal Boyer, ". . . because they had many sophisticated inference systems . . . became vulnerable to a very *restricted* set of supernatural concepts: the ones that jointly activate inference systems for agency, predation, death, morality, social exchange, etc. Only a small range of concepts are such that they reach this aggregate relevance, which is why religion has common features the world over. . . ."[130]

Kaplan's theology would hardly make the cut, for it is deliberately stripped of many of the elements that "seem *designed*," according to Boyer, "to excite the human mind." But if it is the case that our brains are inclined towards certain superstitious concepts — and if it is true, as Ann Eisenstein suggests, that there is a "tenacious human attachment to the personification of God," a personification that is "intrinsically supernatural" — are we not better off *restraining* our religious instinct than indulging it? We see all around us how religion, when unleashed, can be the vessel for fanaticism, torture, terror, war, misogyny, homophobia, delusion, repression and perversity. Just as Judaism urges us (especially men) to "civilize" our sexual instinct for the social good,

---

130. Pascal Boyer, *Religion Explained: The Evolutionary Origins of Religious Thought*, 2001. Boyer is the Luce Professor of Collective Memory and Individual Memory at Washington University.

do we not similarly need to "civilize" our religious instinct? Is this best achieved by rationalistic religion or by "celibacy"? By speaking the language of religion in an enlightened accent, or by speaking the language of the Enlightenment? By worshiping "God" in a language of simultaneous translation, or by finding meaningful alternatives to worship?

SUCH CONCERNS ABOUT THE "SLIPPERY SLOPE" of religion can be stood on their head, of course, for Kaplan's theology has often had the opposite effect, providing thousands of Jews with a lifeline with which to pull themselves *up* the slippery slope, away from untenable superstitious religious belief. If my concern were mainly about the social impact of religion, moreover, I'd be well-advised to continue to participate in religious life and help channel the religious instinct towards constructive forms of fulfillment. Given the biological basis for religion that's been posited in this book, that's where the real social action is.

Leaving my pontificating aside, then, it seems time to ask myself why I still call myself an atheist despite Kaplan's offer to enlarge the tent of religion to embrace all people who believe in the possibility of human transformation, both individual and social. Why am I tempted to check, "Sorry, can't be there," on my RSVP card?

In truth, there are times when I think my resistance to Kaplan's theology is simply rooted in laziness. To stay attuned on a daily basis to Kaplan's God, to stay attuned to states of love, forgiveness, patience, determination, and other "Godly" virtues, takes real effort. It requires overcoming my psychological inertia and my recoil from the impositions on time and schedule that any disciplined spiritual practice requires. It means measuring my ethical decision-making not against the widespread selfishness and corruption that are normative in our world — a standard that makes me feel quite virtuous in my self-directed ethical life — but against idealized human goodness.

A God-infused universe also requires me to be a penitent, for I seem to be a non-believer in "that old time religion," in which the "fear of God" (*yirat shamayim* or *yirat Ha-Shem* in Hebrew) outweighs the love of God. Few Woodstockers would say that their spirituality is informed by the fear of God: What they seem to seek, most of all, is to *get high* on God, high on the spirituality of interconnection. For me, however, the God I don't believe in is a God who makes demands and commands my fear, and whom I would not want to meet in a dark alleyway.

Perhaps I am also an elitist, and my self-esteem is dependent on separating myself from mass sentiment. Let the world chew Bazooka bubble gum; as a kid, I always preferred Dubble Bubble. Let the world listen to Kenny G.; I prefer Dave Douglas or Miles Davis. Let the world struggle with Windows; I prefer my Mac. Let the world express inspiring thoughts through God-talk; I prefer to find other metaphors.

Perhaps I am also unforgiving: of the so-called God who gets thanked for the blessings of our world but never blamed for its torments, and of the religions that contribute so profoundly to those torments in God's name. For my fellow Woodstockers, the question of theodicy — of how we can reconcile the evils of the world with the concept of a God who is Goodness incarnate — seems to be a spiritual nonstarter, perhaps because there is relatively such little suffering and misery in their lives. Led by such theologians as Rabbi Harold Kushner (author of *When Bad Things Happen to Good People*), the Woodstockers have gladly turned away from the God of Job, the God of the whirlwind, the God in whose hands all happiness and all suffering is held, towards a much-reduced Deity whose role is, essentially, to be a motivational speaker, a cheerleader for the good. For me, however, the God in whom I don't believe is the God who is still to be blamed, and no matter how rehabilitated the concept behind the name, I feel no more willing to "praise God," than I am willing to praise Hitler.

In summary, perhaps I deny the existence of even Kaplan's God so as not to be bothered, not to be accountable, not to feel ordinary, not to be set to trembling and rage. Rather than doing the hard work of seeking enlightenment, I deny the possibility of enlightenment and seek, as it were, to kill the Buddha.

IN THIS SELF-FLAGELLATION, perhaps I am not so different from Mordecai Kaplan. According to Reconstructionist leader Daniel Cedarbaum, Kaplan "might better be viewed as an anti-theologian than as a theologian . . . in the midst of a personal crisis of faith, he developed a theology that allowed him to rationalize his passionate commitment to Judaism. . . . [and] 'saved' many of us by teaching that we could do the same."[131] In this sense, Kaplan's Reconstructionist Judaism has been aptly described as "a conceptual bridge between religious and secular Jewishness"[132]— a bridge that enables me to partake in the philosophical wealth of Jewish religious thought, and the community-enhancing rituals of Jewish practice, without having to talk to God, ever.

Unfortunately, however, in my experience of the Reconstructionist movement, elaborate prayer actually seems to be the central focus of synagogue communities, despite Kaplan's belief that "worship should be one of the functions of the synagogue, but by no means the only one, nor even the principal one."[133] At the same time, for many secular Jews, the rejection of God has produced non-affiliation with any and all synagogue communities, and sheer indifference to the many wonderful dimensions of Judaism. This is the outcome of unreconstructed Judaism that Kaplan fears, and that I have spent my career so far trying to address: that the ubiquity of untenable theology will blind the majority of Jews to the philosophical richness and wisdom of Jewish texts and traditions. Kaplan tries to avert that outcome by rejecting a personal God; by rejecting miracles (he insists on "the uniformity of natural law demanded by scientific theory"); by rejecting pie-in-the-sky utopianism (we are to live, he writes, "without illusion and without despair about the future, with clear recognition of the reality of evil and creative faith in the possibility of the good"). In making these affirmations, he steps from the world of religious certainty into the world of creative religious metaphor — and I am glad to follow him through that doorway.

---

131. Daniel Cedarbaum in *The Reconstructionist,* Vol. 70, No. 1, Fall, 2005.

132. Barnett Zumoff, "Secular Jewishness, Then and Now," *Jewish Currents,* March-April, 2006.

133. Mordecai Kaplan, *Judaism as a Civilization.*

Chapter Seven

The Goddess

i thank You God for this most amazing
day: for the leaping greenly spirits of trees
and a bluetrue dream of sky; and for everything
which is natural which is infinite which is yes

(i who have died am alive again today,
and this is the sun's birthday; this is the birth
day of life and of love and wings: and of the gay
great happening illimitably earth) . . .
     — e.e. cummings, "i thank God for this most amazing," 1950

ALTHOUGH MORDECAI KAPLAN's theology/anti-theology has opened
my eyes to many of Judaism's religious metaphors, there remain aspects of my native faith, apart from the superstitious God-idea that
he critiqued, that do seem fossilized to me. Among these is the classic
Jewish principle of *b'tselem elohim,* that human beings are "made in
the image of God." While this precept, as I have earlier noted, can
certainly help breed tolerance, respect and even empathy among human beings — traits that are in short supply in today's world! —it can
also feed an increasingly outdated 'speciesism,' a view of ourselves as
so gosh-darned special as to be *entitled.* Many a religious fundamentalist has opposed the environmental movement, and evolutionary
theory, on precisely those grounds: that human beings are the crown
of creation, *uniquely* created in God's image, and that the world was
created solely for our use, as the book of *Genesis* suggests: "And God
said, 'Let us make man in our image, after our likeness. They shall
rule the fish of the sea, the birds of the sky, the cattle, the whole earth
. . .'" (1: 26). Judaism, like its sister religions, thus creates a wall of

separation between human beings and all other sentient beings — even those like the chimpanzees, with whom we apparently share 99 percent of our genes.

Judaism also erects a wall between nature and God, exemplified by biblical scenes of conquest of the pagan peoples of Canaan by the monotheistic Hebrews, who make war not only to dispossess these peoples but to shatter all traces of their paganism. "Beware of making a covenant with the inhabitants of the land against which you are advancing, lest they be a snare in your midst," commands *Exodus* 34: 12-14. "You must tear down their altars, smash their pillars, and cut down their sacred posts; for you must not worship any other god." While Jewish sacred writings hardly distinguish among the forms of worship that were considered idolatrous, nature worship is certainly counted among them — and while it is indulging in false stereotyping to say that Judaism is somehow "anti-nature" (Judaism began as an agrarian religion and maintains many rapturous scriptural passages about the beauty and order of the natural world), the biblical concern with idolatry and paganism did establish an inhibiting anxiety about confusing Creation and the Creator.

Following Mordecai Kaplan's example, many contemporary Jews have sought to lessen this anxiety in Judaism by developing what Matthew Fox calls "panentheistic" theology, which sees God as immanent in all of creation. Such a theology of immanence is very much a part of Woodstocker spirituality, which is concerned far more with tracing the reality of interconnection than with defending the Heavenly Throne of God. Nevertheless, it has been difficult for mainstream Judaism to rid itself of the fear that panentheism, if given license, will degrade into pantheism, the worship of many gods, and that the unharnessed celebration of nature will produce the kind of idolatry that the Bible and subsequent Jewish commentaries associate with disobedience, self-indulgence, and false consciousness.

Another important form of fossilization that the Jewish community has struggled with over the course of my adult life has been Judaism's gender bias. This bias is especially evident in Orthodoxy's exclusion of women from the central rituals of the religion and from leadership roles within the community — but even in liberal Jewish religious communities, throughout the transformative 1970s and 1980s,[134] it took tremendous effort to win acceptance for women as rabbis, cantors and community leaders, for gender-neutral (or, God forbid, feminine!) prayer language, and for the expansion of the Jewish ritual world to acknowledge such female life-passages as menarche, menopause, divorce, and widowhood.

In fact, the struggle to introduce panentheism to Judaism and the struggle to open the tradition to the full participation of women have been linked in the minds of their opponents. Judith Plaskow, author of the groundbreaking Jewish feminist theology, *Standing Again at Sinai*, points to this linkage in her 1991 essay, "Jewish Anti-Paganism." Jewish feminists, she notes, "who use female or natural metaphors for God have repeatedly been accused of paganizing Judaism, as if women or nature were intrinsically pagan symbols, and as if a variety of images were the same as a variety of gods. Feminist calls for reconsideration of Jewish attitudes toward sexuality have been countered by lurid portraits of pagan licentiousness, as if there were no moral alternative to a patriarchal sexual ethic. Such charges," Plaskow concludes, "conjure and build on unexamined stereotypes in order to strike fear into the hearts of feminists and any who might listen to them."[135]

For some Jewish women of the baby-boom generation, such attacks, and the resistance to innovation that they represented, proved to be

---

134. The first woman rabbi of modern times, Sally Priesand, was ordained by the Reform movement in 1972. The first national Jewish feminist conference took place in New York in 1973 and produced a special issue of *Response* magazine devoted to women's liberation and Judaism. *Lilith* magazine began publishing in 1976. In 1979, the Drisha Institute was founded as the first center for women's advanced study of classical Jewish texts. In 1980, Blu Greenberg began to publicly challenge the constrained role of women in Orthodox Judaism. In 1983, Susannah Heschel published *On Being a Jewish Feminist*. In 1984, Marcia Falk began publishing Hebrew liturgy reflecting feminine representations of God. In 1985, Amy Eilberg became the first woman ordained by the Conservative movement. For more information about these and other feminist developments within the Jewish world, the Jewish Women's Archive in Brookline, Massachusetts is an excellent resource: www.jwa.org/feminism.

135. Judith Plaskow, *The Coming of Lilith, Essays on Feminism, Judaism, and Sexual Ethics, 1972-2003*, 2005.

too alienating. Rather than seeking to heal Judaism of its paranoia about nature worship and women's power, these women simply fled from Judaism and Jewish identity. Susan Brownmiller, for example, who wrote the very influential feminist book about rape, *Against Our Will* (1975), has noted that she realized from a young age that Judaism was a male-dominated religion, and concluded: "So much for Judaism, so much for religion — I became an atheist, a secularist, and never looked back."[136]

Other Jewish women remained faithful to Judaism but also explored traditions of nature-centered spirituality, including Goddess-focused religious practice. In time, they would bring major transformations to Judaism and the Jewish community. As Rabbi Sandy Eisenberg Sasso, the second woman ordained as a rabbi in the U.S., observed in the magazine I edited, *Reconstructionism Today*, on the occasion of her 30th year in the rabbinate,

> Women have helped not only to create new ritual, but to reshape its enactment. . . . They are no longer only silent servers; now they have speaking parts. . . . Women have become interpreters of Torah, writing commentary, creating *midash*. In the process, they have given voices, names and stories to women who had none. . . . Women have also begun to bring their experience to understanding God and to prayer. . . . As the divine moves through the interior world of women, God has become known by names other than Father and King. . . . By adding their voices, women rabbis and other Jewish women teachers and leaders have helped renew and enlarge the Jewish tradition.[137]

The radical changes in Jewish spiritual practice that Eisenberg Sasso cites were primarily shaped by the feminist awakening of the 1970s

---

136. Brownmiller's comment is included at www.jwa.org/feminism.

137. Sandy Eisenberg Sasso, "Celebrating Thirty Years of Women as Rabbis," in *Reconstructionism Today*, Autumn, 2003. Eisenberg Sasso was ordained by the Reconstructionist Rabbinical College in 1973.

and '80s, and were also strongly influenced by women's explorations of non-Jewish spiritual traditions. Throughout those decades, in fact, it sometimes seemed that *all* progressive Jewish women, whether relating to Judaism or not, were circling around the Goddess and those forms of spirituality that would eventually come to be known as Wicca, or modern Witchcraft.

One leader at the center of that circling was Starhawk, neé Miriam Soros, author of the 1979 bestseller, *The Spiral Dance: A Rebirth of the Ancient Religion of the Great Goddess,* among other influential books about the women's spirituality movement. In the late 1980s, Starhawk graced another magazine that I edited, *Genesis 2,* with an article about being a Jewish Witch. She described how her grandmother, who "was never counted in a *minyan* in her life," nevertheless had prayers said over her grave one year after her burial by a *minyan* that included women as full participants. "The event symbolized for me the enormous changes occurring within Judaism," Starhawk noted, describing how twenty years earlier she "had not seen any avenues within Judaism for me to come fully into my power as a woman."

"Walking away from my grandmother's grave," she continued, "I felt the barriers had fallen, or would soon fall." However,

> this insight did not prevent me from grabbing the cheesecloth veiling from my grandmother's headstone for use as an undercloth for the ancestor altar I build every Halloween — the night when, in the Wicca tradition, the beloved dead return to feast and bless us. Each year I set out my collection of old family photos, with plates of apples, nuts and pomegranates. The eyes of the dead gaze at me somewhat quizzically, as if to say, "*Nu?* So what are nice Jewish ancestors doing in a place like this?"[138]

Starhawk has been particularly admired in the Witchcraft and feminist communities as a political activist, environmentalist, ritual-maker and organizer. She is also a charming and accessible writer— and

---

138. Starhawk, "On Being a Jewish Witch," in *Genesis 2*, Vol. 18, No. 4, Winter, 1987/88.

so I recently returned to the 20th anniversary edition of *The Spiral Dance*[139] to try on for size another influential modern theologian who has abstracted God to the point of near-satisfaction for an atheist like me while helping to cultivate certain key aspects of Woodstocker spirituality.

THE WITCHCRAFT MOVEMENT (also known as Wicca, a name derived from the Anglo-Saxon for "to bend or shape" — used here to mean the power to shape reality through consciousness, which is part of the Wiccan definition of magic) has anywhere from 50,000 to 800,000 adherents in the U.S. today.[140] Accurate numbers are hard to come by, since fear of ostracism or persecution inhibits many Witches from publicly admitting their convictions, while a lack of clear definition of who is Wiccan may encourage researchers to count as adherents those who are simply interested in Earth-centered religious concepts but have not committed to the rituals and practice within the coven system that Witchcraft favors.[141]

---

139. Starhawk, *The Spiral Dance: A Rebirth of the Ancient Religion of the Great Goddess,* "Special 20th Anniversary Edition," 1999.

140. Around the world, there are estimated to be nearly a million practitioners of neo-pagan religions, of which Wicca is probably the largest subset. Other varieties include Celtic Druidism and Asatrue (Norse paganism). Traditional forms of "witchcraft" that have endured include Pennsylvania Dutch hexcraft, or "Pow-wow," African-American Hoodoo, Appalachian Folk Magic, Haitian Voodoo, and African witchcraft.

141. Journalist and Witch Margot Adler, author of *Drawing Down the Moon,* estimated in 1986 that there were 50-100,000 active Wiccans in the U.S.; the U.S. Army chaplaincy handbook for dealing with non-traditional religions estimated 50,000 in 1990; the Witches' Voice website (www. witchvox.com) estimated one million Witches in 1999. A poll conducted by Covenant of the Goddess in 1999-2000 estimated a total of 768,400 Witches and Pagans in the U.S. — 33 percent of them under 25 years of age, and another 40 percent between 25 to 39. The Graduate Center of the City University of New York surveyed 50,000 Americans about their religious beliefs in 2001 and estimated there to be 134,000 Wiccans, 140,000 Pagans, and 33,000 Druids in the U.S. These and other data and information about neopaganism are mostly derived from the Ontario Consultants for Religious Tolerance's website, www.religioustolerance.org.

Most Witches trace their movement to ancient Goddess religions, but these origins are clouded in lost history, suppressed history, pre-history, and fictionalized history.[142] At the same time, Witchcraft is a postmodern invention — a "feminist religion of the future," Starhawk writes in *The Spiral Dance*, that "is presently being formed. . ."

> A mode of consciousness that has been dormant for thousands of years is now coming to the fore; we are beginning to see holistically; our model of the cosmos has been changed; we are beginning to value the femi-nine, the life-generative principle, to value humanness, and the existing world.

While there is plenty of ideology popping out of this paragraph, the Witchcraft movement is, according to Starhawk, refreshingly difficult to pin down and generalize about, since it tends to be anarchistic, non-hierarchical, and spontaneous — "a religion of poetry, not theology," she says. Notwithstanding this fluidity, however, modern Witchcraft does share certain ritual aesthetics, metaphysical concepts and organiz-ing principles across the movement.

Witches promote, for example, a view of the natural world as it-self sacred, with "all things — plants, animals, stones, and stars —

---

142. Folklorists, novelists, occultists, anthropologists and scholars, including Charles G. Leland (1824-1903), Robert Graves (1895-1985), and Margaret Murray (1863-1963), among others, helped to promote popular interest in ancient European paganism and its clandestine survival in certain fertility and folk elements of Christianity. British occultist Gerald Gardner (1884-1964), a Freemason and Rosicrucian who was an accomplished amateur archae-ologist and anthropologist in Sri Lanka, Ceylon, Malaysia and Palestine, helped to shape — some say invent — modern Witchcraft through his books, *Witchcraft Today* (1954) and *The Meaning of Witchcraft* (1959). (Starhawk's *The Spiral Dance*, hardly gives a nod to Gardner's influence.) Riane Eisler's bestselling *The Chalice and the Blade* (1988), Merlin Stone's *When God Was a Woman* (1978), Barbara Ehrenreich and Deirdre English's pamphlet, *Witches, Midwives and Nurses: A History of Women Healers* (1972), and Starhawk's *Truth or Dare: Encounters with Power, Authority and Mystery* (1988) were among the works that inspired the expansion of the Witchcraft movement as a religious manifestation of feminism.

L a w r e n c e   B u s h

. . . alive . . . on some level conscious beings," Starhawk writes. "All things are divine, are manifestations of the Goddess. . . . There is no conflict, in Witchcraft, between the spiritual and the material; we do not have to give up one to gain the other."

Witches generally favor a perspective that emphasizes the interconnectness of the world, and view this as more fundamentally real than a perspective of separateness. For Starhawk, this emphasis inspires a commitment to social stewardship, whereas the perspective of separateness feeds the aspiration to dominate. "[W]e are linked," she insists, "with all of the cosmos as parts of one living organism. What affects one of us affects us all. The felling of tropical forests disturbs our weather patterns and destroys the songbirds of the North. No less does the torture of a prisoner in El Salvador or the crying of a homeless child in San Francisco disturb our well-being."

Witchcraft is also a creative and improvisational religion, shaped within the communal structure of the coven — a committed community of witches and witches-in-training. While certain ritual objects are common to many covens, including the wand, athame (a ritual knife), staff, cauldron, candle, chalice, bell and broom, the movement has no set prayer book or liturgy, creeds or doctrines. "What really defines a witch," says Aidan Kelly, a neopagan who has been a subject of controversy in the Wicca movement, "is a type of *experience* people go through. These experiences depend on altered states of consciousness. The Craft is really the Yoga of the West."[143]

The shared spiritual aims of Witches seem to be twofold: first, to affirm through their rituals, language, and relationships the virtues that they associate with positive female consciousness: holism, interconnection, life-giving, love of nature, empathy, cooperation; second, to arouse the symbol-loving mind through active engagement with meta-

---

143. Aidan Kelly, in Margot Adler's *Drawing Down the Moon: Witches, Druids, Goddess-Worshippers and Other Pagans in America Today*, 1986. Kelly returned to his Catholic roots in 1976 in his quest to overcome alcoholism, then reinvolved himself in Witchcraft. His 1991 book, *Crafting the Art of Magic*, stirred up controversy with its assertions that Wicca was not an ancient tradition, as the movement's most prominent contemporary founder, Gerald Gardner, had claimed in the 1940s. See L. Lisa Harris, "Look Back in Controversy: A Samhain Interview with Aidan Kelly," 2006, at: www.widdershins.org/vol8iss5/01.htm.

phors, shapes, colors, and objects, and through the anthropomorphic and anthropopsychic interpretation of nature (the four directions, the four seasons, the four elements, the phases of the waxing and waning moon, and so on). Conscious breathing, singing, chanting, dancing, word association, exercises of relaxation and visualization, nudity, and other techniques of arousal and "letting go" are combined in rituals to heighten sensory awareness, trigger emotions and shift consciousness to what Starhawk calls "starlight vision" —

> [A]ll things are swirls of energy, vortexes of moving forces, currents in an ever-changing sea. Underlying the appearance of separateness, of fixed objects within a linear stream of time, reality is a field of energies that congeal, temporarily, into new forms . . . .

> This view of the universe as an interplay of moving forces — which, incidentally, correspond to an amazing degree with the views of modern physics — is a product of a very special mode of perception . . . that is broad, holistic, and undifferentiated, [and] sees patterns and relationships rather than fixed objects. It is the mode of starlight: dim and silvery, revealing the play of woven branches and the dance of shadows, sensing pathways as spaces in the whole.

Witchcraft, Starhawk sums up, is not so much a belief system as "a constantly self-renewed attitude of joy and wonder to the world." Described a lot more dryly, it seems to be a vigorous form of adult fantasy-play, involving a set of techniques for getting naturally high in an intimate and tightly bonded community. As Aidan Kelly implies, it is far more concerned with shaping consciousness than with shaping a concept of God — and in this particular, it is a classic form of Woodstocker religion.

I GUESS MY ONLY COVEN has been my wife and two kids, but we have certainly shared aspects of "starlight vision" and a sense of "joy and wonder to the world" together. When we hiked in the Grand Canyon, for example . . .

My first time was with Susan in our pre-marital, pre-parenting life, in the summer of 1975. Our hike from the South Rim to the North Rim of the Canyon was a truly wondrous adventure — part of a nine-week hitchhiking tour of the U.S. — an experience of "swirls of energy, vortexes of moving forces, currents in an ever-changing sea"! The second time in the Canyon, summer of 1999, we brought our children, who were then 12 and served as our witnesses as Susan and I performed a twentieth wedding anniversary ceremony, renewing our vows, in the inner canyon along the Bright Angel Trail.

At that time, I remember, the kids were in the habit of using the word "awesome" to describe anything and everything that impressed or pleased them. ("Let's get some ice cream." "Awesome.") My stock reply had become, "No, no, the Grand Canyon is awesome." Now, hiking to the bottom of the Canyon, they understood: "Awesome" meant the monumental sculptural work of wind, water and time; the full moon's light reflecting off a rock wall when there is no other illumination besides a flashlight; the pervasiveness of life beyond the perimeters of civilization (mule deer! rattlesnakes! lizards! cacti! flowers! cicadas!); the fragility of our own bodies in a harsh environment; the intense pleasure of eating when hunger is keen; the blessed relief of shade and flowing water when the temperature climbs above 100°; the infectiousness of mood when people make a tough hike together — and, the upsurge of magical consciousness when the alien rocks suddenly coalesce into faces on the stone ledges above . . .

We would periodically spot these totemic gods and goddesses, and align our fields of vision with spoken coordinates and pointing fingers. Bringing the stone faces into focus evoked great feelings of mystery, revelation and sharpened attention. The more alien qualities of the Canyon would recede: The inconceivable eons of erosion would become mythical lifespans; the geological strata, thrones, palaces, and altars. I knew, of course, that I was simply looking at rocks — yet I found that the search for those faces helped me see *everything* in the Canyon more intimately, in more detail, and with more interest and arousal.

It seems that the pattern-seeking mind is a very alert mind — and is linked to the magical mind, which forms symbols, infers significance and detects agency — even when there is none.[144] Starhawk calls this aspect of mind the "Younger Self," which she describes as one of three states of consciousness identified by Witches —

> It is the Younger Self that directly experiences the world . . . Sensations, emotions, basic drives, image memory, intuition, and diffuse perception are functions of Younger Self. Younger Self's verbal understanding is limited; it communicates through images, emotions, sensations, dreams, visions, and physical symptoms. Classic psychoanalysis developed from attempts to interpret the speech of the Younger Self. Witchcraft not only interprets, but teaches us how to speak back to Younger Self.

Doing so, Starhawk continues, ". . . may sometimes seem silly to very serious-minded people, who fail to realize that ritual is aimed at Younger Self. The sense of humor, of play, is often the key to opening the deepest states of consciousness. . . . A child makes believe that she is a queen; her chair becomes a throne. A Witch makes believe that her wand has magic power, and it becomes a channel for energy."

And an atheistic backpacker in the Grand Canyon makes believe the rocks are beings, and they become guides to the truly awesome.

So is this the stuff that led the Reverend Pat Robertson to include Witchcraft in a denunciatory litany that included feminism, socialism, anti-family policies, marital desertion, the killing of children, the destruction of capitalism, and lesbianism?[145]

---

144. "Our evolutionary heritage," writes Pascal Boyer in *Religion Explained,* "is that of organisms that must deal with both predators and prey. In either situation, it is far more advantageous to overdetect agency than to underdetect it. The expense of false positives (seeing agents where there are non) is minimal, and we can abandon these misguided intuitions quickly. In contrast, the cost of not detecting agents when they are actually around (either predator or prey) could be very high."

145. *The Washington Post,* August 23, 1992.

Is this what other Christian ideologues have linked with "Satanism" and described as "spiritual adultery."[146]

Is this what provoked the U.S. Department of Veteran Affairs to refuse burial at Arlington Cemetery under the sign of the pentacle?[147]

Is this what provoked the writers of the Bible to declare bluntly, "You shall not suffer a witch to live" (*Exodus* 22:17)?

My goodness, is Witchcraft really that threatening to the lords of monotheism?

Indeed it is, for Witchcraft serves to disconnect people from classical religious ideology while keeping them connected to their religious passions and fantasies. The oppositional voice of atheism is feeble compared to the subversive power of a full-blown alternative religion that engages people's religious instincts while undermining their faith in dominant dogmas. As Carol Christ writes in her anthology, *Womanspirit Rising*: "Symbol systems cannot simply be rejected, they must be replaced."[148]

The challenges offered by Witchcraft are manifold:

• Witchcraft undermines the idea that patriarchy, the domination of society by men and its organization into a hierarchy of power, is the

---

146. The "Spiritual Adultery Bible Studies" Series, www.acts17-11.com/witchcraft.html, describes Witchcraft as "rebellion coupled with a desire to 'stay in the game,' to be a spiritual player without submitting to God. . . .Witchcraft works by focusing on a distracter, a lie, which is some technique purported to release power." It "bolsters up [sic] the lie with: mystery, pseudoscience, ancient knowledge, new knowedge, etc. . . . [T]he practitioners of it often think they are serving God, while accessing a power from below (earth) — not from above."

147. According to the July-August, 2006 issue of *Church & State,* the publication of Americans United for Separation of Church and State, Wiccans tried unsuccessfully for many years "to persuade the National Cemetery Administration to add the pentacle to its list of approved emblems for government headstones, markers and plaques." In April, 2007, the Wiccan pentacle was at last added to the list of emblems allowed in national cemeteries and on headstones of soldiers' graves.

148. Carol Christ and Judith Plaskow, eds., *Womanspirit Rising: A Feminist Reader in Religion*, 1979, quoted in Starhawk's *The Spiral Dance*.

only normative organizing principle for the human race. It does so by resurrecting the concept of woman-as-deity (the Goddess), by celebrating the powers to give and nurture life as more potent than the powers to take and dominate life, and by declaring itself to be an ancient form of worship that was displaced through repression and conquest by patriarchal religions. Whether this "herstory" is actual or mythical, it postulates that patriarchal systems are not "God-given" or "just the way it is," but are self-perpetuating outgrowths of historical circumstances. The grip of what seems normative is greatly loosened when the norm is recognized as a social construct rather than an inevitability.

• Just as radically, Witchcraft creates intense, emotional ties between feminist ideology and a religious sense of the good and the sacred. The Witchcraft tradition suggests that the release of women from oppression and enslavement is not only a *political* necessity — vital to the democratization and economic empowerment of impoverished countries,[149] and to curbing war and violence — but also represents the attunement of humanity to the ways of nature, the ways of the life force, the ways of the cosmos.

• Witchcraft also challenges mainstream theological dualism — what Starhawk describes as "the view of a universe composed of warring opposites, which are valued as either good or evil." In Witchcraft, there are no sides to take, no "other" to persecute, no claims to salvation,

---

149. According to *The Asian Enigma*, a 1992 UNICEF report about hunger and malnutrition in developing countries, "equal freedoms, opportunities, and rights for women — including the right to participate in decision-making both inside and outside the home" are a critical ingredient of poverty relief. See Nora Simpson's "Global Development and the United Nations" in the September-October, 2006 issue of *Jewish Currents*. Simpson describes the findings of The Hunger Project that "African women . . . produce 80 percent of Africa's food through small-scale farming. Women also perform 90 percent of the work to process food, collect and transport 90 percent of the water, wood, and fuel used on the continent, and perform 60 percent of the work to market Africa's food. Yet African women own 1 percent of the land, and receive less than 7 percent of farm extension services and less than 10 percent of credit given to small-scale farmers. . . . In addition, 40 percent of women in Africa have never seen the inside of a schoolhouse, much less achieved any sort of education or literacy. With so little attention paid to the people responsible for meeting basic human needs, there is little wonder that the development programs of the last fifty years have not achieved their goals in Africa."

no accusations of damnation. Witches, instead, view "polarities" as being "in balance, not at war. . . . The Goddess is ourselves *and* the world — to link with Her is to engage actively with the world and all its problems." Witchcraft therefore places no value on otherworldliness or on withdrawal from our "wicked" or "illusory" world, nor does it promote what she calls the "Righteousness Syndrome" of religious triumphalism.

• Witchcraft challenges mainstream religion's punishing attitudes towards human sexuality, physical pleasure and sensuality. "Goddess religion identifies sexuality as the expression of the creative life force of the universe," Starhawk writes. "It is not dirty, nor is it merely 'normal'; it is sacred, the manifestation of the Goddess. . . . In orgasm, we share in the force that moves the stars." The perspective she promotes is not one of dissolution or self-indulgence, but rather, of self-expression and self-fulfillment, which she considers to be more difficult to achieve than "the most extreme patriarchal disciplines":

> It is easier to be celibate than to be fully alive sexually.
> It is easier to withdraw from the world than to live in
> it; easier to be a hermit than to raise a child; easier to
> repress emotions than to feel them and express them;
> easier to meditate in solitude than to communicate in
> a group; easier to submit to another's authority than
> place trust in oneself.[150]

• Witchcraft also challenges the classic religious notion that without the authority of an omnipotent God, human sin and misdeed are sure to run rampant. Starhawk formulates the question this way: "By what standards can [we] judge [our] actions, when the external judge is removed from his place as ruler of the cosmos?" The answer she offers is that "love for life in all its forms is the basic ethic of Witchcraft," while "justice is an inner sense that each act brings about consequences that

---

150. This is one passage from *The Spiral Dance* that Starhawk, twenty years later, is inclined to retract. "I've been taken to task by many people for this paragraph," she writes in her notes to the twentieth anniversary edition, "and I have to admit that they are right. Adopting an ascetic tradition is not an escape from engagement with life, but simply a different choice."

must be faced responsibly." Witchcraft "does not foster guilt, the stern, admonishing, self-hating inner voice that cripples action. Instead, it demands responsibility."

Finally, the challenges offered by Witchcraft are not limited to Western religions. Starhawk acknowledges that "Eastern religions offer a radically different approach to spirituality than Judeo-Christian traditions" and "philosophies [that] are very close to that of Witchcraft." However, she cautions against the ego-surrendering, self-transcending teachings of Eastern religions: "women," she writes, "cannot become whole by being yet more passive, gentle, and submissive than we already are. . ."

> We cannot achieve enlightenment through identifying
> with Buddha's wife or Krishna's groupies. . . . If we
> look closely at the symbols, the hierarchical structure,
> the denial of sexuality and emotion purveyed by the
> gurus who do attract popular cults in the West, we can
> only conclude that, while they may be using different
> instruments, they are playing the same old song.

In all of this, Witchcraft directly confronts the intimidating authority of established religions. Like Matthew Fox and Mordecai Kap-lan, Starhawk tries to free our spiritual sensibility by shaking it loose of the fear of death, of holier-than-thou ideologies, of God Almighty imagery, of repressive authoritarianism, so that our spirituality might be associated, instead, with wonder, joy, and the affirmation of life.

Unlike Fox and Kaplan, however, Starhawk is unburdened by religious metaphors that have borne the weight of authoritarian religious ideology for centuries. Yes, she associates Witchcraft with a historical tradition: "more than 35,000 years ago," she avows, "when the temperatures of Europe began to drop and the great sheets of ice crept slowly south in their last advance . . . gifted shamans could attune themselves to the spirits of the herds, and in doing so they became aware of the pulsating rhythm that infuses all life . . ." She also mourns as her own tragic history the "Indo-European invasions [that] swept over Europe from the Bronze Age on . . . [and] drove the Goddess peoples out from the fertile lowlands," and the subsequent execution of hundreds of thousands, perhaps even millions, of women (and young girls and men and children) as Witches by the Catholic and Protestant churches between the 1300s and the 1700s.[151] Yet Starhawk seems to recognize all of this history as speculative — a "mixture of oral tradition, interpretations of physical evidence, and standard scholarship" — and even while she believes the Goddess religion to be "unimaginably old," she admits that it "could just as accurately be called The New Religion . . . undergoing more than a revival; it is experiencing a renaissance, a recreation."

MOST REFRESHINGLY, the "Special Twentieth Anniversary Edition" of *The Spiral Dance* has a remarkable running commentary by the author looking back on her own writing at 10- and 20-year-after junctures. In these notes, Starhawk often second-guesses herself, modifies her statements, adds a new "middle-aged" perspective, even pokes fun at her earlier writings. These are the reflections of a skeptical religious leader who seems doggedly to be avoiding the role of guru, the appearance of being all-wise, and the promotion of religious dogma.

Her skepticism even extends to Witchcraft's own outlandish statements about the nature of reality. Starhawk admits, for example, that "most Witches" believe in reincarnation, though as "not so much a doctrine as a gut feeling growing out of a world view that sees all events as continuing processes." Similarly, she writes that the "myths and stories" of Goddess traditions "are not . . . to be taken literally, any more than we are meant to take literally that 'my love is like a red, red rose.' They are poetry, not theology — meant to speak to Younger Self." Elsewhere, she adds: "Religion becomes dogmatic when it confuses the metaphor with the thing itself."

---

151. The history of witch-hunting and witch-burning has apparently been the subject of a great deal of speculation and fabrication. Writing in *The Crisis*, October 2001, Sandra Meisel, a medievalist and journalist, argues that "nine million women burned is a figure conveniently larger than the Jewish Shoah, yet it was actually invented out of whole cloth by American feminist Matilda Joslyn Gage in 1893. . . . [R]ecent academic research has largely demolished both the old Enlightenment certainties and the new neopagan theories." For Meisel's analysis of "Who Burned the Witches?", see: www.crisismagazine.com/october2001/feature1.htm.

And what about magic, which suffuses the Witchcraft movement? Occultist Dion Fortune's definition of magic — "the art of changing consciousness at will" — is quoted approvingly by Starhawk, but then she warns:

> If Goddess religion is not to become mindless idiocy, we must win clear of the tendency of magic to become superstition. . . . Magical systems are highly elaborated metaphors, not truths. When we say, "There are twelve signs in the Zodiac, " what we really mean is "we will view the infinite variety of human characteristics through this mental screen, because with it we can gain insights." . . . But when we forget that the signs are arbitrary groupings of stars, and start believing that there are large lions, scorpions, and crabs up in the sky, we are in trouble.

Goddess religion should therefore be grounded "firmly," she concludes, "in science, in what we can observe in the physical world."

AFTER A WHILE, HOWEVER, THE FREQUENCY of these rationalistic assertions fosters the suspicion that Starhawk, just like Mordecai Kaplan, is actually quite concerned about the "slippery slope" of magical thinking in her religious movement. In fact, her own rationalism slips quite a few times in *The Spiral Dance,* as she makes affirmations of irrational belief and permits them to go untested and uncontested, leaving this skeptical reader to wonder about the range of nonsense that presumably passes for legitimate belief in the privacy of covens across America.

Regarding the "techniques of magic," for example, while Starhawk plausibly credits them with "creat[ing] states of ecstasy," she also claims that they involve "neurological repatterning . . . the development and then the integration of right-hemisphere, spatial, intuitive, holistic, patterning awareness," which "opens the gates between the unconscious and the conscious minds, between the starlight and flashlight vision." Magical spells thus exercise power not only through psychological suggestion, but "can also influence the external world. Perhaps the job hunter 'just happens' to walk into the right office at the right time. The cancer patient, without knowing that a healing spell was cast, has a spontaneous remission."

Has any aspect of this hodge-podge, combining neurology, psychology, medicine and synchronicity, been subjected to scientific scrutiny? Well, Starhawk suggests,

> This aspect of magic . . . coincides in many ways with the "new [quantum] physics". . . . But I do not offer it as "proof" that magic works — nor do I wish to convince anyone to drop their doubts. (Skeptics make better magicians.) It is simply an elaborate — but extremely useful — metaphor.

This "extremely useful metaphor" may work best, by the way, when the moon is waxing: "Subtle power increases as the moon waxes, so the time of the waxing moon is best for spells involving growth or increase, such as money spells." Other witches, she adds, "make a detailed study of astrology in an effort to plan their magical workings at the optimum times" — this from a woman who insists that magic "functions within natural law, not outside of it."

Whenever she can, Starhawk hitches her spiritual practice to the wagon of science. "Physicists," she writes, "inform us that the atoms and molecules of all things, from an unstable gas to the Rock of Gibraltar, are in constant motion. Underlying that motion is an order, a harmony that is inherent in being. Matter sings, by its very nature." A Witch's power, she goes on, derives from "channeling" this "energy" from the earth, from other people, and from other natural sources. How? Well, "certain stones increase the flow" and it also helps if a Witch "grounds" herself with the earth through visualization techniques that help her "draw on the earth's vitality, rather than depleting [her] own." Magical tools can be helpful, too, though "when buying magical tools," she advises, without further explanation, "never haggle over the price."

When such "scientific" explanations of Witchcraft are simply stretched too thin, Starhawk is perfectly willing to resort to the mystification and impeachment of science itself. "Scientific knowledge, like religious knowledge," she claims, "is a set of metaphors for a reality that can never be completely described or comprehended." Is the calculated speed of light, then, a metaphor — and if so, a metaphor for what? Are accurate scientific predictions about the material world metaphors? Are radio waves metaphors? Are nuclear bombs metaphors? To Starhawk, it seems that anything that has a metaphorical component, or that may have symbolic meaning for the human mind, qualifies as a metaphor.

"Physics, mathematics, ecology, and biochemistry more and more approach the mystical," she insists. Yet spirituality "leaps where science cannot follow, because science must always test and measure, and much of reality and human experience is immeasurable. Without discarding science, we can recognize its limitations. . . "

> There are many modes of consciousness that have not been validated by Western scientific rationalism, in particular what I call "starlight awareness," the holistic, intuitive mode of perception of the right hemisphere of our brains. As a culture, we are experiencing a turn toward the intuitive, the psychic, which have been denied for so long. Astrology, Tarot, palmistry — all the ancient forms of divination are undergoing a revival.

Starhawk thus celebrates the revival of the irrational: those valiant, fascinating, and largely ineffectual practices by which human beings, during the many, many centuries that predated the scientific method, sought to control the unpredictable forces of nature, to systematize their often-incorrect intuitions about material reality, and to probe their own psyches. In essence, she gets away with this romanticization of these pre-scientific "ways of knowing" by mobilizing all of the Woodstocker biases described in this book of mine: our conflation of science with modern capitalism and capitalist alienation; our resort to "holism" as a code-word for love, life, and interconnection; our idealization of the past as more sacred, more pacific, more cooperative, more spiritual than our troubled present; our oppositional-salvational ideology, which deems Western Civilization a monster; our belief that the "high" of the mystical union experience constitutes an actual transcending of the "illusory" or degraded nature of waking consciousness; our belief in the deep psychological significance of coincidence.

And to seal the deal, Starhawk presents her dizzying *Spiral Dance* as the communal dance of feminism, the embodied spirit of resistance to patriarchy, and the path of healing for our species. "If our culture as a whole is to evolve toward life," she concludes, "we need to . . . create a religion of heretics, who refuse to toe any ideological lines or give their allegiances to any doctrines of exclusivity" — or even to rationalism.

AND SO WE ARE HANDED the ideology of *anything is possible. Anything is possible* becomes the mark of open-mindedness, open-heartedness, a capacity for joy, and a properly outraged sense of righteousness about the crimes and narrow perspectives of mainstream religions and mainstream society.

Anything is possible because the Establishment declares so much to be impossible, beyond the pale, improper, heretical, against human nature, or sinful.

Anything is possible because so much is amazing.

Anything is possible because everything is interconnected.

And I sit, arms crossed, on the sidelines saying *No, no, no, no* . . .

Part Three

What Can I Say?

Chapter Eight

A Spiritual Atheist

"Then I saw this ladder on a painting leading up to the ceiling where there was a spyglass hanging down. . . I went up the ladder and I got the spyglass and there was tiny little writing there. You really have to stand on the top of the ladder — you feel like a fool, you could fall any minute — and you look through and it just says 'yes.'"
— John Lennon, describing his first encounter with Yoko Ono's art, in *The Beatles Anthology*[152]

I'm afraid that *No, no, no, no* has been my principal response to Woodstocker spirituality throughout this book, even to the contemporary theologians whom I most respect. My "spiritual explorations" have basically been a series of pendulum swings between the allure of spiritual experience and the *no, no, no, no* of my rational skepticism, which I consistently deploy to ward off the anxieties provoked in me by beckoning gurus, the promise of religious redemption, and the notion of cosmic accountability.

Negatives can have their positives, however. When the great bard of the Woodstock generation, John Lennon, asked us to "imagine" a redeemed world, he talked about "no heaven," "no country, and no religion too," and "no possessions." Lennon perceived that belief in an afterlife, a homeland, a religious ideology, and "mine not yours" was confining to our sense of possibility. In saying *no, no, no, no,* he hoped to unleash the richer and more generous aspects of our humanity: "Imagine all the people living for today . . . living life in peace . . . sharing all the world."[153]

---

152. *The Beatles Anthology*, 2000.

153. John Lennon, "Imagine," 1971.

I like to think that the *no, no, no, no* of my atheism similarly expresses an optimistic sense of our potential for passionate living and transformational acts once our minds are turned loose from belief systems. Years ago, I poured this optimism into a poem, entitled "After the Revolution." Over time, as I periodically reworked the piece, and as the teachings of the Jewish tradition became more and more a part of my intellectual fabric, "After the Revolution" evolved to "When *Moshiakh* Comes." "*Moshiakh*" means "messiah" — the vague but redemptive figure of Jewish lore. It was an important part of the personal evolution of this child of Jewish communists to realize that "After the Revolution" and "When *Moshiakh* Comes" express, for me, virtually the same longings and hopes.

Now, it may be that for every such sigh of hope, a skeptic should also heave a sigh of apprehension, in the knowledge that hope, when thwarted by reality, often mutates into ideology — and that ideology, given the opportunity to avenge itself on reality, often yields atrocity.[154]

---

154. As I have earlier noted (see footnote 74), the rabbis of the Talmud, the rabbis most responsible for the creation of normative Judaism, actually downplayed the significance of *moshiakh*, and the imminence of his arrival, perhaps for fear of unleashing religious zealotry and warfare against the Roman empire that dominated their land. The Jewish people had already been crushed by Rome in two uprisings, ending in 70 C.E. and 135 C.E., that resulted in the killing of hundreds of thousands of Jews and their exile from the land of Israel. When the leader of the second uprising, Simon Bar Kokhba, was declared to be the messiah by the great rabbinic leader Akiva, Rabbi Yohanan ben Torta responded, "Akiva, grass will be growing out of your cheeks and the messiah will still not have come."

 By being coy about the actual identity and arrival time of the messiah and of his herald, the Prophet Elijah, the Jewish tradition encouraged people to regard one another as a potentially holy leader — a classic use of religious metaphor to inspire humanistic ethics.

 Messianic expectations nevertheless persisted throughout Jewish history, giving rise most notably to the birth of Christianity in the 1st century C.E., and to the messianic craze that shook the entire Jewish world in the mid-17th century when Sabbetai Zevi, a charismatic manic-depressive, was widely embraced throughout the Jewish world as the messiah. (Zevi was forcibly converted to Islam by Ottoman leaders when he sought to declare his "throne.") In our own time, the Lubavitcher Hasidic movement (Chabad) was seized in the 1990s by the belief that its leader, Rabbi Menachem Shneerson, was the messiah, a belief that persisted even after his death.

Even with that kind of skepticism perched on my shoulder, however, I have always wanted to belong to John Lennon's league of "dreamers,"[155] and I sought membership when I wrote and rewrote "After the Revolution"/"When *Moshiakh* Comes"[156] . . .

When *Moshiakh* comes . . .

The Pentagon will be a post office.
The President will be in therapy at least once a week.
The average American will speak three languages
when *Moshiakh* comes.

When *Moshiakh* comes . . .
The National Anthem will be a jazz standard.
The White House will be redecorated as the Rainbow Room.
We'll proudly fly the flag
when *Moshiakh* comes.

People will often ask, "What day is today?"
It will be fun to stand in line.
We'll all have Bloomingdale's credit cards
when *Moshiakh* comes.

When *Moshiakh* comes . . .
"Fuck you" will be a friendly greeting.
High school kids will be taught to be attentive lovers.
Tampons and sanitary napkins will be free
when *Moshiakh* comes.

Those who rape
will be taught, by men, to weep.

---

155. "You may say I'm a dreamer, but I'm not the only one" — from the same song, "Imagine," by John Lennon.

156. Published in my book, *American Torah Toons: 54 Illustrated Commentaries*, 1993.

Those who steal
will be given what they want.
Those who abuse
will be held with loving arms
when *Moshiakh* comes.

"How shall we get rid of our dismantled nuclear weapons?"
"Who should be the first inducted into the
Hall of Outstanding Gay Americans?"
How will we apologize to each other
when *Moshiakh* comes?

When *Moshiakh* comes . . .

Russia will be named Glasnostia.
The U.S. will be named the Altered States.
We'll be much, much less afraid
when *Moshiakh* comes.

Africa will host the feast.
Glasnostia will offer the benediction.
The Altered States will receive an invitation
when *Moshiakh* comes.

Israel will build settlements
for endangered animals in reforested lands.
The U.N. will declare that "Zionism ain't all that bad."
There will be no weapons in Jerusalem
when *Moshiakh* comes.

When *Moshiakh* comes . . .

Whales and dolphins will send congratulatory messages.
The only threatened species will be Male Chauvinist Pigs.
We'll still be allowed to kill mosquitos
when *Moshiakh* comes.

We'll proudly display our wrinkles.
We'll notice each other's eyes.
We'll dream less of other worlds
when *Moshiakh* comes.

"I want to share this with my mother."
"I wish my father had lived to see this."
Will there be a resurrection
when *Moshiakh* comes?

When *Moshiakh* comes . . .

We will wonder how long *Moshiakh* intends to stay.
We will try to be brave and stop weeping.
We will forgive
but not forget
when *Moshiakh* comes.

DOES THIS *MOSHIAKH* OF MY DREAMS require an atheistic platform on which to make her or his appearance? Only insofar as my urge to imagine actual solutions to what I regard as unjust and repressive in society is driven by my belief that there is no messiah, has never been a messiah, and never will be a messiah — that redemption is strictly a human affair. The "no" of my atheism thereby helps inspire the "yes" of my poem, in all of its specifics.

Still, I cannot pretend that atheism is defined, or even necessarily accompanied, by such schemes for redemption. Nor can I pretend that my belief in redemption as "strictly a human affair" gives me greater courage, or more activist energy, than the believer who roots his or her political commitment in a relationship with God or the mandates of a religious tradition. Notwithstanding the efforts of atheist philosophers to link their atheism inextricably with positive belief— with "good conduct and wisdom in living" (Paul Kurtz); with "truthfulness" and "social necessity" (Goparaju Ramachandra Rao, known as Gora)[157] — atheism is, in essence, a negation of theological belief, not an affirmation

---

157. Paul Kurz, previously cited several times, is the creator of the humanistic credo that he calls "eupraxsophy." Gora (1902-1975) worked with Gandhi

of alternative belief. It does not necessarily offer alternative symbols, rituals or metaphysical schemata when it says *no, no, no, no* to people's deeply held beliefs; it does not necessarily replace false hope with real hope, false meaning with real meaning, false redemption with real redemption. In the popular mind, in fact, atheism is generally associated with dark pessimism, "absurdity" (Sartre), and what philosopher Walter Kaufman defined as the four basic tenets of existentialism: "dread, despair, death, and dauntlessness."[158]

No, no, no, no. No soul, only body and brain. *No afterlife,* only our reputations, our offspring, and the fruits of our deeds. *No overarching meaning,* only the evolutionary unfolding of the grand accident of life. *No discernible metaphysical architecture,* only the laws of physics and chemistry. These are the classic negations of atheism — and any intimations you have to the contrary, we nonbelievers will inform you, are simply mind tricks, wishful thoughts, metaphors so beautiful that they have hypnotized you.

It's no wonder that atheists, long before we get around to our affirmations, are likely to be denounced as depressed, traitorous, morally rootless, angry and/or intolerant. Indeed, our "intolerance" is barely tolerated: Atheists are discriminated against in child custody cases and legally excluded from the Boy Scouts of America. The constitutions of seven states, Arkansas, Maryland, North Carolina, Pennsylvania, South Carolina, Tennessee and Texas, have vestigial clauses that deny political office to atheists (state supreme courts have consistently struck these down as unconstitutional when test cases are brought)[159], and

---

for the abolition of the caste system in India and created a system of "positive atheism."

158. Walter Kaufman, *Existentialism from Dostoevsky to Sartre,* 1975.

159. In 1997, for example, Herb Silverman, a Jewish atheist from Philadelphia, ran for office in South Carolina explicitly to challenge the state constitution's requirement that candidates believe in a "higher power." After eight years in the courts, the case was decided in Silverman's favor unanimously by the state supreme court. Silverman went on to serve as president of the Secular Coalition of America, which has on its staff Lori Lipman Brown, the only lobbyist in Washington, D.C. representing an atheist organization. For an interview with Herb Silverman, see: www.theinfidels.org/herbsilvermaninterview.htm.

L a w r e n c e   B u s h

President George H.W. Bush, in 1987, described atheists as neither citizens nor patriots.[160]

MOST WOODSTOCKERS, I ASSUME, do not share these biases against atheists. They are, like me, far more concerned about the frightening and growing power of authoritarian Christian and Islamic fundamentalism than with the stubborn skepticism of the atheist minority. Hold a debate between me and a jihadist (with weapons checked at the door), and my Woodstocker brethren would know for whom to root; hold a school board election between me and a Christian Creationist, and they would know for whom to vote.

Afterwards, however, while shaking my hand in the hallway, they might still wonder about the depths of my disbelief, as I often used to wonder about my own father's. *You know that we Woodstockers are the good guys,* they might say, *and that part of what marks us as the good guys is our compassionate, optimistic spirituality and our orientation towards higher consciousness. We have stood together against the God of the Establishment — the God of exclusivity, strict rules, repression, us-versus-them, sexism, sin and salvation. But why say No, no, no, no even to those nontraditional theologians and spiritual teachers who have led our generation beyond the God of No to the Goddess of Yes?*

Why do you care whether Jesus was an actually existing, divine being if the invocation of his "Via Positiva" can help people tune themselves to a sense of blessing, gratitude and environmental responsibility?

Why do you care whether or not the universe is actually structured to "make for redemption" if thinking so helps human communities to strive for redemption?

Why do you care whether the oh-so-distant stars have any effect upon human destiny if astrological metaphors can help people gain insight into themselves?

Why do you care if "magic" is really just a word for social and psychological creativity, if calling it "magic" helps people take their own power seriously?

---

160. Responding to a reporter on August 27, 1987, Bush said, "I don't know that atheists should be considered as citizens, nor should they be considered patriots. This is one nation under God." See *Free Inquiry*, Fall, 1988, Vol. 8, No. 4.

What is gained, after all, by saying no, no, no, no to metaphors, or even superstitions, if they serve to ennoble and embolden us? Isn't it our behavior, rather than our belief systems, that counts?

My first impulse would be to return challenge for challenge:

My fellow Woodstockers, why do you cling to the metaphors of pre-scientific centuries of superstition, suffering and oppression — metaphors that are still actively used as excuses for mayhem and domination — rather than inventing new ones?

Why do you romanticize the past? Why do you imagine that the "old ways of knowing" are somehow superior, less "tainted," than modern paths of knowledge? Don't you think our human species is making progress, however slowly, in the realms of self-knowledge and social understanding? Your God of Yes has been bred of incredible prosperity, unprecedented good health, and tremendous personal freedom — the very accomplishments of Western Civilization, the civilization of reason, science, and materialism that your religious and lifestyle ideologies tend to castigate! So why do you spend your precious time with astrology instead of psychology? With learning to "channel energy" instead of learning about solar energy? With reciting prayers instead of writing songs? With praising God for the wonders of the natural world instead of building a bird feeder? With studying kabbalah instead of studying mathematics? With past-life regression instead of future-life activism?

Why do you prefer getting high to getting real?

Is it so hard to keep hope alive without believing that the entire universe is on your side?

Since you've come this far — knocking God off His throne, shaving off His beard, stripping Him of miracle-making power, removing evil from His hands, making Him female, depersonifying Him, collapsing the walls between "God" and "nature" — why not go the rest of the way? See what it's like to demand proofs of the unlikely, the improbable, the unreasonable, rather than handing out "anything is possible" licenses. See what it's like to challenge your own intuitions, rather than romanticizing them. See what your life is like without any "received" wisdom, dogma, canned happy thoughts, "calculated date of redemption," or senseless behavioral rules. See how you express yourself without relying on familiar scripts of worship. You want to express thankfulness for your abundance? Share it with someone in need! You want to express your joy? Go hug your child or make love to a consenting adult!

My fantasy debate evaporates quickly, however, and feelings of lone-
liness and desperation follow fast in its wake. There is, in fact, no way
that I can intellectually "defeat" the God of my Woodstocker friends,
for they have, indeed, created what philosopher Mitchell Silver calls
"a plausible God"[161] to believe in. I can point to the irrational elements
of Goddess religion as much as I want, or warn about the "magical
thinking" that even Reconstructionist prayer tends to produce, or denounce the grim, Inquisitorial antecedents of Matthew Fox's Christian
liberation theology — but all of this amounts to cheap shots at easy
targets. The fact is that Woodstocker religion is more about achieving
a certain state of consciousness than believing in a particular dogma,
and Woodstocker theology, as Silver notes, simply gives the name
"God" to "whatever there is in nature that makes good things possible.
. . . That is all that this baseline God asks one to believe: that goodness
is not ruled out."

How can such a minimalist theological concept alienate me? Why
don't I celebrate it as the victory of modernism, which has wrung so
very many concessions from the religious world?

THE ANSWER SEEMS TO BE THAT I SIMPLY have a bad case of heredi-
tary allergy to religion, even in minute traces, and most especially to
prayer services. Unless they are improvisational, creative, intimate, and
without the G-word, they strike me, at best, as mediocre theater that
affords participants the kind of easy emotional outlet and identification
that Bertolt Brecht described, rather scornfully, as "dramatic" theater:
"I weep when they weep; I laugh when they laugh. . . . That's great art,
It seems the most obvious thing in the world." (Brecht described his
preference, "epic" theater or the theater of alienation, as "I laugh when
they weep; I weep when they laugh. . . . That's great art — nothing
obvious in it.")[162]

I suppose I have a similarly critical and intellectualized response
to the bulk of mass cultural offerings, yet I am *particularly* galled
by the schizophrenic contradictions of prayer language, the resort to

---

161. Mitchell Silver, *A Plausible God*, as previously cited.

162. "Bertolt Brecht on the Epic Theater," http://oregonstate.edu/instruct/ger341/
brechtet.htm.

time-worn formulae rather than new, fresh expression, the sentimentality and the striving for easy ecstasy that I witness among my peers — because the truth is that I am *deeply* interested in the discussion of morality and ethics, the quest for community, the witnessing of one another's lives, and the profound emotional stirrings that seem, alas, to be almost the exclusive province of Religion, Inc.

Still, I don't believe for a second that there will soon be alternative structures that can successfully contest religion's near-monopoly over issues of meaning and community. Social movements that attempted to overturn the power of religion, such as the French, Russian and Chinese revolutions, have consistently failed at their goal, meanwhile producing atrocities more than new forms of enlightenment. If religious concepts do, indeed, appeal deeply to our instincts and fit quite neatly with our mental architecture, then the construction of some kind of "spiritual atheism" as a replacement would require its deliberate propagation in a fashion that could be successful only under totalitarian conditions — God forbid!

In fact, the very idea of building a compelling, secular alternative to religion seems rather ludicrous in an era when the reality of human community is being transformed by capitalism in most parts of the world. In Western societies, especially, the involuntary bonds of community that were once determined by class, gender, ethnic and caste status, birth order, and so on, have been largely supplanted by the advent of a freewheeling consumer culture in which money does the talking. Powerful identities of class, race, religion, and geography are steadily being replaced by a single identity, that of the consumer, who is offered incredible tools of self-sufficiency that privatize our lives and remove all sense of interdependency from our relationships. This has been, perhaps, the most revolutionary aspect of capitalism: its reduction of community to a purely voluntaristic activity that we can easily do without. Under such circumstances, it is hardly likely that well-established religious communities will soon be supplanted by communal secular alternatives — except, perhaps, during those brief periods of social experimentation that seem to refresh the human experience every couple of generations.

It seems, therefore, that I can't beat 'em and I won't join 'em. It can be lonely, especially around holidays, to live life as a spiritual atheist.

"SPIRITUAL" BECAUSE I DO TREASURE the feelings that surge in me when I am alerted to the reality of my interconnection with other living beings. These feelings, which grant relief from the bounded emotional life of the self, if only for a little while, constitute the essence of what is generally called "spirituality," and seem to provoke us to reach for personal growth and greater self-mastery.

For me, as for many people, the spirituality of interconnection has been most frequently accessed through love — for my wife, my kids, my intimates, the ones who seem truly to know me, recognize me, respond to me, and need me. Love is ennobling; love is a mirror; love is a source of repentance and humility; love fosters self-fulfillment and self-transcendence. All of these aspects of love have been manifested to me in my very fortunate love-life, which has inspired me to try to see all human beings, even the stranger — even the wicked stranger — as having the same multi-dimensionality behind the mask of their appearance that I have behind mine. This effort to encounter other beings as a "Thou" rather than an "It," to use Martin Buber's wonderful phrase,[163] is something I work hard to maintain nearly every day of my life. I don't need, however, to believe that each is "made in God's image" in order to feel my empathy — I need only to remind myself that each shares *my* image, my plight, my needs, my urges, and my potential for what Mordecai Kaplan called "salvation." Interconnection is an earthly reality, and I prefer to experience it directly, without God as my intermediary.

So my love-stoked spirituality remains tethered by atheism. While love has been, for me, the most generative and instructive of human emotions, I have found no reason to believe it to be a cosmic force. That widespread religious impulse to project our great, creative emotion of love onto the universe strikes me as hubristic, if sentimental. When in 1967 the Beatles sang "All You Need Is Love" in the first international satellite television broadcast, I agreed with them and thrilled to the spectacle. Had their lyric been, "all there is is love," or "God is love," I would have clucked my tongue in disappointment.

A SECOND SOURCE OF SPIRITUAL STIRRING for me has been the wonderworld of nature: the strivings and contentions, harmonies and in-

---

163. Martin Buber, *I and Thou*, 1923.

terdependencies, deaths and reproductions — and more reproductions, and more reproductions! — that swirl all around me in a blind, unfolding evolutionary process. To stroll in nature, whether a mile down in the Grand Canyon or right out my door in New York's Mid-Hudson Valley, has been my truest form of meditation, enabling me to escape the clutch of my thoughts while surrendering to my senses, my instincts, my endorphins.

Sometimes on those strolls, I like to awaken my magical mind and try on for size a pagan apprehension of the world. I may pretend that each bird, tree, or moss-covered stone bears a message for me; I may exercise the power of my voice to ward off evil, especially on a moonless night; I may interpret all attention-getting events as omens of meaning. All of this I can fantasize, even with the sound of an airplane overhead — yet I would be very unlikely to participate in rituals of worship meant to cultivate these states of mind.

Why? Because I am an atheist and, in all honesty, I celebrate the fact that the plane is there overhead, contrails and all, permitting human beings to fly, visit, trade, and cross boundaries — while I can walk here below, through woods and meadows, without the anxiety of being either predator or prey, and with a leisurely lifespan of 75+ years, not 35+, thanks to the microbe-conquering rationalism of my species. I treasure being a modern, Western man and I have no nostalgia for the helpless conditions in which my superstitious ancestors lived. Would I ban airplanes from the sky in order to preserve the integrity of the Earth's atmosphere? I would! Would I give up some of my safety in order to repopulate the East Coast with mountain lions and grey wolves? I might. Would I whittle my longevity if it meant extending the longevity of the planet? I would probably do that, too. Still, when I read the spiritual urgings of folks like Thomas Berry —

> The natural world demands a response beyond that of
> rational calculation, beyond philosophical reasoning,
> beyond scientific insight. The natural world demands
> a response that rises from the wild unconscious depths
> of the human soul.[164]

---

164. Thomas Berry, *The Great Work, Our Way Into the Future,* as previously cited.

L a w r e n c e   B u s h

— I am moved by the eloquence, but unconvinced by the sentiment. Enough for me to find aesthetic pleasure, sensory adventure, mental health, and opportunity for day-dreaming in the natural world; all of that seems to me to be sufficient motivation for saving the planet, and a far more trustworthy source of response than "the wild unconscious depths of the human soul."

AFTER LOVE AND NATURE, it is science, with its many "revelations" about the material reality of interconnection, that serves as my third reliable source of spirituality, though I am not at all a trained scientist. The fact that we human beings have been breathing the same oxygen molecules for eons; the fact that all six billion of us have likely descended from a single mitochondrial mother; the fact that our cousins, the animals, consistently display consciousness, complexity and social sensitivity that surprise, impress, and humble us; the fact that we humans are far, far, far more similar than different across all cultures, races, and other group classifications, in our capacities and responses to the world — these are among the "yesses" written on *my* ceiling, the "yesses" perceived through telescopes and microscopes and fieldwork observation and laboratory experiment. They are the revelations of reason, diligent observation, the scientific method, and great collective effort — and they are, for the most part, utterly modern insights.

For me as an atheist, the spirituality of these scientific "revelations" is denigrated by religious portrayals of science as merely "another way of knowing," or what Starhawk calls "a set of metaphors" that are somehow in the same class as religious metaphors. Never mind that the Big Bang theory has some resemblance to the biblical story of creation ("Let there be light") or that our common genetic ancestry seems to have been vaguely foretold in the biblical story of Adam and Eve; for every good guess by our pre-modern scriptural authors, I could offer ten that have been utterly contradicted by scientific findings of fact. These resemblances between religious metaphor and scientific fact are slim reeds that Woodstockers grasp in their desire to lend to their spiritual intuitions and their "alternative" paths of wisdom and healing the undeniable respectability of science — just as the Marxist believers of my parents' generation did by calling their historical theories "scientific" socialism.

I am not suggesting that other "ways of knowing" than the scientific method, or all other paths to wisdom than analytical reasoning, should be dismissed. "Science, bluntly, has no room for human values, purposes, ethics or hopes," concedes Norman Levitt in *Prometheus Bedeviled*[165]— which leaves space and need for many other vital undertakings meant to address those realities. It is not generally atheists, however, who seek to extend science's authority into the realm of religion, ethics, morality, wisdom, etcetera, but rather Woodstockers who trespass by trying to gain the scientific imprimatur for their religious beliefs — or, failing that, to degrade the authority of science.

They really should cut it out! For science is not merely "another way of knowing," it is our *only* reliably accurate way of knowing. Science mobilizes our intuitions, and then successfully transcends them, in order to investigate truth: the truth about material reality, individual and social psychology, health and disease, birth and death, the possible and the impossible. If claims of truth, as opposed to interpretation, are made about these and other realms without scientific evidence, I tend to distrust them; if such claims of truth *contradict* scientific principles, I tend to discount them, and to suspect their purveyors of charlatanism. Had this simple rule of skepticism been embraced by the Woodstockers in the 1970s, many a cult leader might have been bankrupted and many a life might have been spared long, meandering diversions onto paths of religious illusion.

A FOURTH SOURCE OF SPIRITUALITY for me has been great works of art, those embodiments of human creativity that can shift our consciousness so dramatically from monologue to dialogue. Art makes us aware of the exquisite beauty, balance, vitality and complexity of our world, and of the vast scope of human subtlety and expressive power. These are virtues for which many an artist will take little personal credit, seeing them instead as a collective endowment — hence the frequent and sincere protestations by artists that they are but "channels" for some cosmic creativity, that they are freeing the sculpture from the stone, that they are discovering, not inventing, musical themes. All such statements testify to the capacity of great art to make us aware of

---

165. Norman Levitt, *Prometheus Bedeviled: Science and the Contradictions of Contemporary Culture*, as previously cited.

Lawrence Bush

our social connectedness, or what Karl Marx called our "species-be-ing." Oftentimes, as part of my "plotting" against religion (or in my quest for self-justification), I wonder if art, if retrieved from the marketplace and brought back to the center of community life, could not compete with contemporary religious practice as a more dynamic and participatory source of spiritual illumination. We Woodstockers have seen its potential to do so at our own famous Woodstock Festival, at the annual Burning Man Festival in Nevada, at the Bread and Puppet Theater Circus in Vermont, and at other events of mass creativity. By comparison, most religious services are events of mass consumption.

A FIFTH SOURCE of spiritual inspiration for me (my "yesses" thus win over my "no's," 5-4) has been the determined political activism of people, their capacity to be stirred to collective risk-taking and sacrifice in the name of justice. In particular, the nonviolent resistance strategies of Martin Luther King, Jr. and the civil rights heroes and heroines of the 1950s and '60s were inspiring testaments to human interconnection, dependent as these strategies were on the assumption that the great majority of human beings have enough of a moral sensibility and enough feelings of empathy to be susceptible to the transforming power of conscience rather than only to vanquishment by violent insurrection.

Dr. King, of course, rooted his courage and his intense optimism in his Christian belief in "God's triumph over all the forces that seek to block community . . . He who works against community is working against the whole of creation."[166] One needn't have faith that the universe has got your back, however, to believe in the redemptive potential of nonviolent resistance and "love-thine-enemy" conduct. It's enough to know that there's a human instinct for fairness and mutuality at play in most of us — an instinct that even our close cousins, the chimpanzees, seem to have, according to recent research at the Yerkes National Primate Research Center in Atlanta.[167] Because human survival has

---

166. Dr. Martin Luther King, Jr., "An Experiment in Love," in *Jubilee* magazine, September, 1958.

167. www.sciencedaily.com/releases/2005/02/050212191635.htm: The research, by Drs. Sarah Brosnan and Frans de Waal, determined the chimpanzees'

always demanded social cooperation, evolution seems to have finely tuned us to issues of trust, mutuality and justice.[168] We will balk and resist if we feel unfairly disadvantaged (especially by people to whom we are not related), and we will feel anxious if we successfully take advantage of others — or else we will allay that anxiety by convincing ourselves that the disadvantaged ones are less worthy, less related to us, i.e., less human. Injustice therefore produces rationalizations, psychic

---

responses depended "on the strength of their social connections. This is the first demonstration that nonhuman primates' reactions to inequity parallel the variation in human responses to unfair situations based on the quality of the relationship."

168. Human beings are by no means alone among animal species in displaying altruistic and socially cooperative behavior. Most show an instinct to expend more resources and energy for the benefit of their genetic offspring or relatives than for strangers, and many species will also display a reciprocal altruism that is dependent upon survival conditions. Human beings, however, also have a highly developed sense of social morality that is evidenced even in young children. "[E]xperimental studies," writes Pascal Boyer (in *Religion Explained*, as already cited), "show that there is an early-developed specific inference system, a specialized moral sense underlying ethical intuitions." Human beings also tend to display moral behavior even "in a way that does not maximize individuals' benefits," such as "tipping in restaurants one will never again patronize, refraining from undetectable cheating, and so on." Pascal and others attribute this to our need "to demonstrate [our] reliability" in order to gain the cooperation of others, which made it to our evolutionary advantage to develop "clear signals" that make deception difficult — "emotional cues such as facial expressions and gestures that often give people an intuitive feeling that some deception is going on." Seen in an evolutionary light, Pascal concludes, "moral feelings make much more sense. . . . Guilt is a punishment we incur for cheating or generally not living up to our advertised standards of honest cooperation with others. But then a feeling of guilt is also useful if it balances the benefits of cheating, making it less tempting. Prospective guilt provides negative rewards that help us brush aside opportunities to cheat, a capacity that is crucial in organisms that constantly plan future behavior and that must assess its prospective benefits. Gratefulness is a positive emotional reward associated with encountering cooperation in others in situations where cheating was indeed possible. Pride, a positive reward for cooperative behavior, somehow compensates for the frustration of missed opportunities to cheat. All these dispositions area all the more beneficial if we have limited control over their emotional effects."

numbing, dehumanization of the opponent, accumulating injustices, social discontent, and other messy consequences, in a ripple effect across the human, if not the cosmic, landscape — while the resistance, the push for justice, particularly if it is disciplined enough not to incur fresh injustices, feels righteous and restorative, and can win the day because it is in harmony with the ways of the world.

"THE WAYS OF THE WORLD?" Is this phrase appropriate for an atheist to utter?

While I cannot make the leap of faith to affirm "community" as a governing principle of "the whole of creation," as Dr. King believed it to be, I do see interconnection as a human reality principle. It is not the only reality principle at work in our lives, by any means: Our egotism, self-interestedness, and hierarchical competitiveness all have their own evolutionary histories and operational imperatives, and thus we are often tugged in opposite directions by our own instincts. Still, Mordecai Kaplan's observation that human beings are unique among the animals in that our "nature not only makes for the survival of the fittest, but aims to make the greatest possible number fit to survive," is wonderfully accurate: Our capacity to act in common, and to feel elevated by such actions, has been a great motor of human accomplishment.

This is perhaps most obvious in the economic realm, the realm of making a living and surviving here on Earth. The Bible expresses its fundamental economic reality principle very tersely, in the opening of Psalm 24: "The Earth is the Lord's, and all of its fruits." Over the centuries, the rabbis who formulated the fundamentals of Jewish observance used this concept of the "Divine ownership of wealth" as the cornerstone for an admirable body of ethical teachings about sustenance and wealth. While they recognized the role of greed, insecurity and status-seeking in motivating economic activity — "Without the *yetzer hara* (the "evil" or "lustful" urge)," the Midrash declares, "a man would not build a house, take a wife, beget children, or engage in commerce"[169] — the rabbis still considered their belief in God as Landlord to mandate economic policies that emphasize the individual's responsibility to the collective.

---

169. *Genesis Rabbah* 9: 7.

They unpacked this principle with a whole lot of detail. There is the everyday Jewish tradition of *tzedakah*, the mandatory redistribution of wealth in the name of justice, which the Talmud calls "equal to all the other commandments." There is the Torah tradition of the Jubilee year, which assures that the rising of some families into wealth and the sinking of others into poverty will be curbed through the redistribution of land every half century. There are laws about agricultural land that consistently compromise private property rights to allow for the gathering of wood by all, gleaning of harvest remains by the poor, communal access to water and fishing, and other kinds of sharing in nature's resources. There are laws that ban predatory practices from the marketplace, such as false advertising (*geneivat daat*, literally, "stealing the mind"), windfall profiteering, and worker exploitation. There are laws against armaments sales and other forms of assistance to "perpetrators of evil deeds." With such economic laws constituting more than a sixth of the 613 traditional Jewish *mitzvot* (commandments), it is reasonable to see Judaism as, fundamentally, a centuries-long moral discussion of how we can best live together in community, balancing the realities of self-interest and individual urge with the realities of interconnection and interdependence.

All of this good stuff proceeds, however, from the declaration that "the Lord" owns all the world — a statement that most atheists would probably dismiss as a meaningless. For me, however, Judaism's economic philosophy has proved too attractive and too arresting for me not to essay some sort of humanistic translation of its founding principle.

First, I take Psalm 24 and substitute "nature" for "the Lord" — the classic atheistic switcheroo — which leaves me with a simple statement of fact that any sensible person will affirm, that the planetary elements of air, water, soil, sunlight, minerals and life forms exist independently of human achievement. These resources, which are essential for all economic enterprise, are our collective endowment, the gifts of a "greater power" — nature — that enables us to recreate ourselves daily with food and sustenance.

Yet there is far more implicit in Psalm 24 than nature worship. There is also a moral response to the vast human collectivity that undergirds the creation of wealth: the great body of human knowledge and effort, infrastructure and support, innovation and practice. As

Albert Einstein put it — notwithstanding his reputation as the outstanding "lonely genius" of the 20th century — "When we survey our lives and endeavors, we soon observe that almost the whole of our actions and desires is bound up with the existence of other human beings. . . . We eat food that others have produced, wear clothes that others have made, live in houses that others have built. The greater part of our knowledge and beliefs has been communicated to us by other people through . . . a language that others have created. . . ." All of our achievements, Einstein observed, come to us as members of "a great human community."[170]

In particular, economic enterprises of any kind demand, according to political scientist Gar Alperovitz,

> the build-up of highways and waterways, the evolution of overall skill levels, repeated generations of schooling . . . [and] still more fundamentally . . . the much longer and larger community investment which provides centuries of science — from before Newton to after Einstein — and in the development of technologies and inventions among hundreds of thousands of scientists and engineers and millions of skilled working people. . . . When a bright young computer inventor produces an innovation that makes him a millionaire, he commonly thinks he "deserves" all that he receives. His "invention," however, is literally unthinkable without the previous generations — indeed, centuries — of knowledge, skills, wealth. He picks the best fruit of a tree which stands on a huge mountain of human contribution.[171]

To extract real meaning from Psalm 24, then, a second word substitution is needed: "humankind" for "the Lord." *By no longer using the Divine "You" as a proxy for the collective "We," we translate the psalm into*

---

170. Einstein quoted in *Jewish Currents*, May-June, 2005.

171. Gar Alperovitz in *Israel Horizons*, Spring, 1992.

an undeniable reality principle — that wealth is, by nature, a collective product. The ethical and moral implications of this reality may be open to debate, but who would argue against it as fact?

IN GENERAL, HOWEVER, we do the opposite, migrating from the seemingly unaddressable "We" to the "You" who can be addressed through the magical language of prayer. The spirituality of interconnection thus serves as a yeast for theology and religious belief. I expressed this thought in a sermon that I helped to craft with Rabbi Alexander M. Schindler, then president of the Reform synagogue movement, in 1987. Our theme was inspired by a fantasy I'd had of a global project of hand-holding — all of humanity, holding hands around the world, all at once.[172] It would be an impossible feat, of course: There are oceans separating us, time zones and war zones; there are class differences, language differences, gender differences, tribal differences, religious differences, and all the rest of those differences; there are rivalries and hatreds, competitions for money, love, land, propagation; there are babies being born, elders dying, the sheer chaos of our six billion struggles for survival, status, and satisfaction. "We are too far apart," the sermon admitted. "We are spread across the land and across the globe, and though we are all rushing together through the cosmos, and though we are all turning together towards the sun, the appearance is that of separation, of boundaries and time zones." Therefore, "the essential means of encounter available to us, given the human condition, given our multitude, is our shared encounter with God, our shared seeking of the reflected image, our shared language of prayer. . . . we reach out to each other by reaching up. We call out to God above . . . to join us together as one."[173]

I wrote those words for Rabbi Schindler nearly twenty years ago. They all but acknowledge the metaphorical nature of "God" for many liberal religious people. Still, I am not yet satisfied with our conclusion.

---

172. I thought of it as "Mount Sinai writ large." At Sinai, one *midrash* holds, every soul of the 600,000 freed Hebrew slaves was present as witness — and had even one been absent, the Revelation would have been withheld.

173. Rabbi Alexander M. Schindler, "A World in Transition — Reform Judaism in Action," presidential address to the 59th General Assembly of the Union of American Hebrew Congregations, October 29-November 3, 1987.

L a w r e n c e   B u s h

I fear that when human beings settle for the Divine "You" as the stand-in for our collective "We," something very vital gets lost in the translation. At worst, we end up with the exact opposite of the "spirituality of interconnection," namely, religious triumphalism, sectarianism and war, with "God" embodying the worst of our tribal instincts. At best, we end up settling for prayer instead of conversation, for faith instead of critical thinking, for ritual theater and emotional catharsis instead of real-life effort . . .

The effort, say, of lining up all the fleets of the world — all those warships, cruise ships, oil tankers, barges, yachts — in chains across the oceans so that people can stand on them, holding hands . . .

The effort of sending armies of peace onto every continent to feed and fortify populations and alert them to the great day, the great moment . . .

The effort of translating the call into hundreds of spoken and written languages . . .

The effort of removing stumbling blocks from before the blind, and building ramps for the wheelchair-bound, and fitting prosthetics to those whose hands have been cruelly cut off or blown away, as we extend the human chain from hospitals to mansions, from mental wards to presidential palaces, from houses of prostitution to cathedrals, with none forgotten, none too degraded or too exalted to be included . . .

The effort of trekking to the nearest superhighway where thousands are already standing shoulder to shoulder, hand in hand . . .

The effort of trying to do the impossible instead of trying to believe in the impossible.

In one of my favorite tales from that centuries-long Jewish discussion called the Talmud, the rabbis veer awfully close to affirming the collective "We," rather than the Divine "You," as having preeminence in human affairs. The story describes a disagreement between Rabbi Eliezer and a group of his peers about the ritual purity of a clay stove.[174] Eliezer is a minority of one in his opinion, and begins to resort to supernatural proofs that he is correct. "If the Law is with me, this carob tree will prove it," he says — and the tree uproots itself and leaps a hundred feet!

---

174. Babylonian Talmud, *Bava Metzia* 59b.

"No proof can be brought from a carob tree," the others say.

Eliezer next predicts that the stream's current will flow backwards to prove his point — and so it does. He then predicts that the walls of the study house will collapse to prove his point — and they begin to topple. He argues that a voice from heaven will back him up, and all the disputants all hear it: "Why do you argue with Rabbi Eliezer, with whom the law always agrees?"

Still, the rabbis refuse proof by miracle — even by a Divine voice. "The Torah is not in heaven!" one of them proclaims, while another explains, "We pay no attention to a Divine voice because long ago, at Mount Sinai, You [God] wrote in the Torah, 'After the majority must one incline.'"[175]

The men who created this parable seemed to have understood that when the law was "handed over at Mount Sinai," an arc of religious evolution was set in motion. It led from the unpredictable chaos of pagan theologies — so many gods to appease, and so little time! — to the biblical idea of covenantal monotheism, which placed limits on the arbitrary power of the unknown and beckoned humanity to a higher level of security, autonomy, and moral unity. In our own time, that arc of evolution has led much further, at least within the Woodstocker sub-culture, to a purely voluntary, celebratory sense of religion, marked by theologies of awe and wonder that recast God in abstract terms — from a being to a feeling, from a noun to a verb, from the agent of other-worldly salvation to the simple embodiment of worldly goodness.

We have thereby nearly given ourselves permission to ignore the proxy "You" and devote ourselves wholeheartedly to the collective "We." The rabbis of the Talmud were canny enough to predict this outcome and proclaim it as the full arrival to maturity of "God's children." Their

---

175. The rabbis in disputation with Rabbi Eliezer cite *Exodus* 23: 2 as their prooftext: "You shall neither side with the mighty to do wrong — you shall not give perverse testimony in a dispute so as to pervert it in favor of the mighty . . ." This statement is very nearly opposite in meaning to "inclining after the majority," so either the rabbis are misquoting the Torah by taking a phrase out of context (a not uncommon practice) — or they mean to imply that Rabbi Eliezer's heaven-sent miracles constitute "perverse testimony!" For a wide-ranging discussion of this famous Talmudic parable, see David Luban's "The Coiled Serpent of Argument" at: www.law.georgetown.edu/faculty/documents/luban_000.pdf.

Lawrence Bush

story of the stove has a dénouement, in which the prophet Elijah is asked to describe how God reacted to the sages' defiant independence, their disregard for miracles, their insistence on working out their disagreement among themselves.

"God laughed," Elijah reports, "saying, 'My children have defeated Me, my children have won.'"

With that laughter planted in our hearts, we could now turn away — *Goodbye Elijah! Goodbye God!* — and walk forward, hand in hand.

Bibliography

The Beatles Anthology, by the Beatles, 2000, Chronicle Books, San Francisco, CA

The Denial of Death, by Ernest Becker, 1973, The Free Press, New York, NY

Cosmic Adventure, by Bob Berman, 1998, William Morrow, New York, NY

The Great Work: Our Way Into the Future, by Thomas Berry, 1999, Bell Tower Books, New York, NY

Sefer Ha-Aggadah, The Book of Legends, ed. by H.N. Bialik and Y.H. Ravnitzky, 1992, Schocken Books, New York, NY

Religion Explained The Evolutionary Origins of Religious Thought, by Pascal Boyer, 2001, Basic Books, New York, NY

The Spiritual Tourist: A Personal Odyssey Through the Outer Reaches of Belief, by Mick Brown, 1998, Bloomsbury USA, New York, NY

I and Thou, by Martin Buber, 1923, 1958, Charles Scribner's Sons, New York, NY

Contemporary Jewish Religious Thought, edited by Arthur A. Cohen and Paul Mendes-Flohr, 1987, Free Press, New York, NY

Unweaving the Rainbow: Science, Delusion and the Appetite for Wonder, by Richard Dawkins, 1998, Houghton Mifflin, Boston, MA and New York, NY

Albert Einstein, the Human Side, edited by Helen Dukas and Banesh Hoffman, 1981, Princeton University Press, Princeton, New Jersey

Original Blessing, by Matthew Fox, 2000, Jeremy P. Tarcher/Putnam (originally published in 1983), New York, NY

The Future of an Illusion, by Sigmund Freud, 1964, Anchor Books (originally published in 1927), New York, NY

Working on God, by Winifred Gallagher, 1999, Random House, New York, NY

The Legends of the Jews, by Louis Ginsberg, 1935, Jewish Publication Society, Philadelphia, PA

The Sixties: Years of Hope, Days of Rage, by Todd Gitlin, 1987, Bantam Books, New York, NY

The Way of Response: Martin Buber, Selections from His Writings, edited by Nahum Glatzer, 1996, Schocken Books, New York, NY

The Romance of American Communism, by Vivian Gornick, 1977, Basic Books, New York, NY

Money: Who Has How Much and Why, by Andrew Hacker, 1997, Touchstone Books, New York, NY

Rational Mysticism: Spirituality Meets Science in the Search for Enlightenment, by John Horgan, 2003, Mariner Books/Houghton Mifflin, New York, NY

Einstein, History, and Other Passions: The Rebellion Against Science at the End of the 20th Century, by Gerald Horton, 1996, Addison-Wesley Publishing Co., Reading, MA

The Structure and Dynamics of the Psyche, Collected Works, Vol. 8, by Carl Jung, 1978, Princeton University Press, Princeton, NJ

The Meaning of God in Modern Jewish Religion, by Mordecai Kaplan, 1937, the Reconstructionist Press, New York, NY

"Jimmy Higgins" — The Mental World of the American Rank-and-File Communist, by Aileen Kraditor, 1988, Greenwood Press, New York, NY, Westport, CT and London, UK

The Transcendental Temptation: A Critique of Religion and the Paranormal, by Paul Kurtz, 1986, Prometheus Books, Buffalo, NY

The Basic Writings of C.G. Jung, edited by Violet Staub De Laszlo, 1959, Modern Library, New York, NY

The Apocalyptic Premise: Nuclear Arms Debated, ed. by Ernest W. Lefever and E. Stephen Hunt, 1982, Ethics and Public Policy Center, Washington, DC

Prometheus Bedeviled: Science and the Contradictions of Contemporary Culture, by Norman Levitt, 1999, Rutgers University Press, New Brunswick, NJ

Higher Superstition: The Academic Left and Its Quarrels with Science, by Norman Levitt and Paul R. Gross, 1994, Johns Hopkins Press, Baltimore, MD

Indefensible Weapons: The Political and Psychological Case against Nuclearism, by Robert Jay Lifton and Richard Falk, 1982, Basic Books, NY

The Skeptical Environmentalist: Measuring the Real State of the World, by Bjorn Lomborg, 2001, Cambridge University Press, Cambridge, UK and New York, NY

Thomas Berry and the New Cosmology, Anne Lonergan and Caroline Richards, eds., 1988, Twenty-Third Publications, Mystic, CT

Synchronicity, Science and Soul-Making, by Victor Mansfield, 1995, Open Court Publishing Co., Peru, IL

The Drama of the Gifted Child: The Search for the True Self, by Alice Miller, 1979, Basic Books, New York, NY

The Economics of the Mishnah, by Jacob Neusner, 1990, University of Chicago Press, Chicago, IL

Why God Won't Go Away: Brain Science and the Biology of Belief, by Andrew Newberg and Eugene D'Aquili, 2001, Ballantine Books, New York, NY

Why I Am Not a Christian, by Bertrand Russell, 1929, Haldeman-Julius Publications, Girard, Kansas

Golems Among Us: How a Jewish Legend Can Help Us Navigate the Biotech Century, by Byron L. Sherwin, 2004, Ivan R. Dee Publisher, Chicago, IL

A Plausible God: Secular Reflections on Liberal Jewish Theology, by Mitchell Silver, 2006, Fordham University Press, New York, NY

Gods and Beasts: The Nazis and the Occult, by Dusty Sklar, 1977, Cromwell Publishers, New York, NY

The Spiral Dance: A Rebirth of the Ancient Religion of the Great Goddess, by Starhawk, 1999, HarperCollins, New York, NY

God's Funeral, by A.N. Wilson, 1999, W. W. Norton & Co., New York, NY

Consilience, the Unity of Knowledge, by Edward O. Wilson, 1998, Vintage Books, New York, NY

Index

Horton, Gerald, 23-24, 26

human potential movement, 3

humanism, 2-3, 5-6, 22, 29-31, 58-59, 63, 66, 69, 81, 88, 91-92, 127, 133-134, 146-148, 151, 196

Humanist Manifesto, 31

hypostasis, 151-152

ideology, 2, 57-58, 63, 73, 75-77, 80-81, 83, 87, 107, 162, 167-168, 170, 174-175, 179-180

idolatry, 8, 58-59, 64, 68, 86, 136, 157

image of God, 60, 133, 156; see *b'tselem elohim*

immanence, 51, 157

immortality, 20; see afterlife

individuation, 99-101, 111

interconnection, 11, 35, 38, 55-56, 101-104, 107-108, 110, 132-133, 138, 143, 153, 157, 163, 174, 189, 191, 193, 195-196, 198-199

Islamic fundamentalism, 185

Jacob, 93, 100-101, 116

Jacob's ladder, 100

Jesus, 5, 33, 124-127, 133-138, 140, 143-144, 185

Jewish economic philosophy, 8, 79

Jewish identity, 79, 96, 159

Jewish philosophy, 79-80

Jewish Reconstructionism, 7, 10, 146, 150, 151, 154, 155, 159,

187

Judaism, 7, 12, 35, 79-81, 86, 89, 128, 134, 136, 146-147, 150, 152, 154-160, 196

Jung, Carl, 99-101, 107

kabbalah, 51, 102, 136, 186

Kaplan, Mordecai, 2, 10, 30, 145-157, 170, 172, 189, 195

karma, 49, 93

Kaufman, Walter, 184

Keller, Helen, 3

King, Martin Luther Jr., 128, 193

Kraditor, Aileen, *Jimmy Higgins*, 73, 80, 81

Kurtz, Paul, 56, 183

Leary, Timothy, 33, 140

Lennon, John, 121, 138, 179, 181

lesbianism, 78, 166

levitation, 143

Levitt, Norman, *Prometheus Bedeviled*, 65-68, 72, 87-91, 107, 192

liberation theology, 129, 187

Lifton, Robert Jay, 19-22

Lomborg, Bjorn, *The Skeptical Environmentalist*, 69-72, 75, 83-84

LSD, 33-41, 43, 48, 53, 57, 66, 126

magic, 11, 59, 110, 141, 161, 166, 172-173, 185

Maharaj Ji, Guru, see Guru Maharaj Ji

Maharaj Ji (Neem Karoli Baba), 141

Maharishi Mahesh Yogi, 28, 48

Mansfield, Victor, *Syn-*

chronicity, Science, and Soul-Making, 105-109

marijuana, 35, 37-38

Mandela, Nelson, 91

Marx, Karl, 2, 6, 8, 140, 193

Marxism, 31, 55, 77, 79, 127, 135-136, 191

materialism, 2-3, 22, 61, 69, 83, 94, 186

MDMA (Ecstasy), 41-42

medicine, 4, 67, 75, 82, 102, 173

meditation, 4, 29, 31, 33, 40, 46, 48-49, 95, 121-122, 143, 190

messiah, 81, 134, 136, 180, 183

messianism, 33, 80, 127, 137

metaphysics, 11, 33, 48, 94, 103, 105

Miller, Alice , 98,

miracle, 2, 5, 49, 140, 200-201

Mitchell, Joni, 59, 73

Moonies, 50, 124

Mormon, 95

mortality, 115, 129, 142

Moses, 13, 122

Mother Earth, 68, 133

Muratore, Stephen, 139

Murray, Madalyn, 17

Muslims, 5, 64, 129

mystical consciousness, 37, 39-40, 43

mystical union, 34, 40, 45, 47, 56, 174

mysticism, 10, 38, 43-48, 50-51, 54-57, 81, 116, 121, 136, 149

"natural," 23, 29, 33, 40, 49, 57, 60, 62-66, 68, 72-73, 78, 82, 89, 112, 149, 155-158, 162, 173, 186, 190-191

science, 2, 10, 13, 22-
28, 47, 55, 61, 65-69,
71, 82-84, 87-88, 90-
92, 94, 102, 104-107,
111-112, 114, 116,
146, 149, 172-174,
186, 191-192, 197
scientist, 22-23, 71, 89,
151, 191, 197
SDS, 77
secular Jews, 121, 155
separateness, 44, 55,
103, 107, 163-164
sex, 10, 54, 121, 143
sexuality, 67, 86, 110,
158, 169-170
Shelley, Percy Bysshe,
23, 92
"sigh of the afflicted
creature," 140
Silver, Mitchell, *A
Plausible God*, 6, 10,
187
Sinai, 35-36, 134, 136,
158, 198, 200
The Skeptical Inquirer,
56, 83, 104
skepticism, 5, 29, 43,
47, 49-50, 71, 78, 81,
83, 89, 102, 106, 114,
116, 141, 144, 147,
171, 179, 181, 185, 192
socialism, 2, 22, 78-79,
81-82, 135, 149, 166,
191
species-being, 193
speciesism, 156
spirituality, 3, 5, 10,
15, 19, 37-38, 47, 49,
51, 56, 61, 69, 74, 77,
82-83, 91-92, 128,
130-131, 133-135,
138-139, 142-143, 153,
157, 159-161, 170, 174,
179, 185, 189, 191-192,
198-199
Starhawk, 10, 40, 160,

162-164, 166, 168-175,
191
Steiner, Rudolph, 83
Stenger, Victor J., 103-
104, 108-110
supernatural, 5, 11,
103, 147, 150, 152,
199
superstition, 3, 22, 146,
172, 186
survival of the fittest,
149, 195
sustainability, 61
synchronicity, 5, 93-94,
99-101, 104-109, 111-
114, 116, 122, 173
Szasz, Thomas, 116
taboo, 62, 68, 85, 89
Talmud, 7-8, 51, 79,
196, 199-200
technology, 13, 23, 60-
61, 63, 66-69, 82, 84,
89-90, 105
telepathy, 102, 143
terror, 21, 60-61, 115,
152
terrorism, 4, 13
teshuvah, 29
theism, 11, 64, 131, 146
theodicy, 154
theology, 2, 6, 10, 12,
35, 47, 51, 54, 62, 81,
87, 129-130, 139, 143,
147-148, 151-158, 162,
171, 187, 198
Torah, 7, 36, 79, 81,
136, 159, 196, 200
Transcendental Medi-
tation, 48-49
triumphalism, 134,
136-137, 169, 199
Trungpa, Chögyam, 48
Twilight Zone, 21
Unidentified Forces of
Interconnection, 102,
108
United Nations, 27, 85

Vietnam War, 73
virgin birth, 49, 140
Vorspan, Al, 96, 112
War on Drugs, 52-53
Weather Underground,
77
Weiler, Gershon, 10
Western civilization,
3, 48, 64, 68-69, 71,
74, 76-77, 82-83, 140,
142-143, 163, 170,
174, 186, 188, 190
Western medicine, 82
*What the #$@! Do We
Know?*, 104
Wicca, 160-161, 163
Wilson, Edward O.,
11, 45
witchcraft, 4, 160-164,
166-173
witches, 136, 161-163,
166, 169, 171, 173
women, 4, 13, 36, 78,
125, 129, 150, 157-
160, 168, 170-171
Woodstock generation,
44, 75, 77, 83, 93, 138,
179
Woodstock Nation, 10,
35, 73, 81, 128
Woodstockers, 10-11,
19, 22-23, 28, 30, 37-
38, 48, 51, 62, 64, 69,
70-72, 73, 75, 80-83,
88, 104-105, 107, 140,
142, 149, 153-154,
157, 161, 164, 174,
179, 185-186, 187,
191-193
Worldwatch Institute,
69, 75
yetzer hara (evil urge),
195
yin and yang, 110
yoga, 4, 49, 104, 121-
122, 124, 140, 163
Zodiac, 172

About the Author

Lawrence Bush has written several books of Jewish fiction and non-fiction, including *Bessie: A Novel of Love and Revolution.*

Currently editor of the progressive bi-monthly *Jewish Currents*, he is the former editor of *Reconstructionism Today*, the quarterly magazine of the Jewish Reconstructionist movement. He also co-edited *Jews.*, an arts magazine and mail-art experience.

His writings have appeared in the *New York Times, Tikkun, Moment, Reform Judaism, Mad*, and other publications. He recently provided updating and commentary for the millennial edition of Leo Rosten's classic, *The Joys of Yiddish.*

Photo: Penny Coleman

Ben Yehuda Press presents
Jewish Women of the 20th Century

BESSIE SAINER. Bessie's "career" is full of hazards. At the age of twelve, she is exiled to Siberia because of her brothers' anti-czarist activities. At twenty-five, she loses her husband and baby girl to the ravages of civil war in revolutionary Russia.

At forty, she faces down Nazi hoodlums as she tries to disrupt a pro-Hitler rally in Madison Square Garden. At fifty-five, she is driven underground by McCarthyite persecution. At sixty-two, she squares off against racists in the South—and nearly loses the loyalty of her beloved daughter.

At eighty-eight, she is still making trouble and still making jokes.

A profoundly optimistic novel about a remarkable heroine—a rebel, a lover, a mother, a grandmother, a Jew, and an extraordinary human being.

Bessie: A Novel of Love and Revolution by **Lawrence Bush.**

DOROTHY EPSTEIN. Growing up in the immigrant communities of New York, Dorothy Epstein entered the workforce during the worst part of the Depression. The child of activists herself, Dorothy had been loathe to follow in their overburdened, impoverished footsteps.

However, fate intervened, and Dorothy soon became radicalized and spent most of her life working for the advancement of labor unions and human rights. She died in 2006 at the age of 92.

A Song of Social Significance: Memoirs of an Activist by **Dorothy Epstein.**

Printed in the United States
220921BV00005B/5/A